Sponsoring Editors: **Elizabeth Rodenz, Janet Passaro**

Editing Supervisor: **Elizabeth Huffman**

Design and Art Supervisor: **Caryl Valerie Spinka**

Production Supervisor: **Frank Bellantoni**

Production Assistant: **Mary C. Buchanan**

Photo Editor: **Rosemarie Rossi**

Consulting Design Coordinator/Interior Design: **Susan Brorein**
Cover Photography: **Ken Karp**

Photo Credits
Jules Allen: pages 59 (*middle*), 79, 151 (*middle*), 159, 170, 193 (*top*), 216, 241 (*top, bottom*), 262, 286, 287 (*top*), 297, 310, 311 (*middle*), 325. Apple Computer, Inc.: pages 131 (*top*), 138, 171 (*top*), 174. AT&T: page 151 (*bottom*). Control Data Corporation: pages 217 (*middle*), 231. Datapoint Corporation: pages 217 (*top*), 227. J. Elliot/Direct Positive Imagery: page 192. Will Faller: pages 28, 58, 110, 240, 311 (*bottom*). Richard Hackett: pages xii, 90, 91 (*middle*), 104, 130, 171 (*bottom*), 184, 193 (*middle, bottom*), 217 (*bottom*), 241 (*middle*), 287 (*middle, bottom*), 308. Michal Heron: pages 1 (*top, middle*), 19, 24, 29 (*top, middle*), 39, 48, 50 (*top, bottom*), 63, 87, 91 (*top, bottom*), 95, 111, 120, 127, 131 (*bottom*), 171 (*middle*), 179, 263 (*bottom*), 275. Hewlett-Packard: page 150. Honeywell Information Systems, Inc.: pages 151 (*top*), 156. Robert Phillips/Image Bank: page 311 (*top*). Ricoh Corporation: pages 29 (*bottom*), 55. Bob Rogers: pages 1 (*bottom*), 26, 131 (*middle*), 145, 263 (*top, middle*), 269.

Library of Congress Cataloging-in-Publication Data

Zoubek, Charles E., date
   Gregg shorthand. Dictation and transcription.

   Originally published under title: Gregg dictation
and introductory transcription.
   1. Shorthand—Gregg. I. Title. II. Title: Gregg
dictation and introductory transcription.
Z56.2.G7Z69 1990   653'.4270424   89-2311
ISBN 0-07-073671-5

The manuscript for this book was processed electronically.

Gregg Shorthand: Dictation and Transcription, Centennial Edition

Formerly published under the title *Gregg Dictation and Introductory Transcription*.

2 3 4 5 6 7 8 9 0   DOWDOW   8 9 6 5 4 3 2 1 0

ISBN 0-07-073671-5

GREGG
SHORTHAND

DICTATION AND TRANSCRIPTION

CENTENNIAL
EDITION

CHARLES E. ZOUBEK

Gregg Division / McGraw-Hill Publishing Company

New York Atlanta Dallas St. Louis San Francisco Auckland Bogotá Caracas
Hamburg Lisbon London Madrid Mexico Milan Montreal New Delhi
Paris San Juan São Paulo Singapore Sydney Tokyo Toronto

GREGG SHORTHAND

DICTATION AND TRANSCRIPTION

CONTENTS

UNIT III

UNIT IV

UNIT V

TO THE STUDENT

In *Gregg Shorthand: Basic Principles* you learned the alphabet of Gregg Shorthand as well as brief forms, word beginnings, word endings, and phrases. You now have at your command the tools for writing any word in shorthand. Welcome to the world of Gregg writers!

Gregg Shorthand: Basic Principles was devoted to the basics of shorthand and transcription. Those basics are extremely important for further shorthand and transcription development. *Gregg Shorthand: Dictation and Transcription* will continue to stress the basics, but it will also include some guidelines for document preparation—the ultimate goal of your shorthand study.

Not only will *Gregg Shorthand: Dictation and Transcription* be devoted to increasing your dictation speed; it will also help you develop good transcription skills and increase your transcription speed. Just as you take timings in your typing class, you will take timings in your shorthand class—the only difference is that the words are written in shorthand. What a challenge! As you progress through the program, you will discover that it becomes easier and easier to do the transcription exercises and you will see your speed increase.

Features of *Gregg Shorthand: Dictation and Transcription, Centennial Edition*

The appearance of this part of the program continues that of *Gregg Shorthand: Basic Principles*—all shorthand is written on lines and special words and marks of punctuation are highlighted in color.

DICTATION SPEED BUILDING

The opening segment of each lesson beginning with Lesson 13 is an exercise to develop your dictation speed. You will begin by writing the preview words provided before each letter. Your teacher will then dictate the letter at various speeds.

TRANSCRIPTION SKILL DEVELOPMENT

The second segment of each lesson beginning with Lesson 13 contains exercises that will help you build your transcription skill. The Transcription Warmup is an exercise to boost your transcribing speed on the word or phrase level. After you practice transcribing the lines in the Warmup, your teacher will time you for spurts of 10, 15, or 20 seconds on each of the lines. You should try to transcribe as fast as you can without making any errors. The letter or memo that follows should be read in unison prior to transcription. Your goals are to assure transcription accuracy and to increase transcription speed.

After you have read the Transcription Skill Development sentences and letter, your teacher may tell you to practice transcribing the sentences and then the letter for a minute or two or he or she may time you for 15, 20, or 30 seconds on some or all of the lines in the letter. When you are familiar with the content of the letter, your teacher will give you two or three 1-minute timed writings and eventually 2-minute timed writings on the letter. You should verify the accuracy of the transcript and compute your transcription speed. You might also transcribe the entire letter, noting the time you start transcribing and the time you finish. Divide the number of words by the number of minutes to find your words-a-minute transcription rate.

As you transcribe the Transcription letter, you will be expected to insert the missing marks of punctuation in Lessons 13 through 32.

MAILABLE PRODUCTION LETTER

You may be instructed to read and/or write the material for homework. The following class period you will transcribe the letters and memos in mailable format from your textbook or your own shorthand notes. Inside addresses are provided in shorthand.

DICTATION AND TRANSCRIPTION

In Lessons 13 through 48 a Dictation and Transcription Practice will come at the end of each lesson. This material may be assigned for homework as a reading and/or writing assignment. The following class period, the material may be dictated or transcribed.

UNIT I

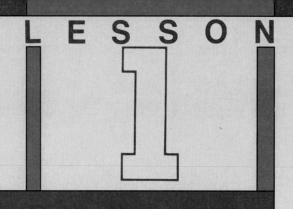

IN LESSON 1

- Word endings *-ing*, *-ings*, *-ly*, *-ingly*, and *-ily*
- Sounds of *ted*, *ded*, and *dit*
- Brief forms and phrases
- Transcription of titles

THEORY REVIEW

Write the following shorthand words until you can write them without difficulty.

Word Ending -ing (Symbol -ing .)

doing	hiring	knowing
hearing	interesting	thinking

Word Ending -ings (Disjoined left s ⌐)

dealings	feelings	meetings
earnings	findings	openings

Word Ending -ly (Symbol e ⌐)

briefly	early	greatly
costly	extremely	highly
daily	fairly	likely

nearly _____   only _____   sincerely _____

Word Ending -ingly (Disjoined e)

accordingly _____   increasingly _____   seemingly _____

exceedingly _____   knowingly _____   willingly _____

Word Ending -ily (Flattened e circle)

easily _____   necessarily _____   steadily _____

family _____   readily _____   temporarily _____

Sound of Ted (Blend of t and d)

accepted _____   completed _____   invested _____

assisted _____   dated _____   listed _____

acted _____   insisted _____   steady, study _____

collected _____   instead _____   today _____

Sound of Ded (Blend of t and d)

added _____   graded _____   needed _____

deduct _____   guided _____   provided _____

Sound of Dit (Blend of t and d)

audit _____   credited ■ _____   edit _____

credit _____   detail _____   editor _____

■ Join *d* to *dit* with a jog.

Theory Practice

Read and write the following sentences and paragraph. For additional practice, dictate the sentences and paragraph to yourself, using the transcript.

1.1

¶ **Charge Account**

[62 words]

BRIEF FORMS AND PHRASES

Write the following brief forms, derivatives, and phrases until you can write them without difficulty.

Brief Forms and Derivatives

a, an

about

acknowledge

acknowledgment

advantage

disadvantage

advertise

advertisement

after

afternoon _[shorthand]_

anniversary _[shorthand]_

appropriately _[shorthand]_

am _[shorthand]_

any _[shorthand]_

are, our, hour _[shorthand]_

and _[shorthand]_

appropriate _[shorthand]_

it, at _[shorthand]_

Brief-Form Phrases

has been _[shorthand]_

I have not been able _[shorthand]_

it will be _[shorthand]_

has been able _[shorthand]_

I will be able _[shorthand]_

we have been _[shorthand]_

has not been able _[shorthand]_

I will not be able _[shorthand]_

we have been able _[shorthand]_

it has been _[shorthand]_

I am _[shorthand]_

we have not been _[shorthand]_

I have been _[shorthand]_

I am glad _[shorthand]_

we have not been able _[shorthand]_

I have not been _[shorthand]_

of our _[shorthand]_

we will be able _[shorthand]_

Brief-Form Practice

Read and write the following sentences and paragraph. For additional
practice, dictate the sentences and paragraph to yourself, using the
transcript.

1.2

1 _[shorthand]_

[shorthand] 15 _[shorthand]_

2 _[shorthand]_

[shorthand]

3 _[shorthand]_

[shorthand]

4 _[shorthand]_

5 _[shorthand]_

[shorthand]

¶ **Policy Changes**

[shorthand]

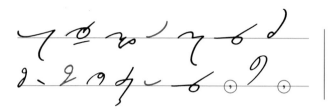

[62 words]

Transcription of Titles

When transcribing the following titles, remember to capitalize and use a period.

⟋ Ms.   ⟋ Dr.
⌒ Mr.   ⌒ Mrs.

The abbreviation *Ms.* is used:

1 When a woman's marital status is not known.
2 When a woman has indicated that she prefers this title.
3 When a woman's marital status is not considered relevant to the situation.

The title *Miss* is capitalized but should not be followed by a period because it is not an abbreviation.

⟋ Miss

Reading and Writing Practice

1.3 Credit Cancellation

1 canceling   2 membership   3 Association
4 prompted

5 failure   6 discontinuing   7 envelope

[115 words]

1.4 Urgent Request

[84 words]

1.5 Credit Approval

[108 words]

8 valuable 9 credential 10 We hope that
11 upset 12 discouraging 13 extra

14 application 15 advantages 16 You will
17 notified 18 general 19 Please 20 It will be
21 welcome 22 customers

LESSON 2

IN LESSON 2

- Sounds of *for* and *fur*
- Word endings *-ful* and *-ification*
- Sounds of *men*, *man*, *min*, and *mon*
- Brief forms and phrases
- Transcription of personal names

THEORY REVIEW

Write the following shorthand words until you can write them without difficulty.

Sounds of For and Fur (Symbol f ⟋)

forget ■

forgive ■

forgot ■

form ■

formal ■

former ■

inform ■

perform ■

forth ■

afford ■

comfort ■

effort ■

force ■

fortunate ■

forever ■

furnish

furniture

further

■ Brief-form derivative.

Word Ending -ful (Symbol f)

careful _____   grateful _____   successful _____

delightful _____   helpful _____   thoughtful _____

doubtful _____   hopeful _____   useful _____

Word Ending -ification (Disjoined f)

classification _____   notification _____   qualifications _____

identification _____   modifications _____   specifications _____

Sounds of Men, Man, Min, and Mon (Blend of m and n _____)

men _____   many _____   minimum _____

meant _____   manage _____   minute _____

mention _____   manager _____   money _____

businessmen _____   manner _____   month _____

women _____   woman _____   monthly _____

Theory Practice

Read and write the following sentences and paragraph. For additional practice, dictate the sentences aparagraph to yourself, using the transcript.

2.1

1 _____

2 _____

3 _____

4 _____

5. *[shorthand outline]* 6. *[shorthand outline]* 50/
[shorthand outline]

¶ **Furniture Sale**

[shorthand outlines]

[shorthand outlines]   [53 words]

BRIEF FORMS AND PHRASES

Write the following brief forms, derivatives, and phrases until you can
write them without difficulty.

Brief Forms and Derivatives

be, by _*[shorthand]*_

before _*[shorthand]*_

between _*[shorthand]*_

business _*[shorthand]*_

businesses _*[shorthand]*_

but _*[shorthand]*_

can _*[shorthand]*_

cannot _*[shorthand]*_

character _*[shorthand]*_

circular _*[shorthand]*_

circumstance _*[shorthand]*_

communicate _*[shorthand]*_

communication _*[shorthand]*_

company _*[shorthand]*_

convenient, convenience _*[shorthand]*_

correspond, correspondence _*[shorthand]*_

corresponded _*[shorthand]*_

could _*[shorthand]*_

difficult _*[shorthand]*_

difficulty _*[shorthand]*_

Brief-Form Phrases

will be able		you have not been able	
you will be able		we would be able	
will not be able		we would not have	
I will be		I might be	
we will not be able		we might be able	
you have been		you might have	
you have not been		I might have	

Brief-Form Practice

Read and write the following sentences and paragraph. For additional practice, dictate the sentences and paragraph to yourself, using the transcript.

2.2

¶ **Supplies Request**

[shorthand outlines]   [64 words]

Transcription of Personal Names

When transcribing personal names, use the following guidelines:

1 Do not abbreviate names.
2 When typing initials in a personal name, follow the period with one space.

[shorthand outlines]

Robert H. Edward   R. H. Edward

Reading and Writing Practice

2.3 Courtesy Thank-You

[shorthand outlines]

1 Thank you for your   2 extended   3 one of our
4 I have   5 your order   6 has been

7 valuable   8 occasions   9 emergency

[106 words]

2.4 Magazine Subscription

[Shorthand outlines]

[94 words]

2.5 Acknowledging Gift

[Shorthand outlines]

[103 words]

---

10 Chicago   11 material   12 It has been
13 especially   14 let us know

15 Dear Mrs.   16 World Atlas   17 Christmas
18 chose   19 excellent   20 example
21 occasions

3

IN LESSON 3

- Word endings *-ure*, *-ual*, *-rity*, and *-lity*
- Sounds of *dev*, *div*, *def*, and *dif*
- Brief forms and phrases
- Transcription of salutations and closings

THEORY REVIEW

Write the following shorthand words until you can write them without difficulty.

Word Ending -ure (Symbol r ‿)

failure	future	procedure
feature	natural	picture

Word Ending -ual (Symbol l ‿)

actual	eventually	individual
annual	factual	manual
equal	gradual	schedule

Word Ending -rity (Disjoined r ‿)

authority	charity	majority
authorities	integrity	security

Word Ending -lity (Disjoined l ⌣)

ability _____ loyalty _____ qualities _____

locality _____ possibilities _____ responsibilities _____

Sounds of Dev and Div (Symbol dev ⌒)

develop _____ devote _____ divide _____

development _____ devise, device _____ division _____

Sounds of Def and Dif (Symbol def ⌒)

defense _____ definite _____ different _____

define _____ difference _____ modified _____

Theory Practice

Read and write the following sentences and paragraph. For additional practice, dictate the sentences and paragraph to yourself, using the transcript.

3.1

1 _(shorthand)_

2 _(shorthand)_

3 _(shorthand)_

4 _(shorthand)_

5 _(shorthand)_

¶ **Successful Businesses**

(shorthand)

(shorthand outlines)

[71 words]

BRIEF FORMS AND PHRASES

Write the following brief forms, derivatives, and phrases until you can write them without difficulty.

Brief Forms and Derivatives

direct *(outline)*	enclosed *(outline)*	ever, every *(outline)*
director *(outline)*	enclosure *(outline)*	executive *(outline)*
doctor, Dr., during *(outline)*	envelope *(outline)*	executives *(outline)*
electric *(outline)*	equip *(outline)*	experience *(outline)*
electrical *(outline)*	equipment *(outline)*	experienced *(outline)*
enclose *(outline)*	equivalent *(outline)*	experiences *(outline)*

Brief-Form Phrases

to do *(outline)*	to know *(outline)*	if you *(outline)*
to do the *(outline)*	about the *(outline)*	if you have *(outline)*
to me *(outline)*	are in, are not *(outline)*	at this time *(outline)*
to make *(outline)*	if the *(outline)*	by this time *(outline)*

Brief-Form Practice

Read and write the following sentences and paragraph. For additional practice, dictate the sentences and paragraph to yourself, using the transcript.

3.2

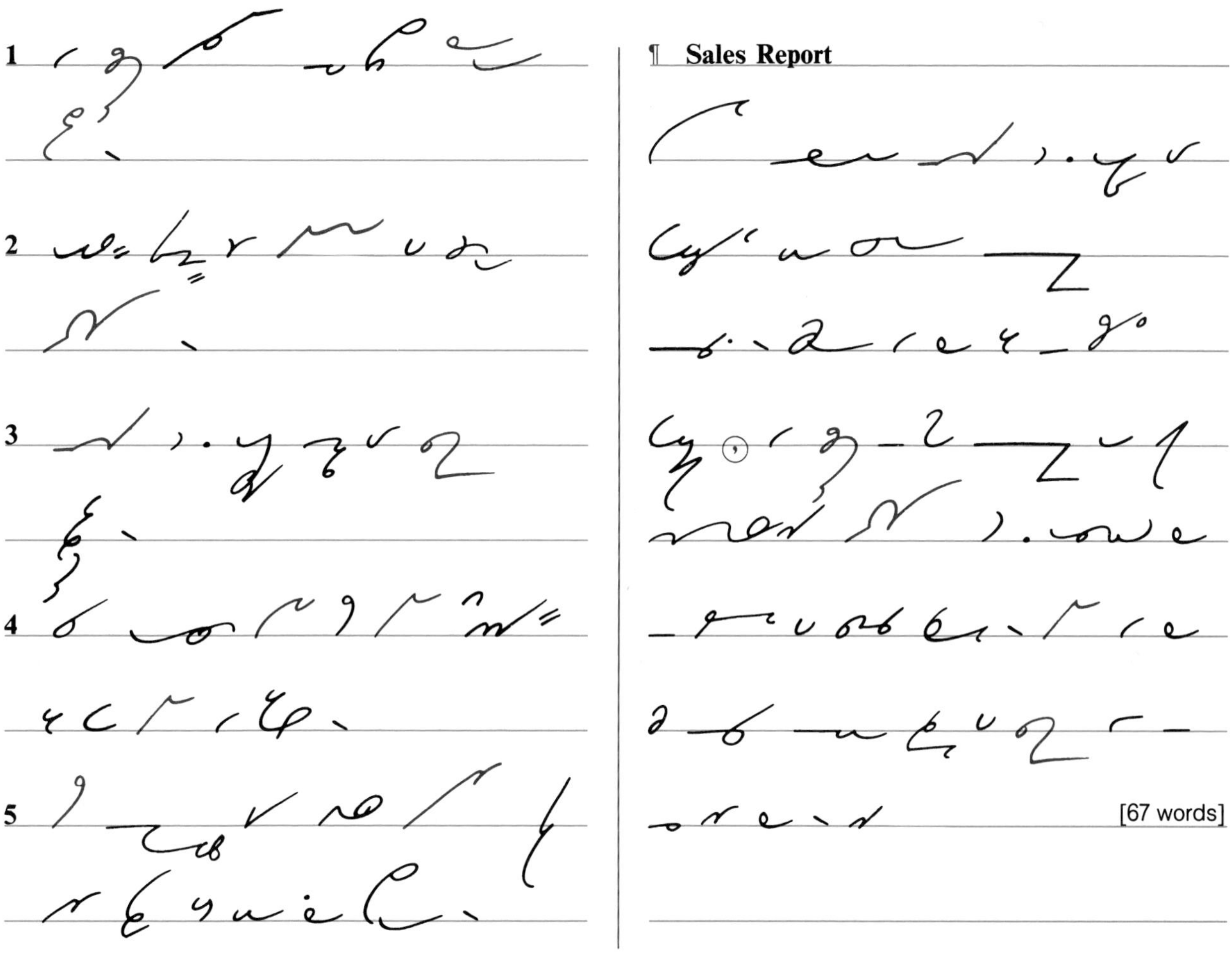

1
2
3
4
5
¶ Sales Report
[67 words]

Transcription of Salutations and Closings

When transcribing salutations, use the following guidelines:

1 Abbreviate the titles *Mr.*, *Ms.*, *Mrs.*, and *Dr.*
2 Capitalize the first word as well as any nouns and titles in the salutation.
3 Place a colon at the end (except when open punctuation is used).

Dear Bob:

Dear Mr. Day:

Ladies and Gentlemen:

Dear Sir or Madam:

When transcribing closings, use the following guidelines:

1 Capitalize only the first word of a complimentary closing.
2 Place a comma at the end of the line (except when open punctuation is used).

Very truly yours,   Cordially yours,

3.3 Telephone Convenience

[shorthand outlines]

1 telephone   2 efficient   3 frustration
4 surprise

[shorthand outlines]

[80 words]

5 impulse   6 gallon   7 frequently   8 efficiently

3.4 Hotel Advertisement

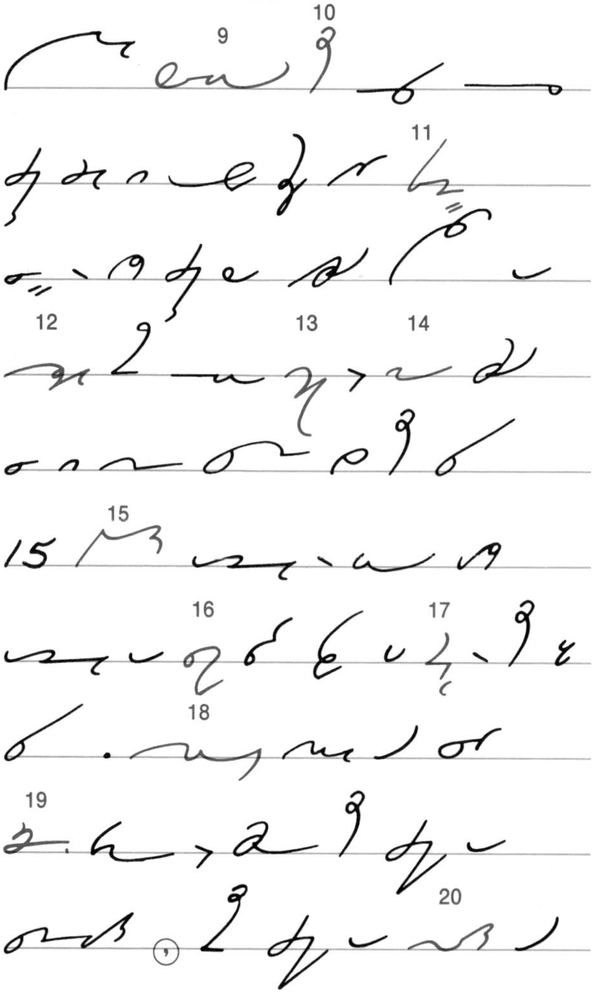

9 Arnold 10 We have 11 Johnson 12 guests 13 comfortable 14 You will 15 deluxe 16 equipped 17 furnishings 18 golf 19 swimming 20 courteous

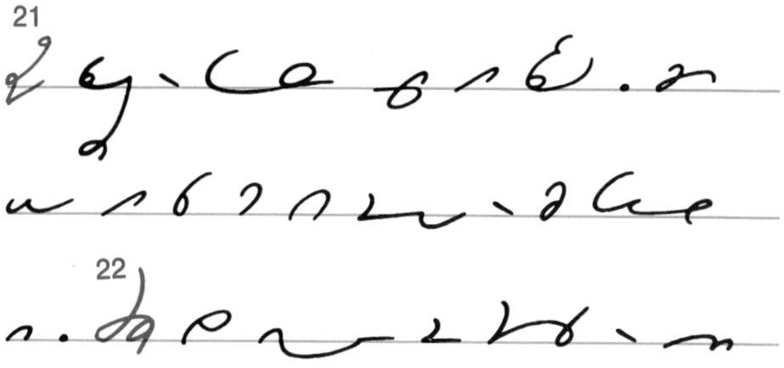

[102 words]

21 efficient 22 vacation

3.5 Business Note

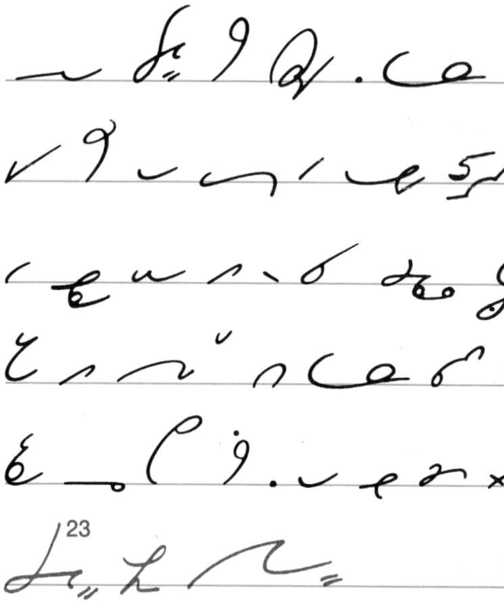

[51 words]

23 James H. Temple

Electronic typewriters often have a linear display above the keyboard that enables the secretary to proofread and correct a document while it is being typed.

LESSON 4

- Sounds of *rd*, *ld*, *nt*, *nd*, *md*, and *mt*
- Word endings -*ment* and -*ble*
- Brief forms and phrases
- Differentiating between *are*, *our* and *to*, *too*, *two*

THEORY REVIEW

Write the following shorthand words until you can write them without
difficulty.

Sound of Rd (Symbol rd ‿)

answered	hired	preferred
appeared	insured	prepared
board	occurred	record
harder	offered	recorded

Sound of Ld (Symbol ld ‿)

billed, build	failed	held
called	filed	settled
canceled	filled	skilled
entitled	handled	told

Sound of Nt (Symbol nt ╱)

account	event	print
agent	entirely	sent
apparent	into	spent
center	plant	urgent
current	prevent	want

Sound of Nd (Symbol nd ╱)

assigned	happened	planned
end	indicate	remind
find	kindly	signed
friendly	opened	spend

Sounds of Md and Mt (Symbol md/mt ╱)

claimed	named	empty
confirmed	performed	prompt
informed	seemed	promptly

Word Ending -ment (Symbol m —)

adjustment	assignment	payment
advertisement	department	settlement
appointment	management	shipment

Word Ending -ble (Symbol b ⟨)

available	eligible	payable
capable	liable	possible

reliable  suitable  valuable 

Theory Practice

Read and write the following sentences and paragraph. For additional practice, dictate the sentences and paragraph to yourself, using the transcript.

4.1

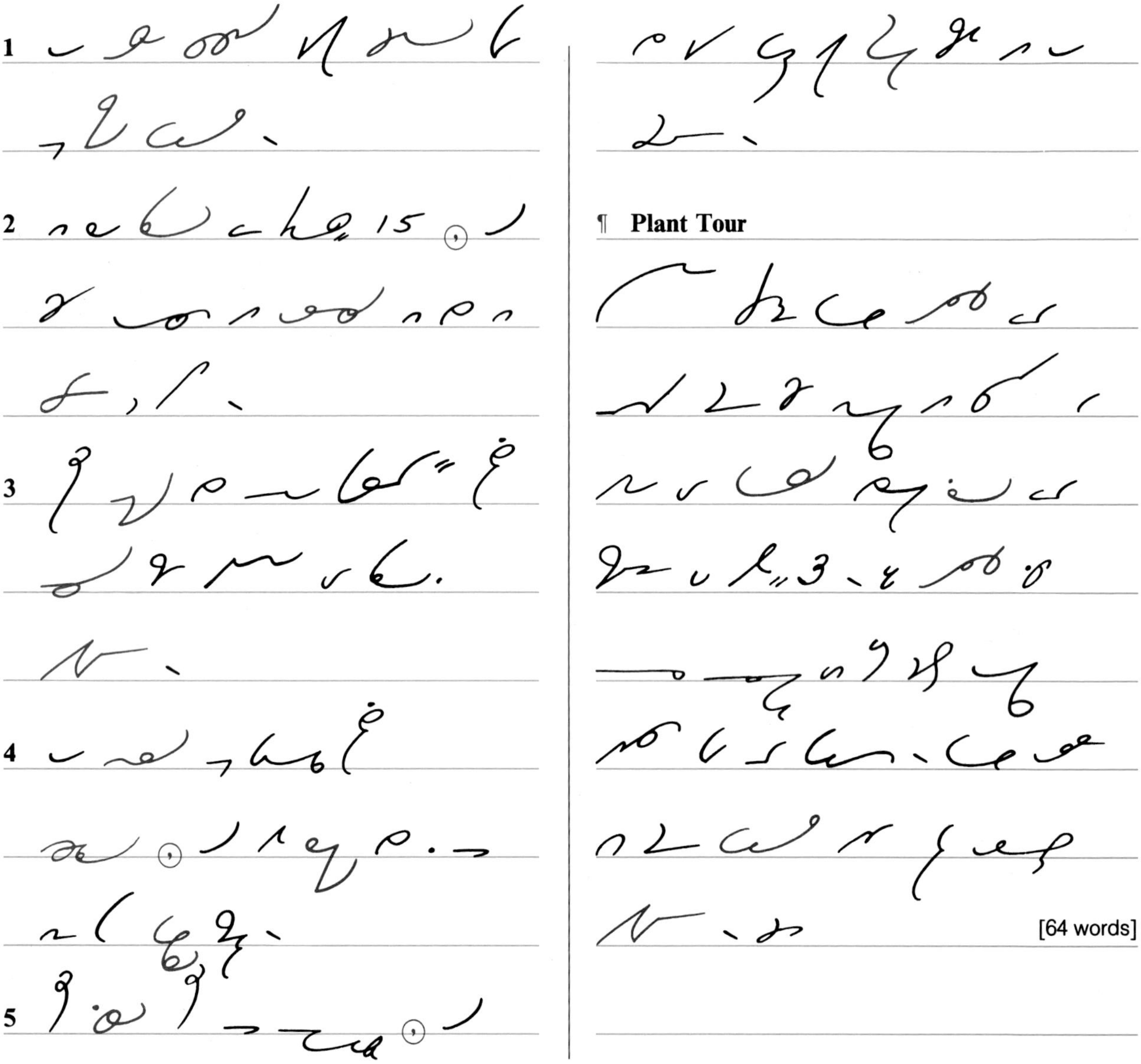
1
2
3
4
5
¶ Plant Tour
[64 words]

Write the following brief forms, derivatives, and phrases until you can write them without difficulty.

Brief Forms and Derivatives

for	glad	however
inform	good	idea
from	govern	ideas
general	government	immediate
generally	have	immediately
Gentlemen	is, his	important, importance

Brief-Form Phrases

can be	for the	I am
can have	for this	I can
can you	for you, for your	I cannot
cannot be	from the	I can be
cannot have	from you, from your	I can have

Brief-Form Practice

Read and write the following sentences and paragraph. For additional practice, dictate the sentences and paragraph to yourself, using the transcript.

4.2

1. [shorthand outlines]

2. [shorthand outlines]

(shorthand outlines)

3

4

5

¶ **Credit Card**

[90 words]

Many employers prefer face-to-face dictation because it allows for questioning and feedback between the dictator and the secretary.

Similar Words: are, our

are: (v.) plural of *is*

our: (adj.) belonging to us

[shorthand]

The secretaries *are* meeting in the conference room.

[shorthand]

We have changed *our* company policy on vacation time.

Similar Words: to, too, two

to: (prep.) toward

too: (adv.) excessive; also

two: a number

[shorthand]

Are your members going *to* a conference?

[shorthand]

The commitment is *too* important *to* him.

[shorthand]

We should appoint *two* members *to* attend.

Reading and Writing Practice

4.3 Recycling Program

[shorthand]

1 You will be

[shorthand]

2 recycling   3 newspapers   4 Wilson

Filing is one of the many skills needed by secretaries in today's electronic office.

[shorthand outlines]

⁵

⁶

⁷

⁸

⁹

¹⁰

¹¹

¹²

[100 words]

4.4 Plant Control

¹³

¹⁴

¹⁵

¹⁶   ¹⁷

¹⁸   ¹⁹

²⁰

²¹

5 magazines	6 pickup	7 burden	8 materials
9 significant	10 ultimate	11 cooperation	
12 collection			

13 industrial	14 controlling	15 I was
16 announcing	17 publication	18 chapters
19 convinced	20 solution	21 impressed

[shorthand outlines] [101 words]

4.5 Dental Appointment

[shorthand outlines]

22 convey   23 congratulations   24 Dear Mr. Sanchez   25 dental

[shorthand outlines] [60 words]

U N I T

II

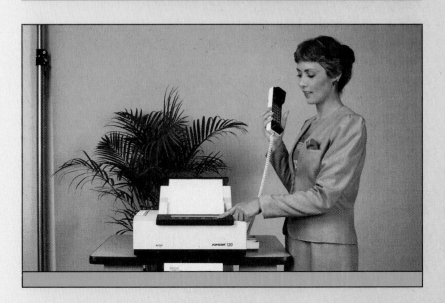

LESSON 5

IN LESSON 5

- Sounds of *ten*, *den*, and *tain*
- Sounds of *tem* and *dem*
- Sound of *th*
- Word ending *-ther*
- Brief forms and phrases
- Differentiating between *cite*, *site*, *sight* and *weather*, *whether*

THEORY REVIEW

Write the following shorthand words until you can write them without difficulty.

Sound of Ten (Symbol ten ⌒)

acceptance	bulletin	outstanding
assistance	competent	remittance
assistant	content	standard
attend	intend	tentative
attention	intends	written

Sound of Den (Symbol ten ⌒)

confidential	deny	evident
confidence	evidence	guidance

30 ▬▬ LESSON 5

identify _____ president _____ student _____

incident _____ resident _____ sudden _____

Sound of Tain (Symbol ten ⌒)

certain _____ maintain _____ obtainable _____

contain _____ obtain _____ retain _____

Sound of Tem (Symbol tem ⌒)

attempt _____ estimate _____ system _____

custom _____ item _____ temporary _____

customer _____ itemized _____ tomorrow _____

Sound of Dem (Symbol tem ⌒)

demand _____ demonstration _____ seldom _____

demonstrate _____ medium _____ damage _____

Sound of Th (Symbol over or under ith ⌒ and ⌒)

method _____ both _____ thorough _____

smooth _____ clothing _____ though _____

then _____ growth _____ through _____

these _____ health _____ throw _____

Word Ending -ther (Symbol over or under ith ⌒ and ⌒)

another _____ gather _____ rather _____

bother _____ neither _____ together _____

either _____ other _____ whether, weather _____

Theory Practice

Read and write the following sentences and paragraph. For additional practice, dictate the sentences and paragraph to yourself, using the transcript.

5.1

1 [shorthand outlines]

2 [shorthand outlines]

3 [shorthand outlines]

4 [shorthand outlines]

5 [shorthand outlines]

¶ **Managers' Meeting**

[shorthand outlines] 16 [shorthand] 19--

[shorthand outlines]

[62 words]

BRIEF FORMS AND PHRASES

Write the following brief forms, derivatives, and phrases until you can write them without difficulty.

Brief Forms and Derivatives

in, not	insured	Mrs.
include	manufacture	Ms.
includes	manufactured	never
incorporate	memorandum	newspaper
incorporated	morning	newspapers
insure, insurance	Mr.	next

Brief-Form Phrases

I cannot be	I will not	in it
I cannot have	I would	in order
I have	I would be	in our
I have not	I would have	in the
I will be	I would not	in this
I will be able	I would not be	in which

Brief-Form Practice

Read and write the following sentences and paragraph. For additional practice, dictate the sentences and paragraph to yourself, using the transcript.

5.2

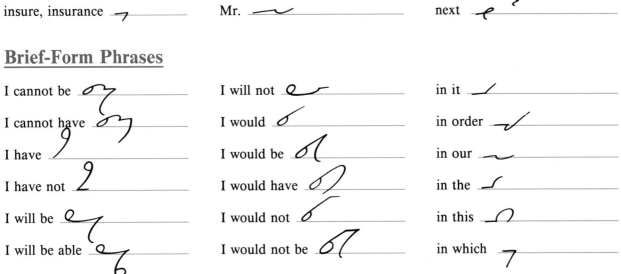

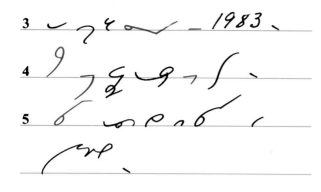

¶ Policy Changes

Communication Skill Builder

Similar Words: cite, site, sight

cite: (v.) to make reference to; to quote

site: a place; a location

sight: having to do with seeing; vision

It is important to *cite* the rule.

A new *site* has not been decided for the office building.

When did you have your *sight* checked?

Similar Words: weather, whether

weather: state of the atmosphere

whether: if

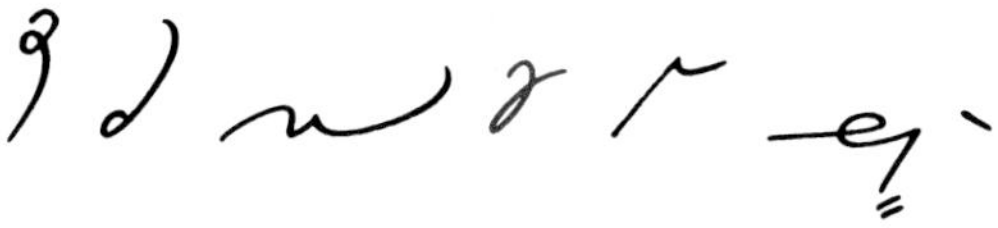

(shorthand)

We have very cold *weather* during March.

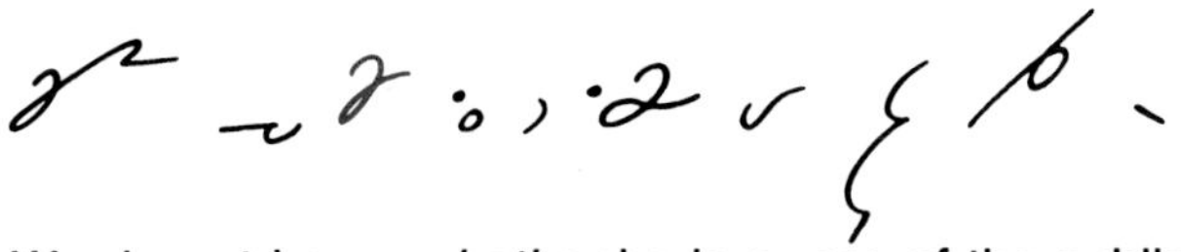

(shorthand)

We do not know *whether* he is aware of the publication date.

5.3 Communications Services

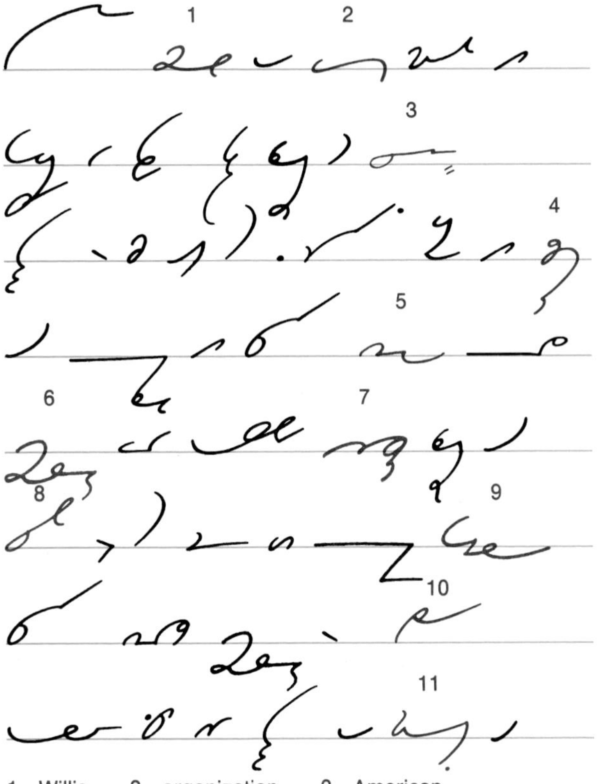

(shorthand outline with numbered markers 1–11)

1 Willis   2 organization   3 American
4 executives   5 one of our   6 conferences
7 communications   8 ideas   9 personnel
10 They will   11 solving

(shorthand outline with numbered markers 12–13)

[114 words]

5.4 Opening-Day Celebration

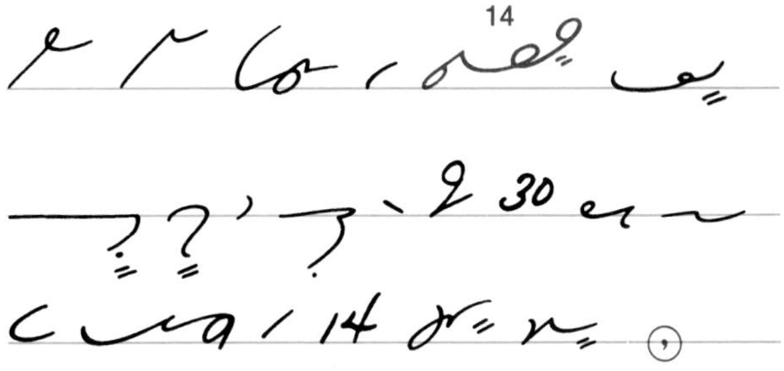

(shorthand outline with numbered marker 14)

12 exchange   13 enclosed   14 Atlanta

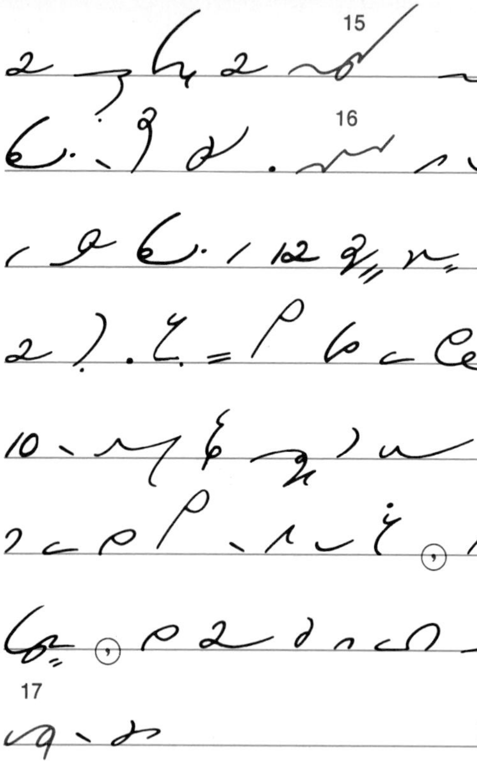

[91 words]

5.5 Sales Seminar

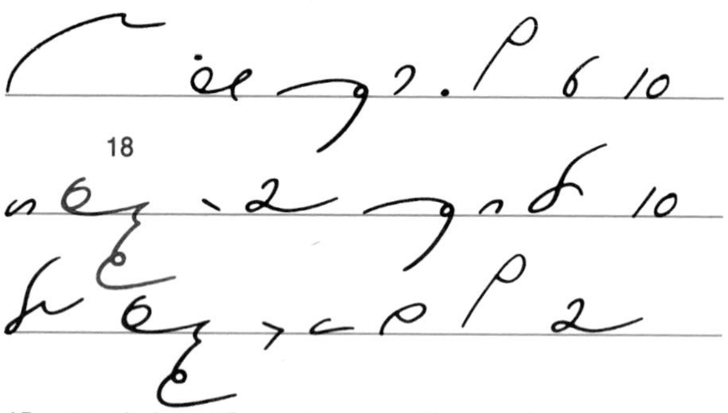

15 crowded 16 contract 17 occasion
18 salespeople

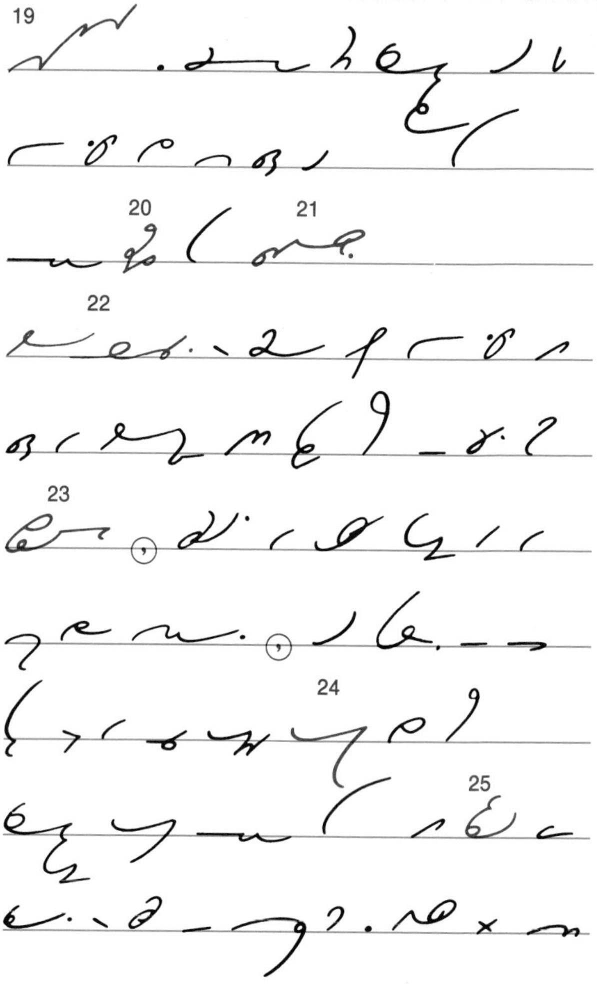

[103 words]

19 conduct 20 efficiently 21 utilizing
22 telemarketing 23 appointments 24 will be
25 spend

L E S S O N

6

IN LESSON 6

- Sounds of *ses* and *sis*
- Word beginnings *super-*, *sub-*, and *self-*
- Word endings *-self* and *-selves*
- Sound of *x*
- Word beginning *ex-*
- Brief forms and phrases
- Differentiating between *advice, advise* and *personal, personnel*

THEORY REVIEW

Write the following shorthand words until you can write them without difficulty.

Sounds of Ses and Sis (Symbol sez $\int$ and $?$)

analysis	increases	process
assist	insist	processes
basis, bases	necessary	reduces
causes	prices	services
chances	produces	sources

Word Beginning Super- (Disjoined comma s ⟩)

superb _____   supervise _____   supervisor _____

superior _____   supervision _____   superintendent _____

Word Beginning Sub- (Symbol s ⟩)

submit _____   subscription _____   substantial _____

subscribe _____   substance _____   suburb _____

Word Beginning Self- (Disjoined left s ⟨)

self-addressed _____   self-assured _____   selfish _____

Word Ending -self (Symbol s ⟨)

herself _____   itself _____   oneself _____

himself _____   myself _____   yourself _____

Word Ending -selves (Symbol sez ⟩)

ourselves _____   themselves _____   yourselves _____

Sound of X (Symbol x ⌐ and ⌣)

tax _____   box _____   approximate _____

taxes _____   fix _____   maximum _____

Word Beginning Ex- (Symbols e, s ⟩ and ⟨)

extra _____   extremely _____   expert _____

exact _____   exist _____   expired _____

examine _____   exception _____   express _____

examination _____   expenses _____   excellent _____

example _____   expensive _____   expect _____

Theory Practice

Read and write the following sentences and paragraph. For additional practice, dictate the sentences and paragraph to yourself, using the transcript.

6.1

1 [shorthand outlines]

2 [shorthand outlines]

3 [shorthand outlines]

4 [shorthand outlines]

5 [shorthand outlines]

¶ **Report**

[shorthand outlines]

[66 words]

Before announcing a visitor, the receptionist should write down essential information. This can be done more quickly and efficiently if written in shorthand.

Write the following brief forms, derivatives, and phrases until you can write them without difficulty.

Brief Forms and Derivatives

object		one, won		ordinary	
objected		opinion		ordinarily	
objective		opportunity		organize	
of		opportunities		organizations	
office		order		out	
offices		ordered		outcome	

Brief-Form Phrases

is in, is not		it will not		of this	
is the		it will not be		of you, of your	
it is		of our		that the	
it was		of the		this is	
it will be		of them		your order	

Brief-Form Practice

Read and write the following sentences and paragraph. For additional practice, dictate the sentences and paragraph to yourself, using the transcript.

6.2

1

2

3

20.

4

5

[77 words]

Communication Skill Builder

Similar Words: advice, advise

advice: (n.) information; recommendation

advise: (v.) to inform; to give counsel

We did not receive sound *advice*.

Mr. Adams will *advise* us of the staff changes.

Similar Words: personal, personnel

personal: belonging to a person; private

personnel: people who make up an organization, such as military personnel; the staff

[shorthand notation]

We need to discuss a *personal* matter.

[shorthand notation]

I received the *personnel* report.

Reading and Writing Practice

6.3   Enrollment Solicitation

[shorthand notation]

1 Carter   2 ability   3 keyboard   4 professional
5 methods   6 techniques   7 quickly   8 easily
9 schedules

[shorthand notation]

[106 words]

6.4   Self-Improvement Course

[shorthand notation]

10 convenient   11 demonstration   12 obligation

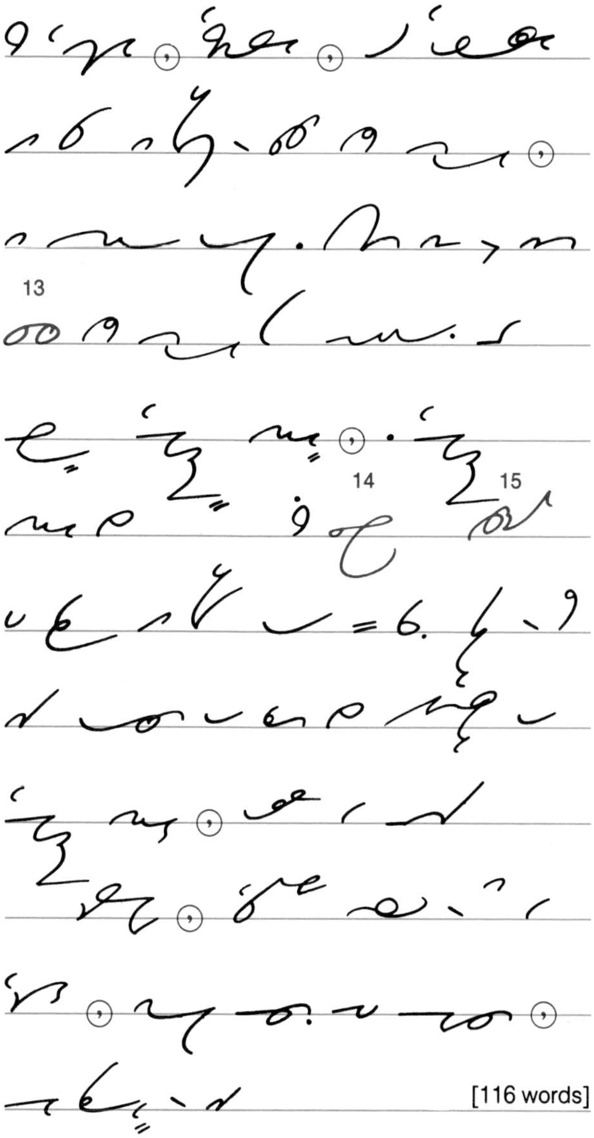

[116 words]

6.5 Editorial Meeting

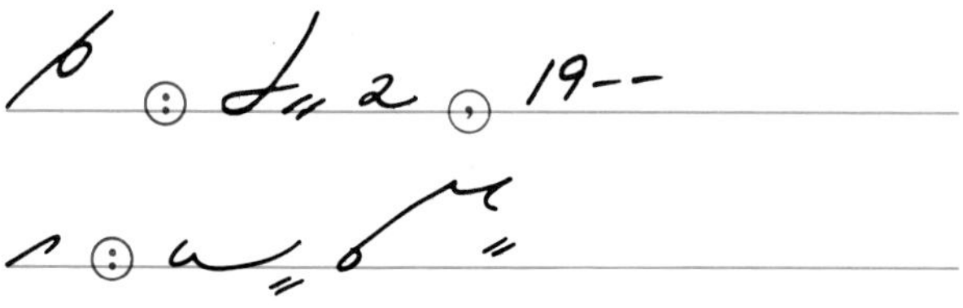

13 acquire 14 enabled 15 thousands

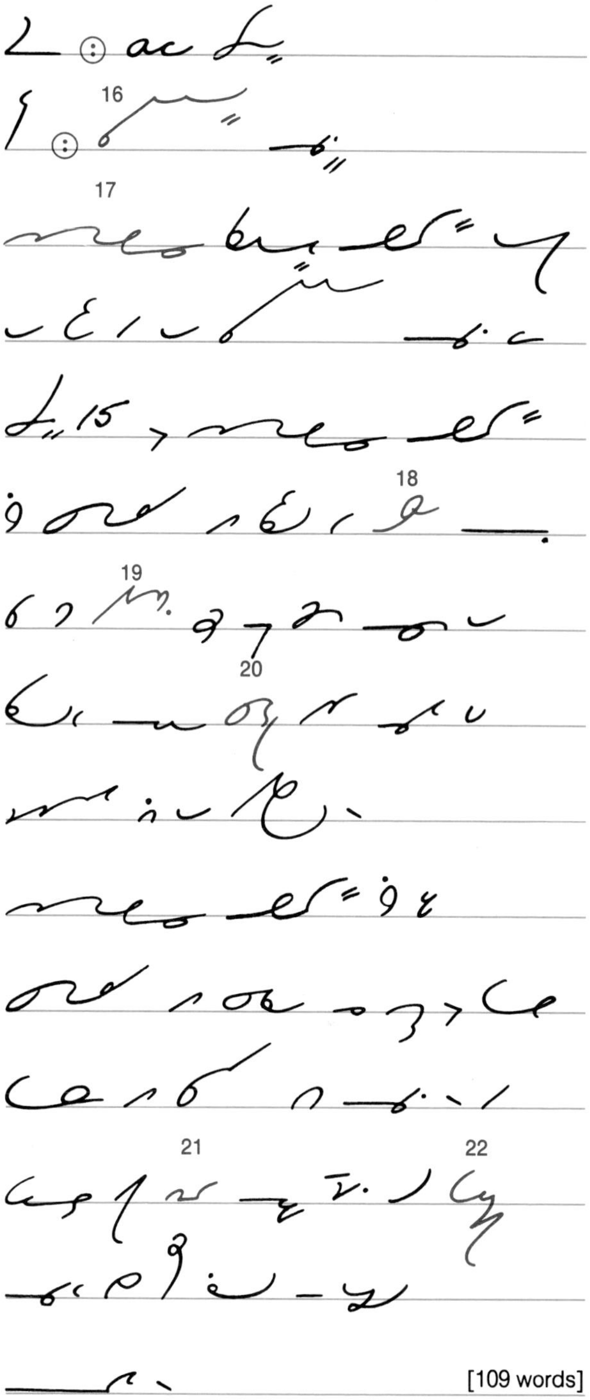

[109 words]

16 Editorial 17 Congressman 18 entire
19 discussing 20 accessible 21 one of the
22 profitable

IN LESSON 7

- Sound of *sh*
- Word endings *-tion*, *-sion*, *-tial*, *-cial*, *-cient*, *-ciency*, and *-ship*
- Brief forms and phrases
- Differentiating between *billed*, *build* and *assistance*, *assistants*

THEORY REVIEW

Write the following shorthand words until you can write them without difficulty.

Sound of Sh (Symbol ish ∕)

sure _____   assure _____   pleasure _____

pressure _____   brochure _____   issue _____

Word Endings -tion and -sion (Symbol ish ∕)

action _____   corporation _____   section _____

application _____   location _____   addition _____

collection _____   national _____   additional _____

operation _____   position _____   competition _____

cooperation _____   promotion _____   condition _____

commission
edition
invitation

estimation
quotation
reputation

stationery
occasion
permission

Word Endings -tial and -cial (Symbol ish /)

beneficial
especially
essential

financial
initial
official

partial
social
special

Word Endings -cient and -ciency (Symbols ish, t and ish, s, e / and ʃ)

efficient
efficiency

patient
proficient

proficiency
sufficient

Word Ending -ship (Disjoined ish /)

friendship
hardship

leadership
membership

partnership
relationship

Theory Practice

Read and write the following sentences and paragraph. For additional practice, dictate the sentences and paragraph to yourself, using the transcript.

7.1

1

2

3

4

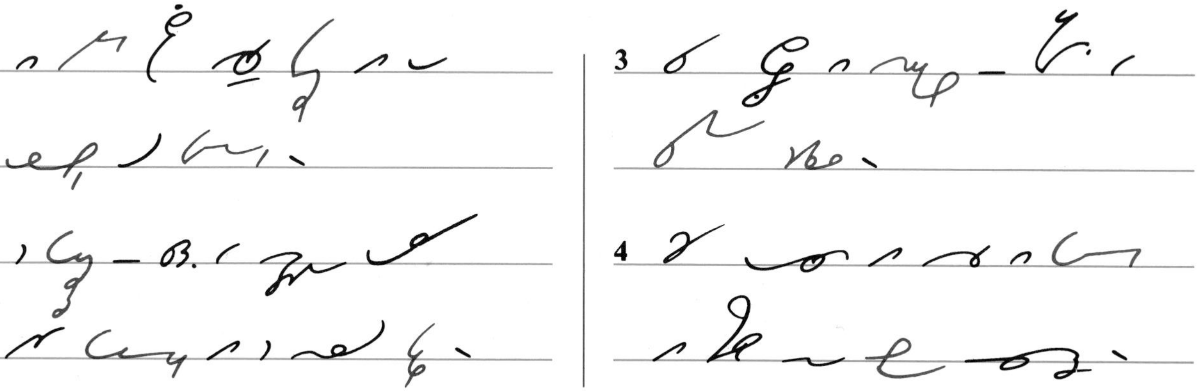

5 *[shorthand outlines]*

¶ **Textbook Publication**

[shorthand outlines]

[84 words]

BRIEF FORMS AND PHRASES

Write the following brief forms, derivatives, and phrases until you can write them without difficulty.

Brief Forms and Derivatives

over _____

overdue _____

overhead _____

part _____

partly _____

partner _____

department _____

particular _____

particularly _____

present _____

presently _____

represent _____

representative _____

privilege _____

privileged _____

probable _____

probably _____

product _____

production _____

program _____

programs _____

Brief-Form Phrases

there are _____

there is _____

there was _____

they are _____

they will _____

this is _____

this is the	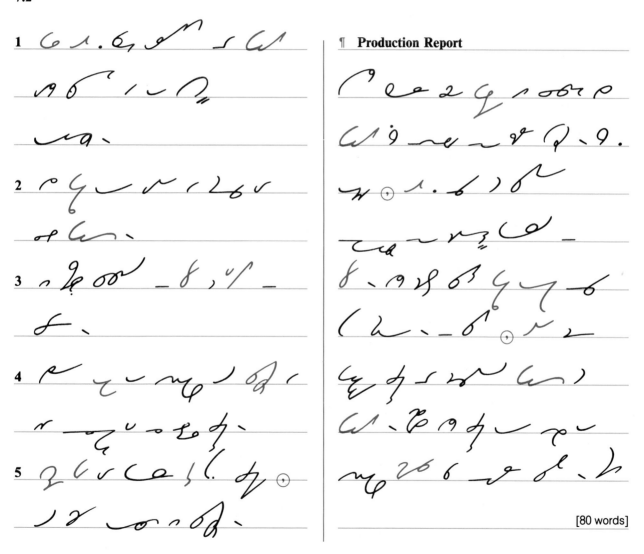	will be		with our	
this will		will not		with the	
which is		I will not be		with you, with your	

Brief-Form Practice

Read and write the following sentences and paragraph. For additional practice, dictate the sentences and paragraph to yourself, using the transcript.

7.2

¶ **Production Report**

[80 words]

Similar Words: billed, build

billed: charged
build: to construct

The James Manufacturing Company was *billed* for the month of April.

It is important to *build* a strong marketing plan.

Similar Words: assistance, assistants

assistance: help
assistants: those who help

Assistance will be needed to complete the report on time.

Our office hired several *assistants* for the summer months.

Electronic typewriters help to increase transcription efficiency because certain functions—such as centering—are automated.

Reading and Writing Practice

7.3 Job Offer

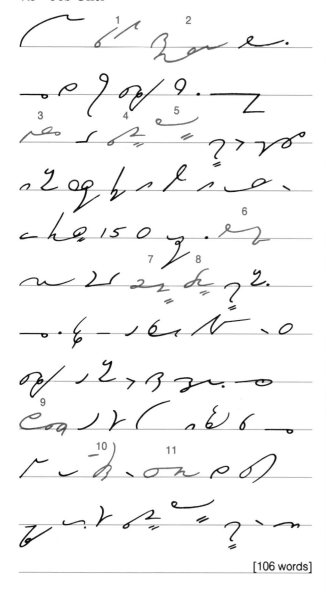

[106 words]

7.4 Membership in Association

[97 words]

7.5 Education Offer

---

1 Edwards   2 Thank you for your letter   3 trainee
4 Edison   5 Electric   6 telephone   7 Wilson
8 Power   9 application   10 interviews
11 I am sure

12 International   13 Perhaps   14 continue
15 knowledge

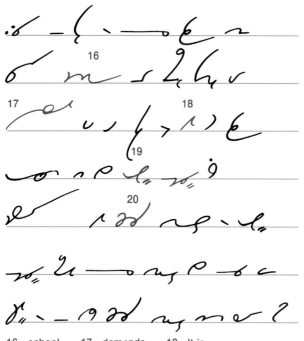

16 school   17 demands   18 It is
19 Reese Institute   20 weekend

21 semester

[108 words]

L E S S O N
8

IN LESSON 8

- Sounds of *oo*, *u*, and *ul*
- Word ending *-ulate*
- Omission of *e* from *oo*
- Sounds of *w*, *wh*, and *sw*
- Sound of *oo* for *w*
- Brief forms and phrases
- Differentiating between *stationary*, *stationery* and *lose*, *loose*, *loss*

THEORY REVIEW

Write the following shorthand words until you can write them without difficulty.

Sound of OO (Symbol oo ⌒)

do, due

reduce

fulfill

knew, new

who

look

lose, loose

whose

pull

move

book

put

noon

booklet

stood

produce

full

took

Sound of U (Symbol oo ⌐)

color _____   generous _____   none _____

cover _____   industry _____   number _____

does _____   just _____   trust _____

enough _____   must _____   us _____

Sound of Ul (Symbol oo ⌐)

adult _____   consultant _____   result _____

consult _____   insult _____   ultimate _____

Word Ending -ulate (Disjoined oo ⌐)

accumulate _____   formulate _____   congratulate _____

calculate _____   regulated _____   congratulations _____

calculator _____   tabulate _____   population _____

Omission of E from OO (Symbol oo ⌐)

community _____   discontinue _____   municipal _____

continue _____   manuscript _____   mutual _____

Sounds of W, Wh, and Sw (Symbol oo ⌐)

we _____   while _____   why _____

way _____   white _____   sweet _____

Sound of OO for W (Disjoined w dash —)

always _____   quit _____   quoted _____

qualify _____   quite _____   quotas _____

quickly _____   quote _____   twice _____

Theory Practice

Read and write the following sentences and paragraph. For additional practice, dictate the sentences and paragraph to yourself, using the transcript.

8.1

[Shorthand outlines — sentences 1 through 5 and paragraph]

1 [shorthand] 25,

2 [shorthand]

3 [shorthand] 22, 26

4 [shorthand]

5 [shorthand]

¶ **Promotion**

[shorthand paragraph]

[60 words]

Write the following brief forms, derivatives, and phrases until you can write them without difficulty.

Brief Forms and Derivatives

progress		recognize	
property		recognition	
public		recommend	
publish, publication		recommendations	
quantity		regard	
quantities		regardless	
question		regular	
questioned		regularly	
questionnaire		reluctant, reluctance	

Brief-Form Phrases

you are	you can be	you will have
you are not	you cannot	you will not be
you can	you will be	you would be

Brief-Form Practice

Read and write the following sentences and paragraph. For additional practice, dictate the sentences and paragraph to yourself, using the transcript.

8.2

3 4 5

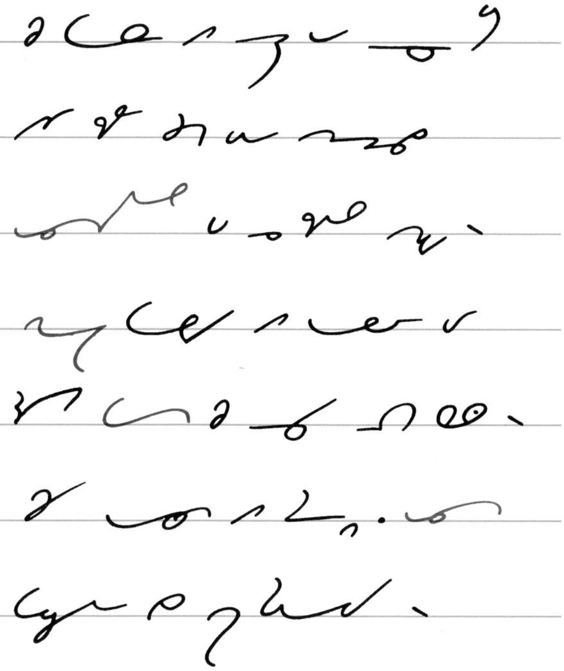

¶ Speech

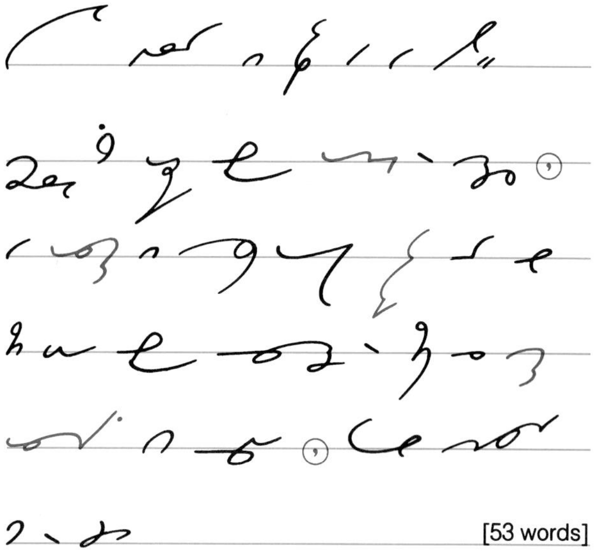

[53 words]

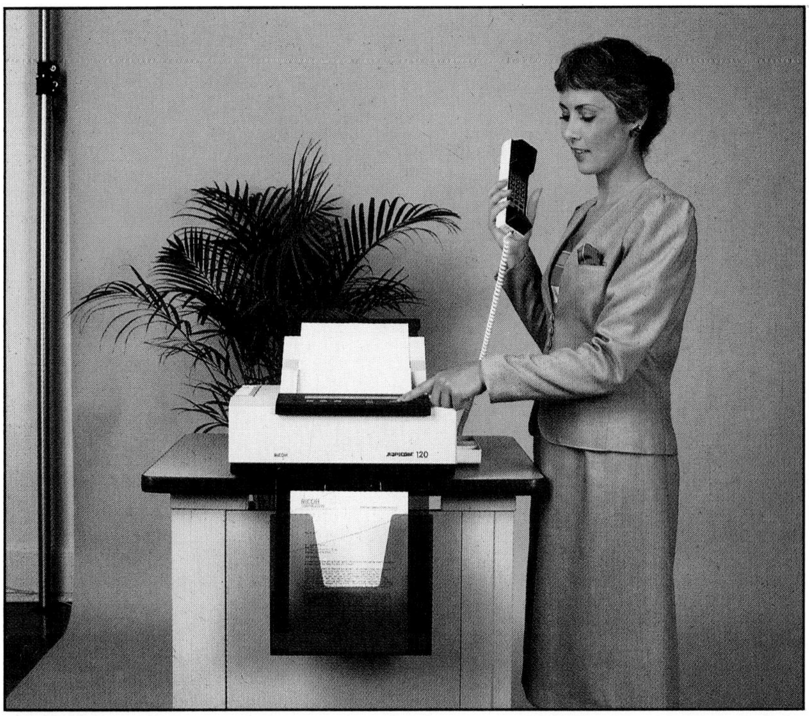

Secretaries use facsimile machines regularly to make copies of contracts, drawings, charts, and photographs.

Communication Skill Builder

Similar Words: stationary, stationery

stationary: fixed; not movable

stationery: writing materials

(shorthand)

The publishing procedures have been *stationary* for years.

(shorthand)

Please list our telephone number on our *stationery*.

Similar Words: lose, loose, loss

lose: (v.) to be deprived of

loose: (adj.) not fastened

loss: (n.) that which one is deprived of

(shorthand)

We did not *lose* the account.

(shorthand)

It is possible that the binder is *loose*.

(shorthand)

The *loss* that we incurred is not known.

Reading and Writing Practice

8.3   Editorial Speech

(shorthand)

1 Thank you for

(shorthand)

2 busy   3 University

[78 words]

[76 words]

8.4 Assembly Plant Project

8.5 Congratulatory Letter

[77 words]

4 policy 5 for the 6 appreciation
7 Thank you for the 8 assembly 9 Birmingham
10 specifications

11 preparation 12 entertaining

U N I T

III

LESSON

IN LESSON 9

- Word beginnings *un-*, *en-*, *em-*, and *im-*
- Sounds of *ng* and *nk*
- Word beginnings *trans-*, *enter-*, and *inter-*
- Word endings *-hood* and *-ward*
- Brief forms and phrases
- Differentiating between *complement*, *compliment* and *principal*, *principle*

THEORY REVIEW

Write the following shorthand words until you can write them without difficulty.

Word Beginning Un- (Symbol n ⌒)

uncertain _____   unjust _____   until _____

unfair _____   unless _____   unable ■ _____

unlisted _____   unpaid _____   unsatisfactory _____

- The symbols *oo, n* are used for *un* because a vowel follows.

Word Beginning En- (Symbol n ⌣)

encourage _____   engage _____   enjoyable _____

endeavor _____   enjoy _____   enlarge _____

Word Beginnings Em- and Im- (Symbol m ——)

embarrass _____

emphasis _____

emphasize _____

employ _____

employee _____

employees _____

employer _____

impartial _____

import _____

impossible _____

impress _____

improve _____

Sound of NG (Symbol n at angle ⌣)

along _____

belong _____

bring _____

bringing _____

length _____

long _____

longer _____

single _____

strength _____

strong _____

wrong _____

young _____

Sound of NK (Symbol m at angle ⌣)

anxious _____

bank _____

banquet _____

blank _____

frank _____

rank _____

Word Beginning Trans- (Disjoined t ╱)

transact _____

transaction _____

transcribe _____

transcript _____

transfer _____

transferred _____

translate _____

transmit _____

transportation _____

Word Beginnings Enter- and Inter- (Disjoined n ‗)

enter _____

entered _____

enterprise _____

entertain _____

entrance _____

interest _____

interested _____

interfere _____

international _____

interpret _____

interrupt _____

interval _____

interview _____

introduce _____

introduction _____

Word Ending -hood (Disjoined d )

childhood 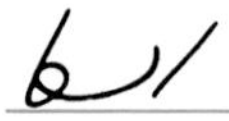 likelihood 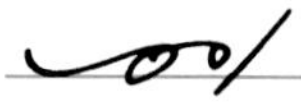 neighborhood 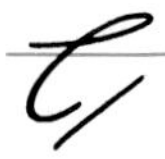

Word Ending -ward (Disjoined d )

backward 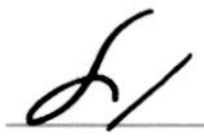 reward 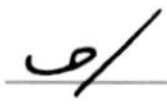 forwarded 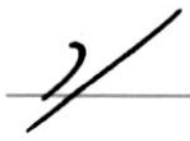

Theory Practice

Read and write the following sentences and paragraph. For additional practice, dictate the sentences and paragraph to yourself, using the transcript.

9.1

1
2
3
4
5

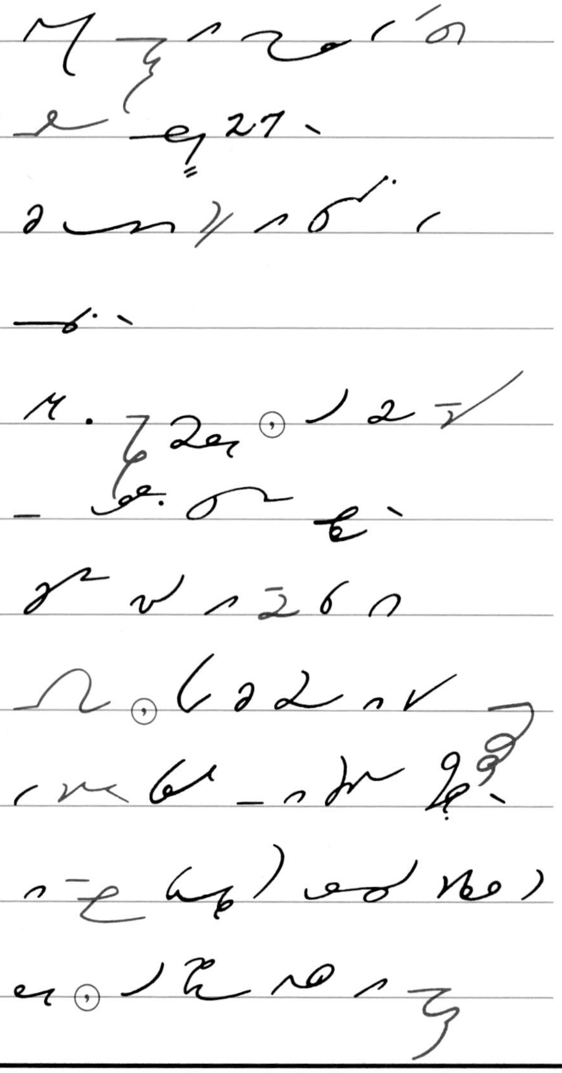

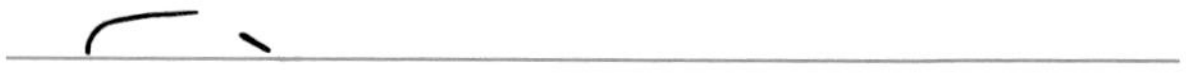

¶ **Employee Promotions**

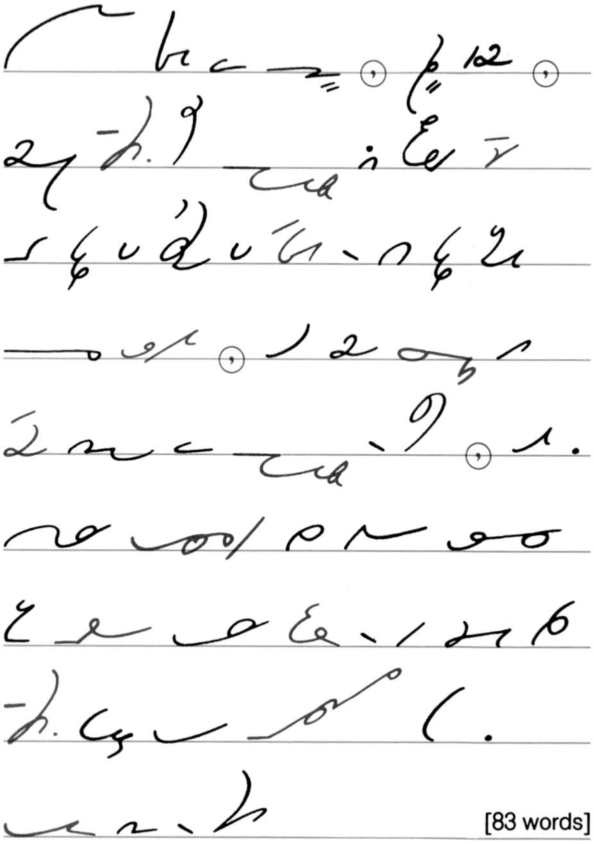

[83 words]

When the manager is unable to see an unexpected visitor, the secretary should ask the visitor for enough information to arrange a future appointment.

BRIEF FORMS AND PHRASES

Write the following brief forms, derivatives, and phrases until you can write them without difficulty.

Brief Forms and Derivatives

request _____

responsible _____

send _____

satisfy, satisfactory _____

several _____

short _____

should _____

significant, significance _____

significantly _____

soon _____

sooner _____

speak _____

speaker _____

state _____

stated _____

statement _____

Brief-Form Phrases

you would not _____

you would not be _____

one of the _____

one of them _____

one of our _____

some of the _____

some of them _____

some of our _____

I hope _____

I hope that *[shorthand]*   we hope that the *[shorthand]*   as soon as possible *[shorthand]*

I hope that the *[shorthand]*   we hope you will *[shorthand]*   of course *[shorthand]*

we hope *[shorthand]*   as soon as *[shorthand]*   to us *[shorthand]*

Brief-Form Practice

Read and write the following sentences and paragraph. For additional practice, dictate the sentences and paragraph to yourself, using the transcript.

9.2

1 *[shorthand outlines]*

2 *[shorthand outlines]*

3 *[shorthand outlines]*

4 *[shorthand outlines]*

5 *[shorthand outlines]*

¶ **Statement**

[shorthand outlines]

[62 words]

Communication Skill Builder

Similar Words: complement, compliment

complement: something that completes

compliment: (n.) praise; (v.) to comment favorably

This scarf will *complement* your outfit.

We received a *compliment* from our manager this morning.

Similar Words: principal, principle

principal: (adj.) chief; (n.) sum of money that earns interest; chief official of a school

principle: a rule or fundamental belief

The *principal* reason for the change was not given.

The *principal* on the loan is $500.

The *principal* of the high school was appointed in August.

There is not one *principle* we did not follow.

9.3 Approval of Credit Application

(shorthand outlines)

[75 words]

9.4 Billing Error

(shorthand outlines)

[127 words]

1 You will be	2 to know	3 We hope that
4 frequently	5 purchases	6 within
7 next time	8 personally	9 oversight

10 exception	11 losing	12 delivered
13 adjustment	14 payment	

LESSON 10

IN LESSON 10

- Sounds of *short i* and *ye*
- Sounds of *long i*, *iety*, and *itis*
- Sounds of *o*, *aw*, and *al*
- Sound of *u*
- Word ending *-ology*
- Quantities and amounts
- Brief forms and phrases
- Differentiating between *than*, *then* and *accept*, *except*

THEORY REVIEW

Write the following shorthand words until you can write them without difficulty.

Sound of Short I (Symbol e ᴏ)

if _____   bill _____   city _____

service _____   did _____   give _____

Sound of Ye (Symbol e ᴏ)

year _____   yet _____   yield _____

Sounds of Long I, Iety, Itis (Symbol i ⊘)

drive	night	variety
hire	rely	appendicitis
light	society	tonsillitis

Sounds of O, Aw, Al (Symbol o ∪)

know	offer	author
own	policy	almost
vote	stock	already
catalog	bought	also
copy	all	although
cooperate	call	alter

Sound of U (Blend of e and oo ℰ)

few	unique	use
refuse	unit	used
review	unite	uses

Word Ending -ology (Symbols o, l ∪)

apology	biology	psychology
apologize	physiology	technology

Quantities and Amounts

$5	$800,000	200
$250	$2 million	8,000
$600	$5 billion	100,000
$3,000	$2.50	5 million

10 a.m. _10 ⊙_   6 pounds _6_   a million _._

5 feet _5,_   a dollar _:/_   7 percent _7,_

Theory Practice

Read and write the following sentences and paragraph. For additional practice, dictate the sentences and paragraph to yourself, using the transcript.

10.1

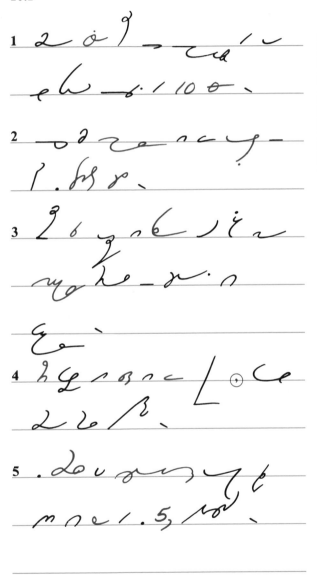

¶ **Refund Policies**

[98 words]

Write the following brief forms, derivatives, and phrases until you can write them without difficulty.

Brief Forms and Derivatives

statistic	successfully	thanking
statistical	suggest	thanks
street	suggestion	that
subject	than	the
success	thank	there, their

Brief-Form Phrases

to be	as you, as your
to have	as you know
to the	do not
thank you for	do you
thank you for the	do you know
thank you for your letter	if you are
as the	I may have

Brief-Form Practice

Read and write the following sentences and paragraph. For additional practice, dictate the sentences and paragraph to yourself, using the transcript.

10.2

1 [shorthand outlines]

2 [shorthand outlines]

3 [shorthand outlines]

4 [shorthand outlines]

5 [shorthand outlines]

¶ **Spring Conference**

[shorthand outlines]

[shorthand outlines]

[84 words]

Communication Skill Builder

Similar Words: than, then

than: conjunction of comparison
then: at that time

[shorthand outlines]

It is more important to complete the report *than* to type the letter.

[shorthand outlines]

Type the letter quickly; *then* send it express mail.

Similar Words: accept, except

accept: to agree to; to receive

except: (prep.) other than; excluding

[shorthand]

The judge did not *accept* the statement of the officer.

[shorthand]

We have a conference every month *except* March.

Reading and Writing Practice

10.3 Employment Interview

[shorthand outlines]

[shorthand] [96 words]

10.4 Moving Arrangements

[shorthand outlines]

1 Parker   2 interviews   3 of our   4 executives
5 knowledge   6 I think

7 director   8 recommending   9 Daily Tribune
10 unique

(shorthand outlines)

555-1796 [131 words]

10.5 Report Information

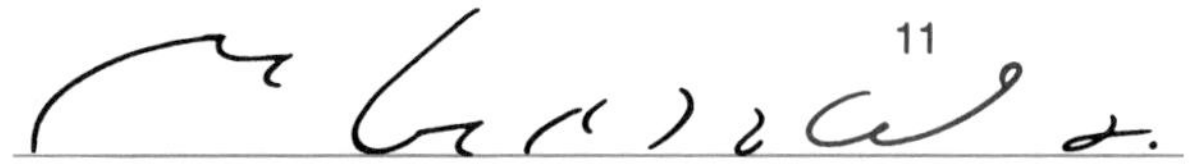

(shorthand outlines)

11 promptly

(shorthand outlines)

15

[76 words]

12 requested

IN LESSON 11

- Sounds of *ern*, *erm*, and *ort*
- Word endings *-quire*, *-titute*, and *-titude*
- Word endings *-tribute* and *-quent*
- Word ending *-ical*
- Cities
- Brief forms and phrases
- Transcription of articles *a* and *an*

THEORY REVIEW

Write the following shorthand words until you can write them without difficulty.

Sound of Ern (Omit r)

turn	eastern	attorney
turned	western	pattern
return	southern	alternate
returned	northern	modern

Sound of Erm (Omit r)

term	terminate	determine

Sound of Ort (Omit r)

port _____ reports _____ resort _____

portable _____ support _____ court _____

airport _____ sort _____ quart _____

report _____ assort _____ quarterly _____

Word Ending -quire (Symbols k, i ⟋)

acquire _____ inquired _____ require _____

acquired _____ inquires _____ requires _____

inquire _____ inquiry _____ requirement _____

Word Endings -titute and -titude (Symbols t, e, t ⟋)

constitute _____ institution _____ substituted _____

constitution _____ substitute _____ aptitude _____

institute _____ substitution _____ attitude _____

Word Ending -tribute (Symbols t, r, e, b ⟋)

tribute _____ contributed _____ distribute _____

attribute _____ contribution _____ distributed _____

contribute _____ contributor _____ distribution _____

Word Ending -quent (Symbol k ⌒)

consequent _____ eloquent _____ frequently _____

consequently _____ frequent _____ subsequent _____

Word Ending -ical (Disjoined k ⌒)

article _[shorthand]_   logical _[shorthand]_   practical _[shorthand]_

identical _[shorthand]_   particle _[shorthand]_   technical _[shorthand]_

Cities

Washington _[shorthand]_   Jacksonville _[shorthand]_   Los Angeles _[shorthand]_

Lexington _[shorthand]_   Pittsburgh _[shorthand]_   San Francisco _[shorthand]_

Framingham _[shorthand]_   Denver _[shorthand]_   Atlanta _[shorthand]_

Theory Practice

Read and write the following sentences and paragraph. For additional practice, dictate the sentences and paragraph to yourself, using the transcript.

11.1

1 _[shorthand]_

2 _[shorthand]_

3 _[shorthand]_

4 _[shorthand]_

5 _[shorthand]_

¶ **Charity Donations**

[shorthand]

[shorthand text]

[110 words]

Write the following brief forms, derivatives, and phrases until you can
write them without difficulty.

Brief Forms and Derivatives

what	willingness	worker
when	wish	world
whenever	wished	worth
where	with	would
which	without	yesterday
will, well	work	you, your

Brief-Form Phrases

we are	we cannot be	we will not
we can	we do	we will not be
we can be	we have	we will not have
we can have	we will	we would
we cannot	we will be	we would be

we would not [shorthand outline]   we would not be [shorthand outline]   with you [shorthand outline]

Brief-Form Practice

Read and write the following sentences and paragraph. For additional practice, dictate the sentences and paragraph to yourself, using the transcript.

11.2

1 [shorthand outlines]

2 [shorthand outlines]

3 [shorthand outlines]

4 [shorthand outlines]

5 [shorthand outlines]

55 [shorthand outlines]

¶ **Plant Closing**

[shorthand outlines]

[77 words]

Transcription of Articles A and An

The shorthand outline for *a* and *an* is the *dot*. Since the outlines are the same, it is important to choose the correct article when transcribing.

In choosing *a* or *an*, consider the sound (not the spelling) of the following word.

Use the article *a* before all consonant sounds, including *sounded h*, *long u*, and *o* with the sound of *w*.

. ⟋ a day　　. ⟋ a unit

. ⟍ a home　　. ⟍ a 1-hour ride

Use *an* before all vowel sounds except *long u* and before words beginning with *silent h*.

. ⟋ an account　　. ⟋ an upward move

. ⟋ an estate　　. ⟍ an hour

. ⟋ an inquiry　　. ⟍ an 8-hour day

. ⟋ an outcome　　. ⟍ an extra ■

■ *Ex* is pronounced *x*.

Making notes in files is one of the many responsibilities of an administrative assistant.

Reading and Writing Practice

11.3 Sales Training Videotapes

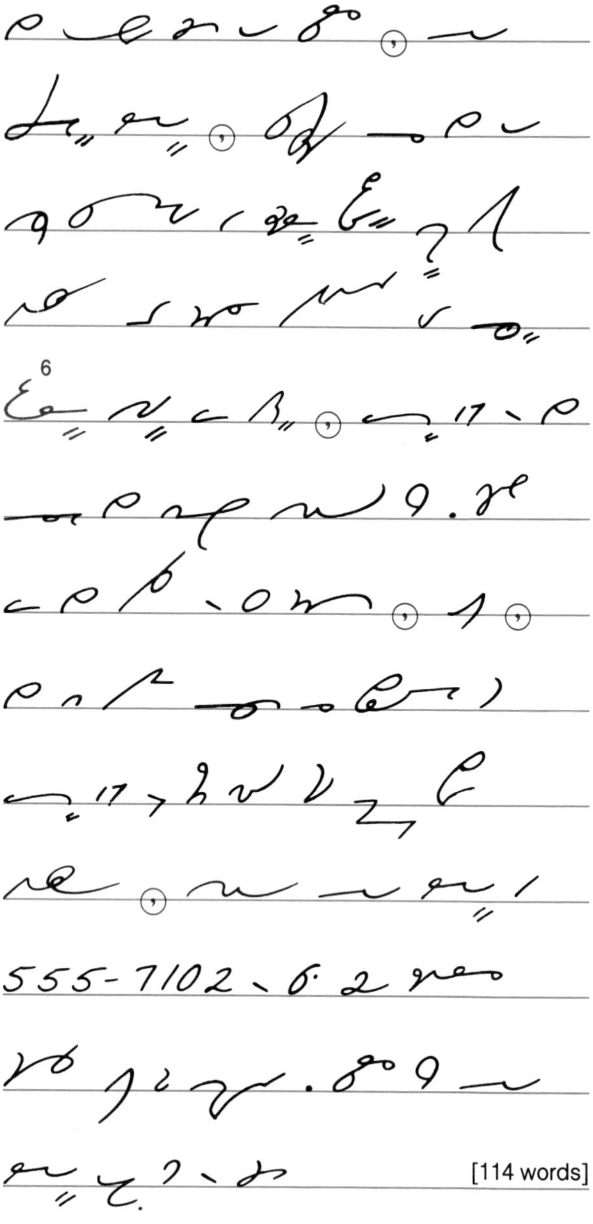

(shorthand outlines)

[103 words]

(shorthand outlines)

[114 words]

11.4 Court Case

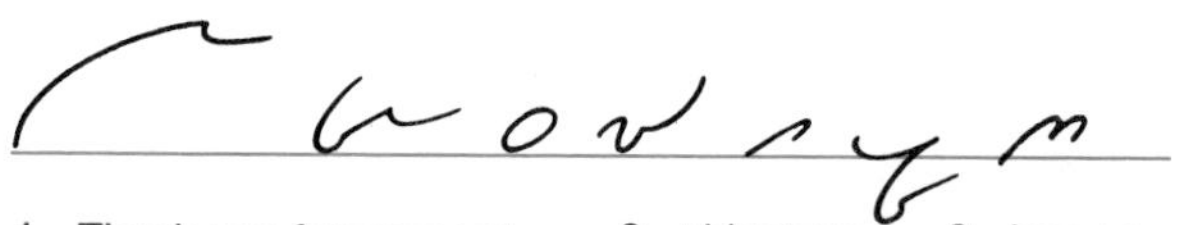

(shorthand outline)

1 Thank you for your letter   2 videotape   3 lawyer
4 collecting   5 misplaced

11.5 Manuscript Publication

(shorthand outline)

6 Supreme

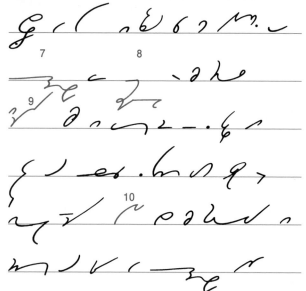

7 manuscript   8 investments   9 understand
10 to know

11 National   12 Publishing   13 editor   14 will
be   15 market

[100 words]

IN LESSON 12

- Vowels coming together: *long i and vowel, ea, ow,* and *oi*
- Word beginnings *con-* and *com-*
- Brief forms and phrases
- Differentiating between *council*, *counsel* and *affect*, *effect*

THEORY REVIEW (VOWELS COMING TOGETHER)

Write the following shorthand words until you can write them without difficulty.

Symbol for Long I and Vowel (Symbol i with e inside ⊘)

client _____   science _____   reliance _____

prior _____   trial _____   appliance _____

quiet _____   via _____   riot _____

Sound of Ea (Symbol a with dot inside ⊘)

appreciate _____   brilliant _____   depreciate _____

area _____   create _____   negotiate _____

associate _____   piano _____   negotiated _____

associates _____   pianist _____   Peoria _____

Sound of Ow (Symbols a, oo ℴ)

now

how

count

account

accountant

allow

amount

announce

around

council, counsel

doubt

doubtful

found

proud

south

Sound of Oi (Symbols o, e ℓ)

annoy

avoid

choice

join

joint, joined

royal

lawyer

point

appoint

appointment

Boyd

invoice

Word Beginning Con- (Symbol k ⌢)

concern

conference

confirm

confuse

consider

considerable

consist

consumer

contract

control

convince

connect ■

Word Beginning Com- (Symbol k ⌢)

accommodate

combine

comment

common

■ Transcription Alert.

compare

compete

complete

computer

committee ■

complex

complain

accomplish

Theory Practice

Read and write the following sentences and paragraph. For additional practice, dictate the sentences and paragraph to yourself, using the transcript.

12.1

1 [shorthand outlines]

2 [shorthand outlines]

3 [shorthand outlines]

4 [shorthand outlines]

5 [shorthand outlines]

¶ **Computers**

[shorthand outlines]

[91 words]

BRIEF FORMS AND PHRASES

Write the following brief forms, derivatives, and phrases until you write them without difficulty.

Brief Forms and Derivatives

them _____

themselves _____

they _____

thing, think _____

thinking _____

things, thinks _____

this _____

throughout _____

time _____

under _____

underneath _____

usual _____

usually _____

value _____

valuable _____

very _____

was _____

were _____

Brief-Form Phrases

we may have _____

you may have _____

I may be _____

you may be _____

I might have _____

I might be _____

you might be _____

on our _____

on the _____

on this _____

to the _____

to you, to your _____

Brief-Form Practice

Read and write the following sentences and paragraph. For additional practice, dictate the sentences and paragraph to yourself, using the transcript.

12.2

1 _____

2 _____

3 _____

(shorthand outlines)

4 *(shorthand outlines)*

5 *(shorthand outlines)*

¶ **Life Insurance Policy**

[79 words]

(shorthand outline)

Communication Skill Builder

Similar Words: council, counsel

council: (n.) an assembly
counsel: (n.): an attorney; advice; (v.) to give advice

(shorthand outline)

The members of the city *council* voted on the merger.

(shorthand outline)

It is necessary to check with our corporate *counsel*.

[shorthand outline]

The teacher did not *counsel* the foreign students.

Similar Words: affect, effect

affect: (v.) to influence; to change

effect: (n.) result; impression

[shorthand outline]

We need to *affect* policy decisions.

[shorthand outline]

The *effect* of the advertisement is not known.

To assist them in developing major reports, managers often ask their secretaries to do research. Shorthand makes this job easier and more efficient.

12.3 Personal Note

(shorthand outlines)

[91 words]

12.4 Piano Recital

(shorthand outlines)

[101 words]

12.5 Newspaper Advertisement

(shorthand outlines)

1 to know   2 application   3 aptitude
4 successfully   5 collect   6 Peoria   7 Theater

8 accomplished   9 pianist   10 newspaper
11 pleasure

(shorthand outlines)

12 unusual   13 We hope that the

14 encourage

[97 words]

U N I T

IV

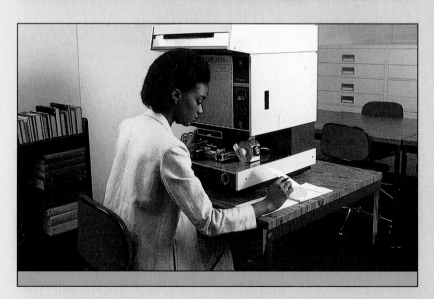

LESSON
13

IN LESSON 13

- ■ **Dictation speed building**
- ■ **Transcription skill development**
- ■ **Series comma**

DICTATION SPEED BUILDING

The preview words below appear in the speed dictation practice which
follows. Practice writing these words using the shorthand outlines.
Then, using the key below, dictate the words to yourself.

Dictation Preview Words

Key: Grant, recruiting, donors, blood, bank, yesterday, collected,
400 units, performance, contributions, thank you for your,
for the,

Speed Dictation Practice

13.1 Blood Drive

[64 words]

Transcribe the following words and phrases, noting spelling and capitalization. Then transcribe the sentences and transcription letter in unarranged format.

Transcription Preview Words
13.2

Transcription Warmup
13.3

Transcription Practice

13.4 Personnel Problem

[shorthand notation]

[92 words]

Series Comma

A series consists of three or more items in sequence. The items may be words, phrases, or clauses, and the last item is preceded by *and*, *or*, or *nor*. A comma is placed before the words *and*, *or*, or *nor* as well as between the other items.

[shorthand notation]

Our meetings will be held on November 6, December 7, *and* January 10.

[shorthand notation]

James did not like the red, blue, *or* green sweater.

It is easy to double-check the content while proofreading when shorthand is the input medium—the notes are right at hand.

13.5 "To Do" List for the Boss

[shorthand outlines]

[45 words]

13.6 Insurance Questions

[shorthand outlines]

1 insurance   2 policy   3 borrowing   4 exact
5 decision

[shorthand outline]

[98 words]

13.7 Publication Correction

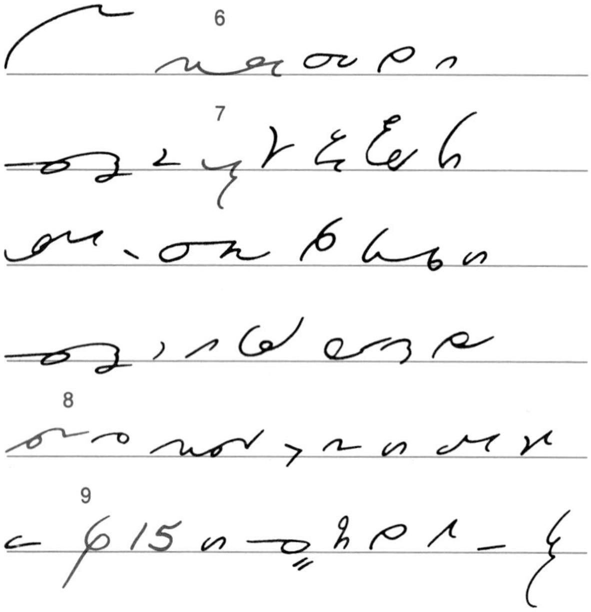

[shorthand outlines]

6 Collins   7 responsible   8 technically
9 page 15

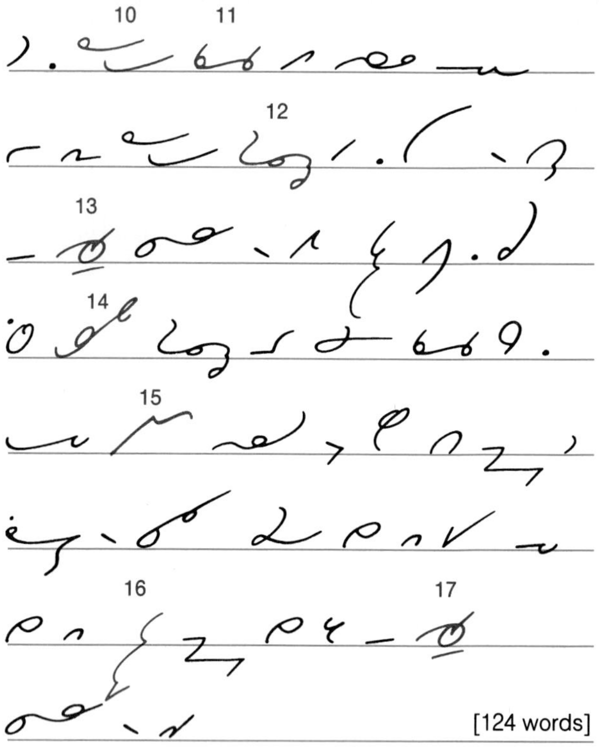

[shorthand outlines]

[124 words]

10 electrical   11 circuit   12 frequency   13 quite
14 radio   15 direct   16 published   17 quite

LESSON 14

IN LESSON 14

- Dictation speed building
- Transcription skill development
- Transcription of numbers

DICTATION SPEED BUILDING

The preview words below appear in the speed dictation practice which follows. Practice writing these words using the shorthand outlines. Then, using the key below, dictate the words to yourself.

Dictation Preview Words

Key: Smith, music, lovers, Connelley, compact, disc, market, dollars, ordinary, that the, do not, you would have, you will be glad

Speed Dictation Practice

14.1 Sales Letter

[69 words]

TRANSCRIPTION SKILL DEVELOPMENT

Transcribe the following words and phrases, noting spelling and capitalization. Then transcribe the sentences and transcription letter in unarranged format.

Transcription Preview Words
14.2

Transcription Warmup
14.3

Transcription Practice

14.4 Career Move

[94 words]

Transcription of Numbers

The basic number rule specifies that the numbers from one through ten are to be spelled out, while the numbers higher than ten are to be written in figures.

When transcribing *thousands*, use comma and ciphers to express *thousand*.

When transcribing *million* and *billion*, replace the commas and ciphers with the word *million* or *billion*.

He will not be available for *two* days.

Our course lasts for *18* weeks.

Did you receive *5,000* booklets?

Over *2 million* people visited our state capital.

14.5 Purchase Information

[82 words]

14.6 Catalogs

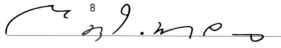

[88 words]

1 Thank you for your order   2 materials
3 promptly   4 factory   5 represents
6 purchase   7 representative   8 Weeks

9 operation   10 branch   11 catalog   12 75
13 printing   14 increasing   15 microfilm
16 published

IN LESSON 15

- Dictation speed building
- Transcription skill development
- *As*, *if*, and *when* clauses

DICTATION SPEED BUILDING

The preview words below appear in the speed dictation practice which follows. Practice writing these words using the shorthand outlines. Then, using the key below, dictate the words to yourself.

Dictation Preview Words

[shorthand outlines]

Key: Harris, pleasure, opportunity, discuss, future, investment, prepared, shortly, proposal, detail, to have, with you, thank you for, I am, will be

Speed Dictation Practice

15.1 Investment Program

[shorthand outlines]

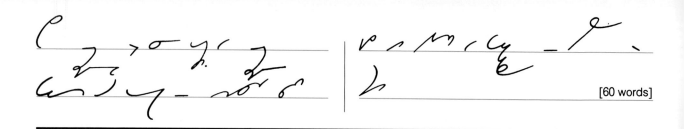

[60 words]

TRANSCRIPTION SKILL DEVELOPMENT

Transcribe the following words and phrases, noting spelling and capitalization. Then transcribe the sentences and transcription letter in unarranged format.

Transcription Preview Words
15.2

Transcription Warmup
15.3

1

2

3

4

5

Transcription Practice

15.4 Publication Material

[Shorthand notation]

[96 words]

As, If, When Clauses

A dependent clause introduced by *as*, *if*, or *when* and followed by a main clause is separated from the main clause with a comma.

[Shorthand notation with "as" and comma marked]

As I told you yesterday, I will not attend the meeting.

[Shorthand notation with "if" and comma marked]

If you would like to come to the party, please let me know.

[Shorthand notation with "when" and comma marked]

When you arrive in Atlanta, please call me.

Office workers find shorthand a valuable tool for recording information.

Dictation and Transcription Practice

15.5 Instructions

[shorthand notation] [36 words]

15.6 Response to Request

[shorthand notation]

1 Santos   2 congratulations   3 exciting

[shorthand notation] [85 words]

4 award   5 excellent   6 typical   7 quality

15.7 Speaker Request

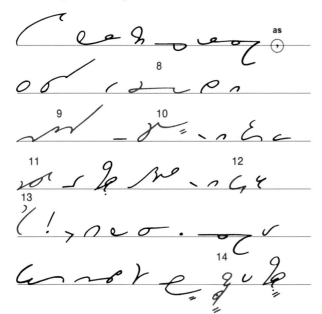

8 seminar   9 conducted   10 Seattle
11 statistics   12 presentation   13 superb
14 Association

15 convention   16 expenses   17 additional

[123 words]

IN LESSON 16

- Dictation speed building
- Transcription skill development
- Number as first word of sentence

DICTATION SPEED BUILDING

The preview words below appear in the speed dictation practice which follows. Practice writing these words using the shorthand outlines. Then, using the key below, dictate the words to yourself.

Dictation Preview Words

Key: Goldman, immediate, service, shipment, 1,500, envelopes, purchase, inconvenience, necessary, thank you for the, to you, I am, to me, it is

Speed Dictation Practice

16.1 Purchase Order

(shorthand outlines)

[90 words]

TRANSCRIPTION SKILL DEVELOPMENT

Transcribe the following words d phrases, noting spelling and capitalization. Then transcribe the sentences and transcription letter in unarranged format. Provide all necessary punctuation.

Transcription Preview Words
16.2

(shorthand outlines)

Transcription Warmup
16.3

1 *(shorthand outline)*

2 *(shorthand outline)*

3 *(shorthand outline)*

4 *(shorthand outline)*

5 *(shorthand outline)*

Transcription Practice

16.4 Campus Information

(shorthand outlines)

[74 words]

Number as First Word of Sentence

Spell out a number that begins a sentence, as well as any related numbers that appear in the sentence.

(shorthand outline)

Five years have passed since we signed the contract.

(shorthand outline)

Sixteen men and *twenty* women have signed up for the conference.

(shorthand outline)

Forty people will attend the class.

Dictation and Transcription Practice

16.5 Instructions

[shorthand]

[38 words]

16.6 Employee Vacations

[shorthand]

[80 words]

16.7 Banking Services

[shorthand]

[102 words]

1 quotas 2 Gleason 3 employees
4 vacations 5 to do so 6 avoid

7 Solomon 8 Southern 9 Atlanta
10 executive 11 profitable 12 provides
13 banking 14 account

UNIT

V

LESSON

IN LESSON 17

- Dictation speed building
- Transcription skill development
- Apposition comma

DICTATION SPEED BUILDING

The preview words below appear in the speed dictation practice which follows. Practice writing these words using the shorthand outlines. Then, using the key below, dictate the words to yourself.

Dictation Preview Words

Key: Hayes, government, benefits, directly, deposited, stolen, mislaid, neighborhood, short, authorizing, if you, you can have, you will, you are

Speed Dictation Practice

17.1 Direct Deposit

(shorthand outlines)

ser **ser**

when

[85 words]

TRANSCRIPTION SKILL DEVELOPMENT

Transcribe the following words and phrases, noting spelling and capitalization. Then transcribe the sentences and transcription letter in unarranged format.

Transcription Preview Words
17.2

(shorthand outlines)

Transcription Warmup
17.3

1 *(shorthand outline)*

2 *(shorthand outline)*

3 *(shorthand outline)*

4 *(shorthand outline)*

5 *(shorthand outline)*

Transcription Practice

17.4 Energy Conservation

[Shorthand content]

[87 words]

Apposition Comma

The appositive is a word or a group of words that provides additional information about a preceding word or phrase. The appositive is indicated by commas.

[Shorthand content]

The conference date has been set for Wednesday, *April 2.*

[Shorthand content]

Larry Smith, *treasurer*, will now give his report.

[Shorthand content]

I would like would like for you to meet the vice president, *Nancy Carlson*.

17.5 "To Do" List

[shorthand notation]

[40 words]

17.6 Home Building

[shorthand notation]

[74 words]

17.7 Grand Opening

[shorthand notation]

[88 words]

1 Roman	2 promised	3 discussed
4 completion	5 easily	6 You will be	7 finish

8 If you have	9 Monday	10 May 5
11 facilities	12 checking	13 We will be glad

LESSON

18

IN LESSON 18

- Dictation speed building
- Transcription skill development
- Mixed numbers

DICTATION SPEED BUILDING

The preview words below appear in the speed dictation practice which follows. Practice writing these words using the shorthand outlines. Then, using the key below, dictate the words to yourself.

Dictation Preview Words

[shorthand outlines]

Key: employed, students, secretaries, organization, highly, performance, complete, training, school, joining, interview, we have, we are, if you have, might be

Speed Dictation Practice

18.1 Job Placement

[shorthand outlines]

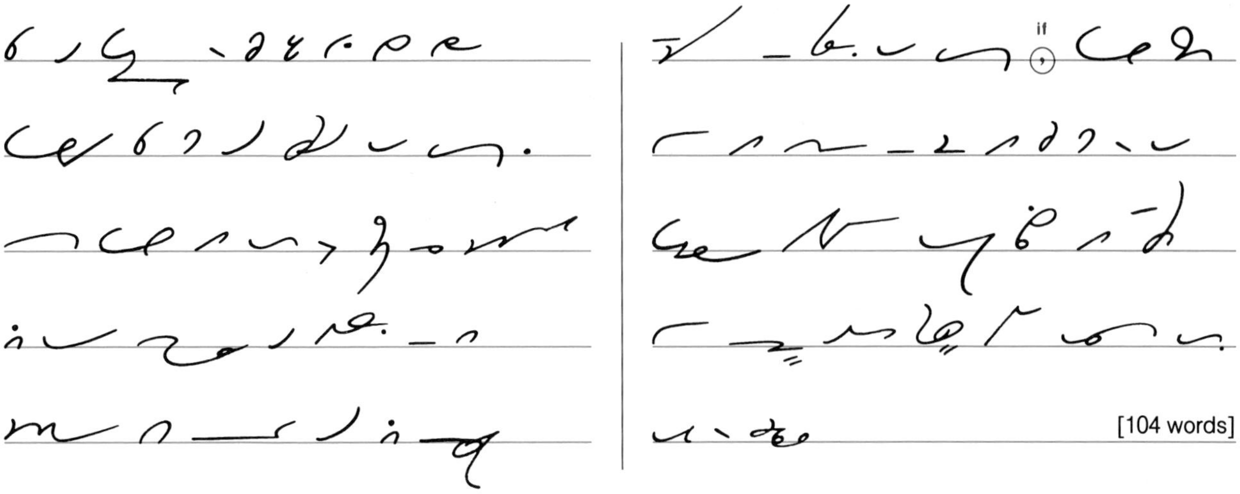

[104 words]

TRANSCRIPTION SKILL DEVELOPMENT

Transcribe the following words and phrases, noting spelling and capitalization. Then transcribe the sentences and transcription letter in unarranged format.

Transcription Preview Words

18.2

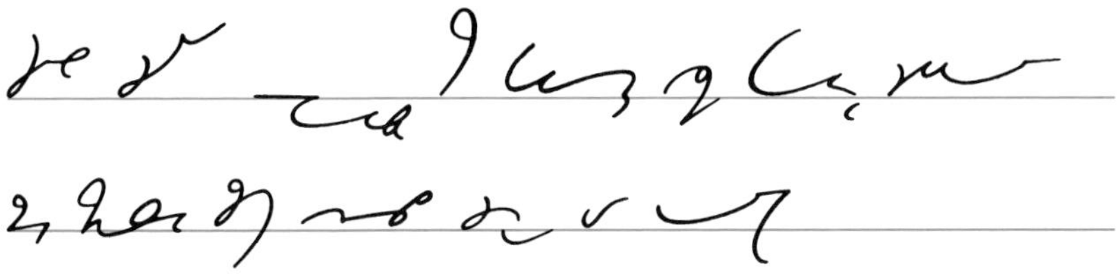

Transcription Warmup

18.3

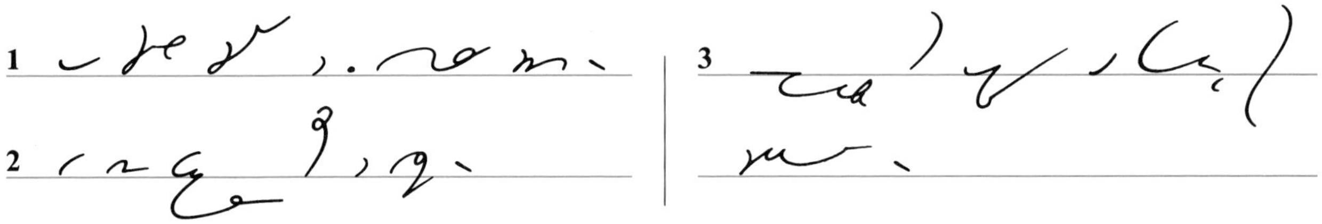

4 [shorthand]

5 [shorthand]

Transcription Practice

18.4 Fitness Center

[shorthand outline] 15 [shorthand] 19-- [shorthand]

[shorthand outlines]

[shorthand outlines]

[shorthand outlines]

[shorthand outlines]

[shorthand outlines]

[shorthand outlines]

[shorthand outlines]

[shorthand outlines]

[shorthand outlines]

[shorthand outlines]

[109 words]

Mixed Numbers

The numbers one through ten are expressed in figures if the sentence also contains numbers higher than ten describing the same kind of data. It is necessary to look at the data carefully to determine whether items are similar. For example, *boys* and *girls* would be considered the same kind of data as would *pens* and *paperclips*. *Telephones* and *delivery trucks* would not be considered the same kind of data.

[shorthand] 5 [shorthand] 12 [shorthand]

The school bus contained *5* boys and *12* girls.

(shorthand)

The application file contains *8* letters of application and *11* data sheets.

(shorthand)

We have tried to get service from *four* different repair people on *12* different occasions.

Dictation and Transcription Practice

18.5 Meeting Schedule

(shorthand) [31 words]

18.6 Thank-You Letter

(shorthand)

1 wonderful

(shorthand) [96 words]

18.7 Incomplete Order

(shorthand)

2 subscription   3 Ladies and Gentlemen

(shorthand outlines)

4 school   5 instead   6 indicates   7 would
have been   8 possibility   9 shipping

10 happened   11 additional   12 appreciate

[122 words]

An executive who needs a document transcribed immediately often gives on-the-spot dictation.

IN LESSON 19

- **Dictation speed building**
- **Transcription skill development**
- **Conjunction comma**

DICTATION SPEED BUILDING

The preview words below appear in the speed dictation practice which follows. Practice writing these words using the shorthand outlines. Then, using the key below, dictate the words to yourself.

Dictation Preview Words

Key: invitation, region, opportunity, development, communications, exact, idea, subjects, it is, I am glad, to have, with you, of your, of the

Speed Dictation Practice

19.1 Speech Acceptance

(shorthand outline)

(shorthand outline) [73 words]

TRANSCRIPTION SKILL DEVELOPMENT

Transcribe the following words and phrases, noting spelling and capitalization. Then transcribe the sentences and transcription letter in unarranged format. Provide all necessary punctuation.

Transcription Preview Words
19.2

(shorthand outlines)

Transcription Warmup
19.3

1 *(shorthand outline)*

2 *(shorthand outline)*

3 *(shorthand outline)*

4 *(shorthand outline)*

5 *(shorthand outline)*

Transcription Practice

19.4 Subscription Renewal

[shorthand content]

[85 words]

Conjunction Comma

Two complete sentences may be joined by a connecting word such as *and*, *but*, *or*, or *nor*. This connecting word is called a *conjunction* and is preceded by a comma.

[shorthand content]

You did not answer our notice, *and* now we are worried you did not receive your policy.

[shorthand content]

Unit sales decreased sharply in September, *but* net income was down only slightly.

[shorthand content]

Show this to Miss Adams, *and* ask for her response.

Dictation and Transcription Practice

19.5 Personal Shopping List

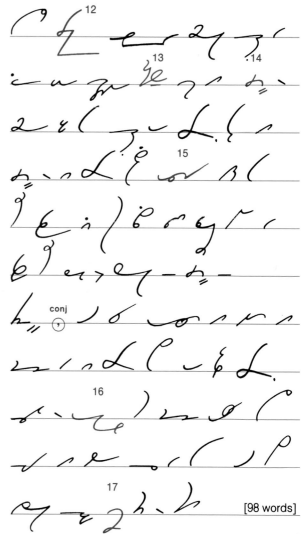

[16 words]

19.6 Insurance Claim

[93 words]

19.7 Banking Services

[98 words]

1 train   2 Boyd   3 As you know   4 blizzard
5 icy   6 electrical   7 control   8 damage
9 extensive   10 let me

11 contractor   12 Benjamin   13 software
14 Chicago   15 recommended   16 Will you please
17 convenient

LESSON
20

IN LESSON 20

- Dictation speed building
- Transcription skill development
- Amounts of money

DICTATION SPEED BUILDING

The preview words below appear in the speed dictation practice which follows. Practice writing these words using the shorthand outlines. Then, using the key below, dictate the words to yourself.

Dictation Preview Words

Key: Rich, registration, conference, $50, canceled, July, information, immediately, it has been, with the, from the, I have not, on the, as you know, will you please

Speed Dictation Practice

20.1 Conference Registration

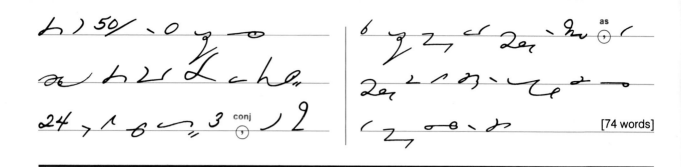

[74 words]

TRANSCRIPTION SKILL DEVELOPMENT

Transcribe the following words and phrases, noting spelling and capitalization. Then transcribe the sentences and transcription letter in unarranged format. Provide all necessary punctuation.

Transcription Preview Words
20.2

Transcription Warmup
20.3

Transcription Practice

20.4 Law Publication

[shorthand notes]

[92 words]

After completing the research for a business report, the secretary is preparing the first draft in shorthand.

Amounts of Money

Numerals are used to express exact amounts of money. A decimal point and zeroes are not used with whole-dollar amounts.

[shorthand]

The price of the book is *$24*.

[shorthand]

The amount owed is *$4.95*.

When transcribing, use a comma to express *thousand dollars*.

[shorthand]

David received an order for *$3,000*.

[shorthand]

We will send a check for *$2,200*.

When transcribing *million dollars* or *billion dollars*, replace the commas and ciphers with the word *million* or *billion*.

[shorthand]

The factory was purchased for *$10 million*.

[shorthand]

We project sales of over *$2 billion* for five years.

20.5   Office "To Do" List

[shorthand]

[47 words]

20.6 Job Placement

[shorthand outlines]

20.7 Relocation

[shorthand outlines]

[103 words]

[93 words]

1 manual   2 Cunningham   3 Thank you   4 very much   5 flattering   6 comments   7 students   8 succeeding   9 graduating   10 expressed   11 announced   12 I am sure

13 Martinez   14 Los Angeles   15 electrical   16 property   17 whether   18 9 a.m.

LESSON 21

IN LESSON 21

- Dictation speed building
- Transcription skill development
- Introductory comma

DICTATION SPEED BUILDING

The preview words below appear in the speed dictation practice which follows. Practice writing these words using the shorthand outlines. Then, using the key below, dictate the words to yourself.

Dictation Preview Words

Key: Dear Mr., Graham, realize, ordinary, insufficient, coverage, Merit Insurance, materials, representative, current, obligation, we can, with you

Speed Dictation Practice

21.1 Life Insurance

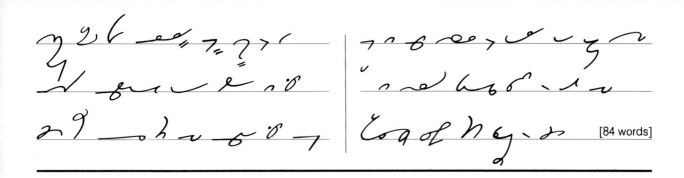

[84 words]

Transcribe the following words and phrases, noting spelling and capitalization. Then transcribe the sentences and transcription letter in unarranged format. Provide all necessary punctuation.

Transcription Preview Words
21.2

Transcription Warmup
21.3

Transcription Practice

21.4 Customer Payment

[shorthand notation] 250/

[shorthand notation] [82 words]

Introductory Comma

Use a comma after introductory words such as *accordingly*, *however*, *therefore*, or a similar word.

[shorthand notation]

Therefore, we cannot come to an agreement at this time.

[shorthand notation]

No, we cannot deliver your order on Saturday.

Use a comma after a dependent clause at the beginning of a sentence.

[shorthand notation]

After you review my report, please return it.

[shorthand notation]

Before we draft the agreement, we need information.

21.5 Luggage Order

[shorthand outlines]

[104 words]

1 O'Hara　2 luggage　3 description　4 travel
5 we have　6 to you　7 express　8 of the
9 for the　10 personal　11 If you have

21.6 Annual Convention

[shorthand outlines]

[103 words]

12 Once　13 National　14 Association
15 Jacksonville　16 departure　17 convention
18 brochure　19 sessions

LESSON 22

IN LESSON 22

- Dictation speed building
- Transcription skill development
- Expressions of time

DICTATION SPEED BUILDING

The preview words below appear in the speed dictation practice which follows. Practice writing these words using the shorthand outlines. Then, using the key below, dictate the words to yourself.

Dictation Preview Words

[shorthand outlines]

Key: Kate, discussed, yesterday, employee, manual, appreciate, willingness, update, benefits, sections, enjoyed, work, it is, of our, with you

Speed Dictation Practice

22.1   Employee Manual

[shorthand outlines]

[83 words]

TRANSCRIPTION SKILL DEVELOPMENT

Transcribe the following words and phrases, noting spelling and capitalization. Then transcribe the sentences and transcription letter in unarranged format. Provide all necessary punctuation.

Transcription Preview Words
22.2

Transcription Warmup
22.3

Transcription Practice

22.4 Employment Opportunities

[shorthand notation] 25 [shorthand notation]

[shorthand notation] [96 words]

Administrative assistants and secretaries work with microcomputers in offices of all sizes, even small ones.

Expressions of Time

Time is expressed in figures when used with *o'clock*, *a.m.*, and *p.m.*

(shorthand characters)

Please meet me at *9 a.m.* on Monday.

(shorthand characters)

I will call at *3 o'clock* this afternoon.

Dictation and Transcription Practice

22.5 Suggestion About Dictation

(shorthand characters)

[40 words]

22.6 Telephone Confirmation

(shorthand characters)

1 changes   2 processor   3 Williams
4 telephone   5 conversation

(shorthand characters)

6 We have   7 briefcase   8 selecting
9 approval   10 expect

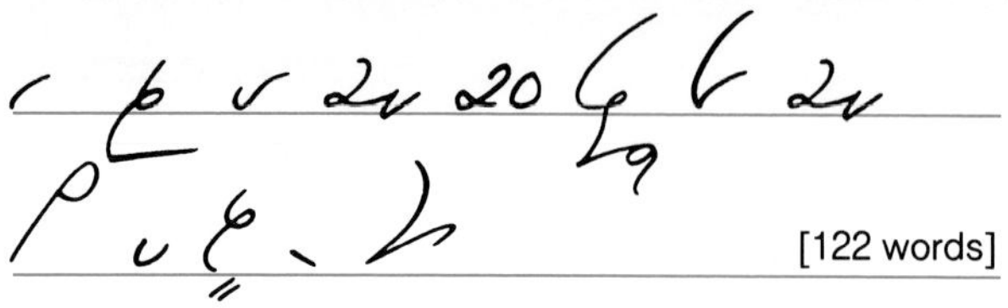

[shorthand outlines]

[122 words]

22.7 New Home

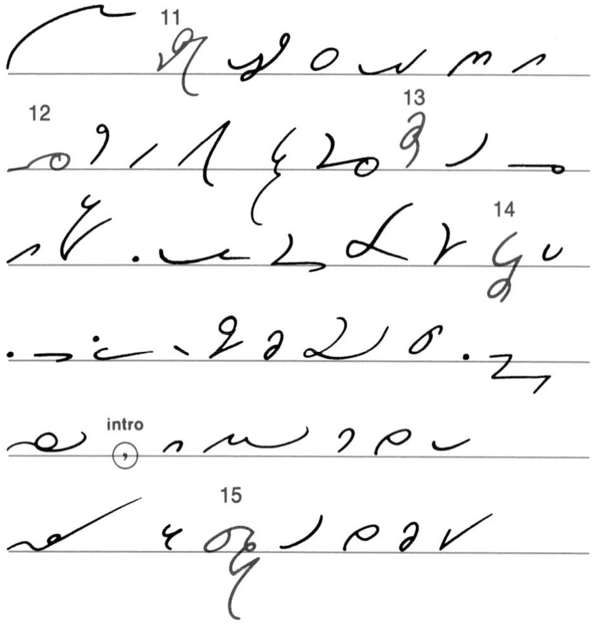

[shorthand outlines]

[120 words]

11 Steinberg   12 inquire   13 wife   14 purchase
15 acceptable

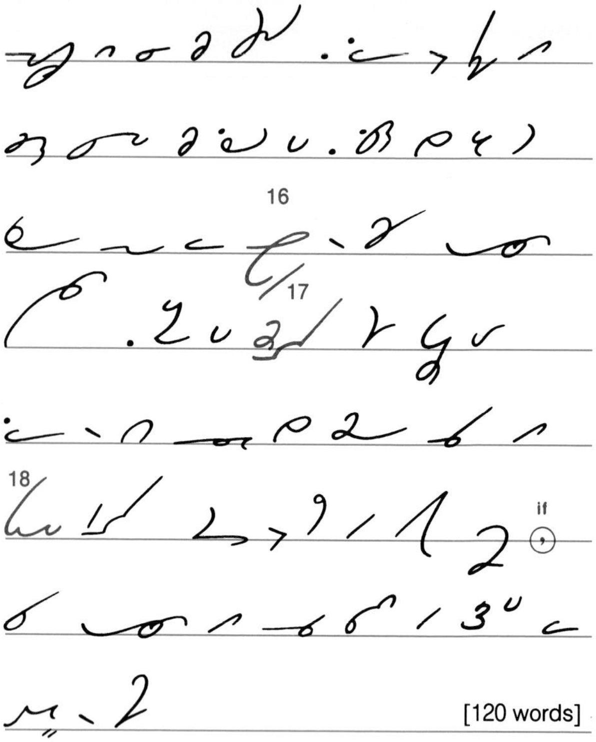

16 neighborhood   17 $200,000   18 borrow

IN LESSON 23

- Dictation speed building
- Transcription skill development
- Parenthetical comma

DICTATION SPEED BUILDING

The preview words below appear in the speed dictation practice which follows. Practice writing these words using the shorthand outlines. Then, using the key below, dictate the words to yourself.

Dictation Preview Words

Key: Ed, after, comments, invitation, annual, conference, humor, Los Angeles, to your, I am, for that, I would be, from you

Speed Dictation Practice

23.1   Invitation Acceptance

[71 words]

TRANSCRIPTION SKILL DEVELOPMENT

Transcribe the following words and phrases, noting spelling and capitalization. Then transcribe the sentences and transcription letter in unarranged format. Provide all necessary punctuation.

Transcription Preview Words
23.2

Transcription Warmup
23.3

Transcription Practice

23.4 Computer Demonstration

[shorthand outlines]

[86 words]

Parenthetical Comma

A parenthetical expression is a word or phrase within a sentence that does not contain any factual information but is an expression of emphasis. The word or phrase *can be omitted* without changing the meaning of the sentence. Therefore, it should be set off by commas.

[shorthand outline with par ⊙ *and* par ⊙ *marks]*

It is important, *therefore*, that Edward complete the research.

[shorthand outline with par ⊙ *and* par ⊙ *marks]*

Fred, *on the other hand*, sometimes makes quick judgments.

[shorthand outline with par ⊙ *and* par ⊙ *marks]*

Her typing skill is, *of course*, very impressive.

23.5 Outline for a Letter

[56 words]

23.6 Book Order

23.7 Closing of Bank Account

[116 words]

1 Eleanor   2 Browning   3 Tuesday   4 Dale School   5 I have been   6 communications

7 finally   8 market   9 copies   10 receive
11 Therefore   12 delay   13 insurance
14 agency   15 San Francisco   16 offered

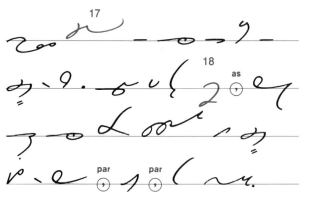

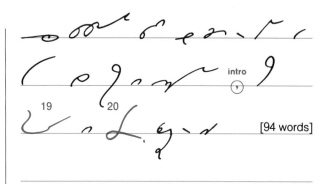

17 settled   18 convenience

19 valued   20 banking

[94 words]

The telecommuter works with a home-based computer that is linked to the company computer. Telecommuters enjoy flexible hours and freedom from the distractions of an office, but they may miss the interactions with coworkers.

LESSON 24

IN LESSON 24

- Dictation speed building
- Transcription skill development
- Days of the week and months of the year

DICTATION SPEED BUILDING

The preview words below appear in the speed dictation practice which follows. Practice writing these words using the shorthand outlines. Then, using the key below, dictate the words to yourself.

Dictation Preview Words

Key: Gray, staff, northern, bank, retired, remember, special, friendships, retirement, party, lovely, thank you for the, it is, I am

Speed Dictation Practice

24.1 Retirement

[68 words]

TRANSCRIPTION SKILL DEVELOPMENT

Transcribe the following words and phrases, noting spelling and capitalization. Then transcribe the sentences and transcription letter in unarranged format. Provide all necessary punctuation.

Transcription Preview Words
24.2

Transcription Warmup
24.3

Transcription Practice

24.4 Design Conference

[shorthand notation]

[80 words]

Days of the Week and Months of the Year

Always capitalize and spell out days of the week and months of the year. Use figures to express the day of the month.

[shorthand: Wednesday]   *[shorthand: February 20]*

Wednesday   February 20

24.5 Phone Message

[shorthand notation]

[41 words]

1 Claire Hall   2 message

3 friendly

24.6 Account Closing

[Shorthand outlines] [96 words]

24.7 Sale of Books

[Shorthand outlines]

4 travel 5 Chicago 6 outstanding
7 completely 8 I will be 9 closing 10 I have
been 11 Washington

[Shorthand outlines] [112 words]

12 successful 13 Nashville 14 accounting
15 transfer 16 magazine 17 Accounting Today

IN LESSON 25

- **Dictation speed building**
- **Transcription skill development**
- **Geographic expressions**

DICTATION SPEED BUILDING

The preview words below appear in the speed dictation practice which follows. Practice writing these words using the shorthand outlines. Then, using the key below, dictate the words to yourself.

Dictation Preview Words

Key: Owens, homeowners, $5,000, carpeting, wear, worldwide, reputation, reliable, manufacturer, exactly, it is, we have, you will, Sincerely yours

Speed Dictation Practice

25.1 Carpeting Purchase

[80 words]

TRANSCRIPTION SKILL DEVELOPMENT

Transcribe the following words and phrases, noting spelling and capitalization. Then transcribe the sentences and transcription letter in unarranged format. Provide all necessary punctuation.

Transcription Preview Words
25.2

Transcription Warmup
25.3

Transcription Practice

25.4 Interview

[shorthand outlines]

[93 words]

Geographic Expressions

A comma is used to separate the name of a city from the name of a state. A comma is also used to separate the name of a foreign city from the name of a country. Since the state or country is actually an appositive modifying the city, a comma follows the state or country as well.

[shorthand outlines]

Dave will visit New Orleans, *Louisiana*, during the summer.

[shorthand outlines]

Our newest branch office is in Atlanta, *Georgia*.

[shorthand outlines]

Her next vacation will be in Paris, *France*.

25.5 Personal "To Do" List

[49 words]

25.6 Notes From a Visitor

[40 words]

25.7 Transportation Needs

[98 words]

1 statistics

2 Larson   3 Sometime   4 Seattle
5 Washington   6 St. Paul   7 Minnesota
8 transportation   9 furniture   10 to take
11 inventory   12 someone

25.8 Student Loan

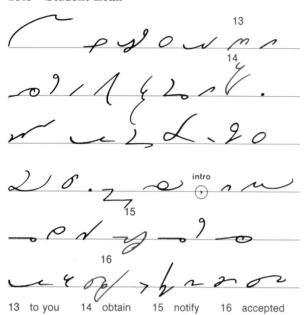

13 to you   14 obtain   15 notify   16 accepted

17 let me   18 scholarship   19 finances

[86 words]

Secretarial responsibilities continually change to reflect the skills required in today's office.

LESSON 26

IN LESSON 26

- ■ Dictation speed building
- ■ Transcription skill development
- ■ Block-style letter

DICTATION SPEED BUILDING

The preview words below appear in the speed dictation practice which follows. Practice writing these words using the shorthand outlines. Then, using the key below, dictate the words to yourself.

Dictation Preview Words

[shorthand outlines]

Key: Aunt Helen, passed, courses, believe, math, achieve, pleasure, diploma, June 4, California, incentive, investment, Amy, you will be

Speed Dictation Practice

26.1   Graduation

[shorthand outlines]

[shorthand outline] conj

[shorthand outline] [74 words]

TRANSCRIPTION SKILL DEVELOPMENT

Transcribe the following words and phrases, noting spelling and capitalization. Then transcribe the sentences and transcription letter in unarranged format. Provide all necessary punctuation.

Transcription Preview Words
26.2

[shorthand outlines]

Transcription Warmup
26.3

1 *[shorthand outline]*

2 *[shorthand outline]*

3 *[shorthand outline]*

4 *[shorthand outline]*

5 *[shorthand outline]*

Transcription Practice

26.4 Late Payment

[shorthand notation]

[82 words]

Automation can increase the productivity by decreasing the time.

Block-Style Letter

The following is an illustration of a block-style letter. Every letter part of the block-style letter begins at the left margin. The date should begin 15 lines from the top edge. Letters should always be single-spaced with a double space between paragraphs.

1890 West Edgewater Avenue, Chicago, IL 60660

February 14, 19--

Miss Judy Taylor
616 Navarre Place
Detroit, MI 48214

Dear Judy

Thank you for sending me a copy of your research study. The findings of your study about the use of shorthand in the modern business office are most interesting to me. As I am sure you realize, your study agrees with several other studies that have been done recently. Basically, all of these studies have found that the best way for a secretary to be hired and to be promoted is for that secretary to know shorthand.

As you know, our company is one of the largest temporary office help agencies in the nation. We find jobs for hundreds of secretaries in cities all across the nation each year. For those secretaries who wish to improve their skills, we offer classes in shorthand, typewriting, and word processing. Also, we publish a magazine for secretaries.

I would like to have you write an article for our magazine based upon the findings of your study. I know that our readers would be as interested in your study as I am. May I expect an article from you soon?

Sincerely

Helen Goldman

Mrs. Helen Goldman
Manager

FL

26.5 Outline for a Business Letter

[shorthand outlines]

[32 words]

26.6 Convention Invitation

[shorthand outlines]

[80 words]

26.7 Quartz Watch

[shorthand outlines]

[102 words]

1 Doctors   2 convention   3 Portland   4 year
5 departure   6 brochure

7 sessions   8 Oliver   9 quartz   10 According
11 description   12 watch   13 first-class
14 usually   15 express   16 collect   17 delivery

IN LESSON 27

- ■ Dictation speed building
- ■ Transcription skill development
- ■ Percentages

DICTATION SPEED BUILDING

The preview words below appear in the speed dictation practice which follows. Practice writing these words using the shorthand outlines. Then, using the key below, dictate the words to yourself.

Dictation Preview Words

Key: Wayne, welcome, opportunity, growth, area, eager, positions, Denver, salary, increases, demonstrate, interests, we are, we have, if you are

Speed Dictation Practice

27.1 College Position

[80 words]

TRANSCRIPTION SKILL DEVELOPMENT

Transcribe the following words and phrases, noting spelling and capitalization. Then transcribe the sentences and transcription letter in unarranged format. Provide all necessary punctuation.

Transcription Preview Words
27.2

Transcription Warmup
27.3

Transcription Practice

27.4 Credit Card

[shorthand outlines] [100 words]

Percentages

The number preceding the word *percent* is always expressed in figures in sentences, and the word *percent* is spelled out.

[shorthand outline]

Nearly *3 percent* of our accounts are considered bad debts.

[shorthand outline]

We offer our customers a discount of *10 percent*.

[shorthand outline]

The money was borrowed at an interest rate of *7½ percent*.

Dictation and Transcription Practice

27.5 House Hunting

(shorthand outline)

1 Martin   2 Providence   3 consultant
4 available   5 somewhat   6 I think   7 mortgage

[109 words]

27.6 Publication of Book

(shorthand outline)

8 Hartman   9 enjoyed   10 terms   11 contract
12 According   13 50,000   14 manuscript

[103 words]

LESSON 28

IN LESSON 28

- Dictation speed building
- Transcription skill development
- Date line

DICTATION SPEED BUILDING

The preview words below appear in the speed dictation practice which follows. Practice writing these words using the shorthand outlines. Then, using the key below, dictate the words to yourself.

Dictation Preview Words

Key: Scott, worthwhile, things, employees, fitness, premises, centers, industry, ability, provide, one of the, for your, we have, we can

Speed Dictation Practice

28.1 Fitness Center

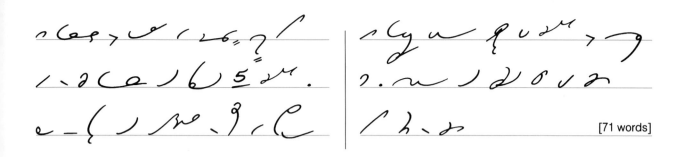

[71 words]

TRANSCRIPTION SKILL DEVELOPMENT

Transcribe the following words and phrases, noting spelling and capitalization. Then transcribe the sentences and transcription letter in unarranged format. Provide all necessary punctuation.

Transcription Preview Words
28.2

Transcription Warmup
28.3

Transcription Practice

28.4 Invitation

(shorthand outlines)

[95 words]

Date Line

The date line consists of the *month*, the *day*, and the *year*. The month is never abbreviated or represented by figures. The day is written in figures, followed by a comma. The date line is typed 15 lines from the top of the paper.

(shorthand outline) 1990

July 4, 1990

---

4   5

28.5 Satisfied Customer

(shorthand outlines with numbered markers 1, 2, 3)

1 Grant   2 Yesterday   3 Arnold Jones

4 luncheon   5 inquire

(shorthand outlines)

[96 words]

28.6 Banking Needs

(shorthand outlines)

6 operated   7 rates   8 quality   9 trucks
10 Baker   11 manufacturing

(shorthand outlines)

[96 words]

12 Birmingham   13 recommended   14 someone

UNIT VIII

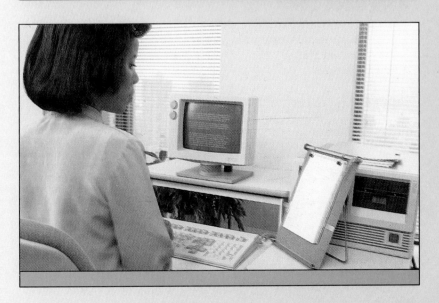

LESSON

29

IN LESSON 29

- Dictation speed building
- Transcription skill development
- Inside address for letters to individuals

DICTATION SPEED BUILDING

The preview words below appear in the speed dictation practice which follows. Practice writing these words using the shorthand outlines. Then, using the key below, dictate the words to yourself.

Dictation Preview Words

(shorthand outlines)

Key: Blake, typing, citizens, extraordinary, ability, achievement, proof, winner, examining, congratulations, I have been, it has been, on this

Speed Dictation Practice

29.1 Typing Class

(shorthand outlines)

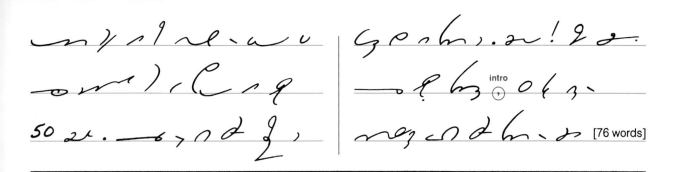

[76 words]

TRANSCRIPTION SKILL DEVELOPMENT

Transcribe the following words and phrases, noting spelling and capitalization. Then transcribe the sentences and transcription letter in unarranged format. Provide all necessary punctuation.

Transcription Preview Words
29.2

Transcription Warmup
29.3

Transcription Practice

29.4 Tennis Group

It is important that people participate in the implementation of office automation and understand its effect on their contribution to the organization.

[81 words]

Inside Address for Letters to Individuals

The inside address should include:

1 The name of the person who will receive the letter.
2 The street address, the post office box number, or the rural delivery (abbreviated R.D.). If the person lives in an apartment building, the apartment number appears on the line above the street address.
3 The city, state, and ZIP Code.

When transcribing, single-space the inside address and place it at the left margin.

Mr. James Martin
767 Lexington Avenue
New York, NY 10020

Dr. Grace Bates
Apartment 51C
405 Market Street
Cleveland, OH 44305

Notice that the proper nouns in the inside address do not contain capitalization marks when written in shorthand. However, the name, title, street address, city, and state are capitalized when they are transcribed.

Dictation and Transcription Practice

29.5 Reminder

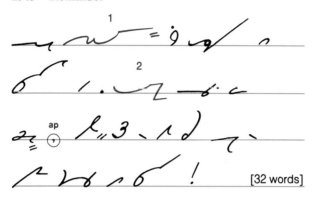

[32 words]

29.6 Investment Inquiry

1 Goldman 2 luncheon 3 Thank you for your letter
4 will be glad 5 financial 6 assets 7 debts
8 accurate 9 picture

[87 words]

29.7 Textbook Shipment

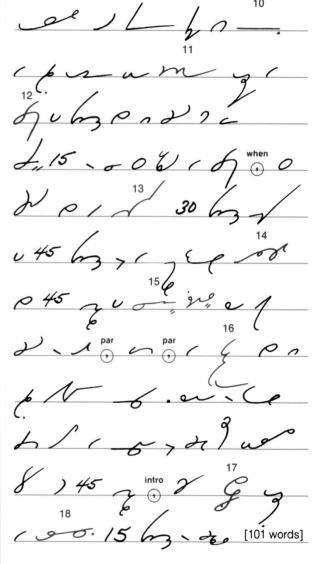

[101 words]

10 morning 11 school 12 package
13 contained 14 indicates 15 American History
16 possibility 17 appreciate 18 remaining

176 LESSON 29

IN LESSON 30

- **Dictation speed building**
- **Transcription skill development**
- **Inside address for letters to organizations**

DICTATION SPEED BUILDING

The preview words below appear in the speed dictation practice which follows. Practice writing these words using the shorthand outlines. Then, using the key below, dictate the words to yourself.

Dictation Preview Words

Key: Larson, David Knapp, inquired, qualifications, programmer, impressed, attitude, dedication, assistant, competent, by the, about the, we would

Speed Dictation Practice

30.1 Job Applicant

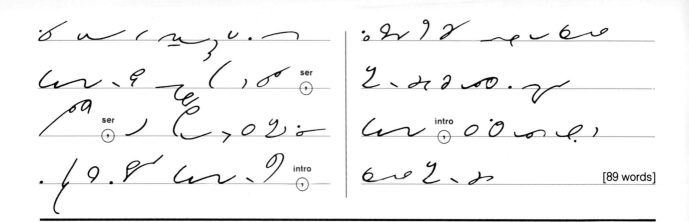

[89 words]

TRANSCRIPTION SKILL DEVELOPMENT

Transcribe the following words and phrases, noting spelling and capitalization. Then transcribe the sentences and transcription letter in unarranged format. Provide all necessary punctuation.

Transcription Preview Words
30.2

Transcription Warmup
30.3

Transcription Practice

30.4 Article Reprint

[shorthand notation]

[84 words]

Word processing software can aid in improving accuracy and increasing speed of transcription.

Inside Address for Letters to Organizations

The inside address should include:

1 (Optional) The name of a specific person, including job title and department if known. If you do not know the name of a specific person, use a title, such as Personnel Director.
2 The name of the business or organization.
3 The street address or post office box number.
4 The city, state, and ZIP Code.

When transcribing, single-space the inside address and place it at the left margin.

Mrs. Janet Jackson, Manager
Accounting Department
Worth Manufacturing Company
732 West Lane
Dallas, TX 75247

Personnel Director
General Publishing Company
327 James Avenue
Chicago, IL 60624

The proper nouns in the inside address will not contain capitalization marks when written in shorthand. However, all proper nouns are capitalized when they are transcribed.

Dictation and Transcription Practice

30.5 Notes From Staff Meeting

[71 words]

1 weekly   2 outline   3 proposal

4 determine   5 systems

30.6 Grand Opening

(shorthand outline)

6 Black Avenue   7 officially   8 located
9 neighborhood   10 opportunity   11 favorite
12 personal   13 You will be glad

30.7 Book Publication

(shorthand outline)

14 Roman   15 discussed   16 facilities
17 Consequently   18 advance   19 25,000

LESSON 31

IN LESSON 31

- Dictation speed building
- Transcription skill development
- Salutation

DICTATION SPEED BUILDING

The preview words below appear in the speed dictation practice which follows. Practice writing these words using the shorthand outlines. Then, using the key below, dictate the words to yourself.

Dictation Preview Words

(shorthand outlines)

Key: Taylor, Johnson Institute, aptitude, appointment, substitute, available, grateful, I would be, if you can, as soon as possible

Speed Dictation Practice

31.1 Request

(shorthand outlines, with "intro" marked)

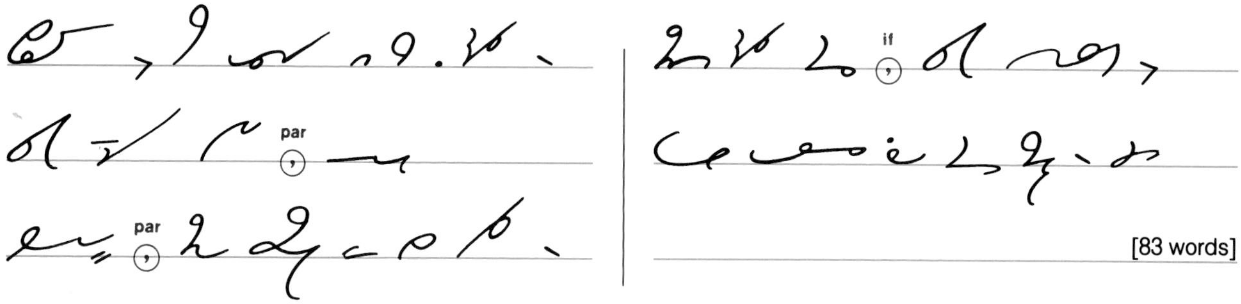

TRANSCRIPTION SKILL DEVELOPMENT

Transcribe the following words and phrases, noting spelling and capitalization. Then transcribe the sentences and transcription letter in unarranged format. Provide all necessary punctuation.

Transcription Preview Words

31.2

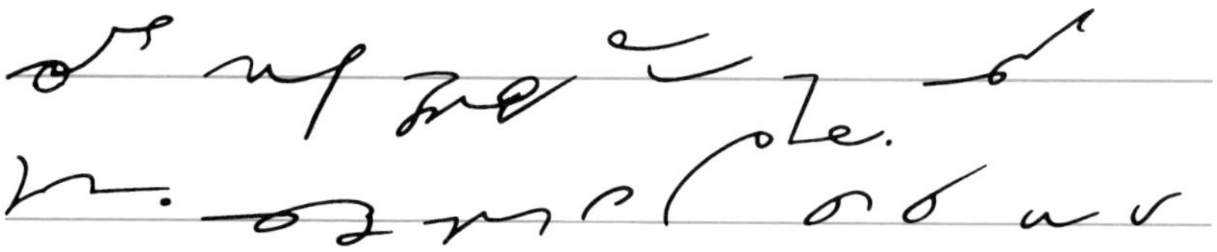

Transcription Warmup

31.3

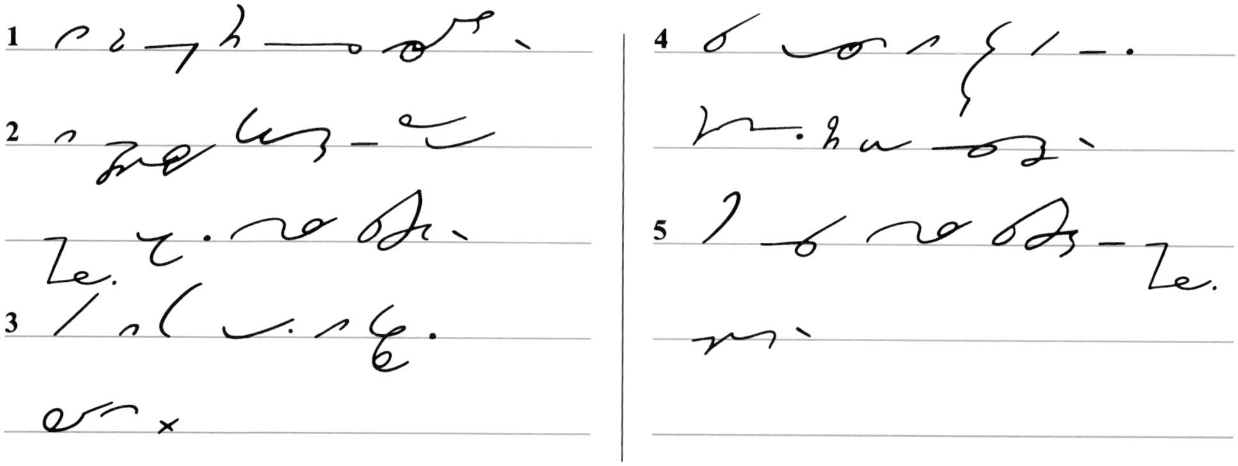

Transcription Practice

31.4 Article Publication

[shorthand notation]

[103 words]

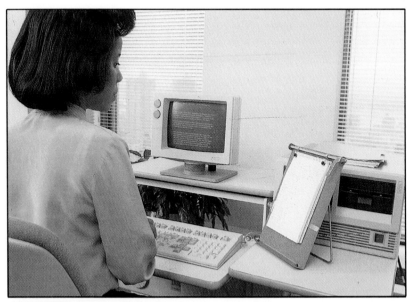

The word processor enables the secretary to edit the work while transcribing and then again while proofreading it.

Salutation

The following guidelines should be used for the salutation:

1 Be sure the spelling of the name in the salutation matches the spelling in the inside address.
2 Abbreviate the titles *Mr.*, *Mrs.*, *Ms.*, *Messrs.*, and *Dr.* Spell out all other titles.
3 Capitalize the first word as well as any nouns and titles.

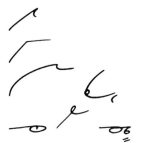

Dear Sir

Dear Madam

Dear Mr. Billings

My dear Nancy

4 Use *Gentlemen* for an organization composed entirely of men.
5 Use the full name for a person whose gender is unknown. For example, use *Dear Robin Samuels* or *Dear E. H. Fox*.
6 Use *Dear Sir* or *Dear Madam* for a person whose gender is known but whose name is not.
7 Type the salutation a double space below the inside address.

Dictation and Transcription Practice

31.5 Important Reminder

[29 words]

1 Kelly

31.6 Building of House

2 Powers   3 house   4 Baker   5 Harris Brothers

(shorthand outline)

[81 words]

31.7 Banking

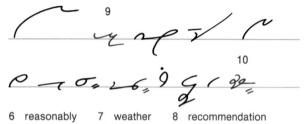

(shorthand outline)

[80 words]

6 reasonably   7 weather   8 recommendation
9 Rosen   10 Western

11 Data   12 successful   13 executive
14 doubt   15 profitable   16 obtaining

IN LESSON 32

- Dictation speed building
- Transcription skill development
- Closing lines

DICTATION SPEED BUILDING

The preview words below appear in the speed dictation practice which follows. Practice writing these words using the shorthand outlines. Then, using the key below, dictate the words to yourself.

Dictation Preview Words

Key: depend, competent, employees, excellent, opportunities, agencies, recruit, applicants, if you are, is the, to the, that will, of your, Yours very truly

Speed Dictation Practice

32.1 Employment

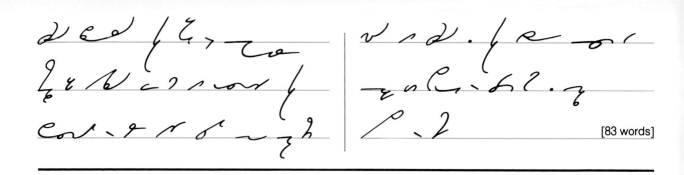

[83 words]

Transcribe the following words and phrases, noting spelling and capitalization. Then transcribe the sentences and transcription letter in unarranged format. Provide all necessary punctuation.

Transcription Preview Words
32.2

Transcription Warmup
32.3

1

2

3

4

5

Transcription Practice

32.4 Training Program

[86 words]

Closing Lines

The following guidelines should be used for the closing lines:

1 Capitalize only the first word of the complimentary closing.

Very truly yours

2 Type the complimentary closing at the left margin a double space below the last line of the body of the letter.

3 Arrange the writer's name, title, and department to achieve good visual balance. If a title takes two or more lines, block all the lines at the left.

Charles Parker   or   Charles Parker, Manager
Manager

Charles Parker, Manager
Accounting Department

Elizabeth Adams
Assistant Vice President
Marketing Division

4 Ordinarily the writer's name is typed on the fourth line below the complimentary closing. However, if the letter is running short, you can leave up to six blank lines. If the letter is running long, you can reduce the spacing for the handwritten signature to two blank lines.

5 Type the reference initials at the left margin on the second line below the writer's name, title, and department.

6 Type the reference initials in capital letters or small letters.

Very truly yours

Mark R. Samuels
Assistant Manager

urs

32.5 Outline for a Letter

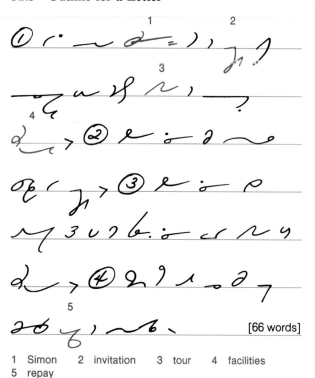

[66 words]

1 Simon   2 invitation   3 tour   4 facilities
5 repay

32.6 Order Information

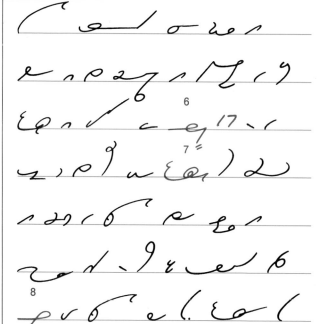

6 March 17   7 suppliers   8 majority

[131 words]

32.7 Convention Invitation

9 advice   10 either   11 another   12 touch

[94 words]

13 privilege   14 seminar   15 conducted
16 Chicago   17 presentation   18 superb
19 Association   20 Representatives   21 convention

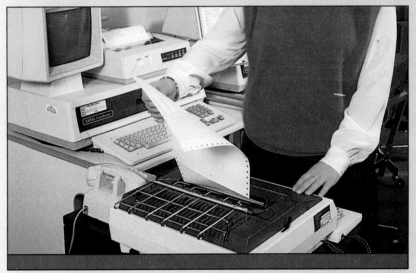

IN LESSON 33

- Dictation speed building
- Transcription skill development
- Mailable production letter
- Interoffice memos

DICTATION SPEED BUILDING

The preview words below appear in the speed dictation practice which follows. Practice writing these words using the shorthand outlines. Then, using the key below, dictate the words to yourself.

Dictation Preview Words

Key: Bond, enrolled, relations, objective, representative, Armstrong, achieved, persuade, recommend, with the, of the, in the, Sincerely yours

Speed Dictation Practice

33.1 Positive Response

[Shorthand outlines]

[90 words]

TRANSCRIPTION SKILL DEVELOPMENT

Transcribe the following words and phrases, noting spelling and capitalization. Then transcribe the transcription letter in unarranged format. A word count is provided to begin recording transcription speed.

Transcription Preview Words
33.2

Shorthand	Word Count
[Shorthand outlines]	10
[Shorthand outlines]	10
[Shorthand outlines]	10

Transcription Practice

33.3 Magazine Subscription

Word Count

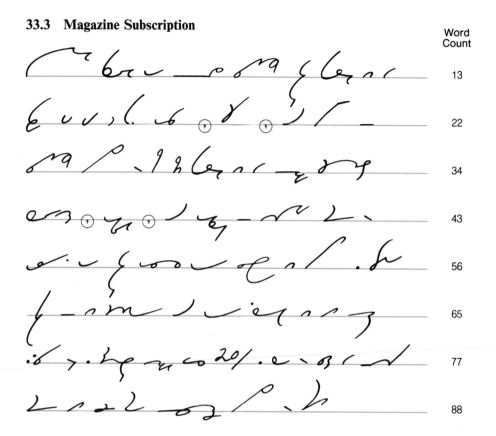

	13
	22
	34
	43
	56
	65
	77
	88

Mailable Production Letter

Transcribe the following mailable production letter in block style, assuring proper placement of the date, inside address, salutation, closing, writer's name, title, and reference initials. Insert all punctuation prior to transcribing. Capitalize proper nouns in the address and closing lines, and be sure to place a comma between the day and the year in the date.

33.4 Catalog Advertising

[shorthand outlines] 57

[shorthand outlines]

[87 words]

Interoffice Memos

An interoffice memo is intended to facilitate the exchange of written information within an organization.

It is customary for many organizations to provide printed forms that standardize all the information that should be contained in the heading. However, there are times when a memo will be typed on plain paper. When typing a memo on plain paper, use the following procedure:

1 Type the heading *MEMORANDUM*, centered in all-capital letters on line 7 from the top.
2 On the third line below the heading *MEMORANDUM*, start typing the guide words *DATE:*, *TO:*, *FROM:*, *SUBJECT:*, and any other items that may be appropriate.
3 Double-space the guide words and type them in blocked format at the left margin. Use all-capital letters. Type a colon after each guide word.
4 If the word *SUBJECT:* is the longest guide word, you can set a tab ten spaces in from the left margin for proper placement.

It is important to type all the guide words before you begin filling in the information that follows since you want all the entries to be blocked at the left, two spaces after the longest guide word. See the illustration on page 198.

```
                        MEMORANDUM

        DATE:    May 20, 19--

        TO:      B. A. Larson, Personnel Department

        FROM:    S. G. Mitchell, Marketing

        SUBJECT:  Job Replacement

        One of my employees, Ms. Ann Davis, has just told me that she has accepted
        a position with another company and will be leaving July 1.  If it is pos-
        sible, I would like to get someone to fill the vacancy immediately so that
        Ms. Davis can help train a new person.

        As you know, some of our business is with customers in South America and
        Central America.  Consequently, it would be a great help to me if you
        could find a person who has some degree of proficiency in Spanish.

        I will be out of town on May 21 and 22, but I will be back on the morning
        of May 23.  I will, therefore, be able to interview applicants beginning
        May 23.

        RM
```

Dictation and Transcription Practice

33.5 Phone Message

1 Graham   2 laboratory   3 apology   4 inconvenience

[47 words]

33.6 Personnel Performance Review

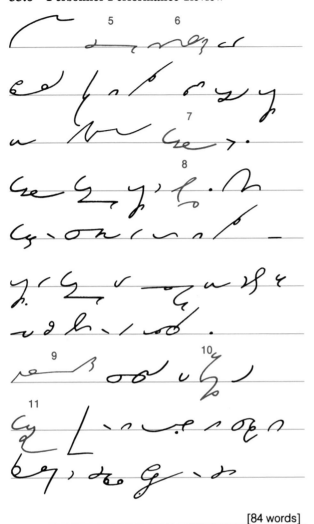

[84 words]

5 Simmons 6 Congratulations 7 personnel
8 typically 9 tremendous 10 objectivity
11 professional

33.7 New Customer

[88 words]

12 Cruz 13 Thank you for your order 14 flooring
15 materials 16 promptly 17 factory
18 represents 19 purchase 20 As you
21 quite 22 hire 23 expert 24 yourself
25 with your

IN LESSON 34

- Dictation speed building
- Transcription skill development
- Mailable production letter
- *And* omitted comma

DICTATION SPEED BUILDING

The preview words below appear in the speed dictation practice which follows. Practice writing these words using the shorthand outlines. Then, using the key below, dictate the words to yourself.

Dictation Preview Words

Key: Kirk, satisfied, electric, system, warm, economical, natural, emission, representative, demonstrate, alteration, it is, will be glad, can be

Speed Dictation Practice

34.1 Heating System

[shorthand notation]

[79 words]

TRANSCRIPTION SKILL DEVELOPMENT

Transcribe the following words and phrases, noting spelling and capitalization. Then transcribe the transcription letter in unarranged format. A word count is provided to begin recording transcription speed.

Transcription Preview Words

34.2

	Word Count
[shorthand notation]	10
[shorthand notation]	10
[shorthand notation]	10

Transcription Practice

34.3   Office Closing

[Shorthand notation] 16 19 — — 4

[Shorthand notation] 6

[Shorthand notation] 9

[Shorthand notation] 14

[Shorthand notation] 25

[Shorthand notation] 36

[Shorthand notation] 48

[Shorthand notation] 24 31 59

[Shorthand notation] 15 71

[Shorthand notation] 83

[Shorthand notation] 95

Mailable Production Letter

Transcribe the following mailable production letter in block style, assuring proper placement of the date, inside address, salutation, closing, writer's name, title, and reference initials. Insert all punctuation prior to transcribing. Capitalize proper nouns in the address and closing lines, and be sure to place a comma between the day and year in the date.

34.4 Company Meeting

[shorthand notes]

[95 words]

And Omitted Comma

When two or more consecutive adjectives modify the same noun and the word *and* has been omitted, the adjectives are separated by commas.

The *and* omitted comma is indicated by *[symbol]*

[shorthand notes]

He found that she was a *competent, efficient* worker.

You can easily determine whether to insert a comma between two consecutive adjectives by mentally placing *and* between them. If the sentence makes sense with *and* inserted between the adjectives, then the comma is used.

(shorthand outline)

He found that she was a *competent and efficient* worker.

Note: In the example above, the comma is not used when the adjectives are connected by *and*.
    The comma is not used if the first adjective modifies the combined idea of the second adjective plus the noun.

(shorthand outline)

The colors in her living room consisted of *beautiful blue* fabrics.

In the example above, although *blue* is an adjective modifying the noun *fabrics*, *blue fabrics* is one thought.

34.5 Party Arrangements

(shorthand outline)

[37 words]

1 available   2 together

34.6 Research Conference

(shorthand outline)

3 approaches   4 enthusiasm   5 airport
6 Denver

[92 words]

34.7 Insurance Policy

[105 words]

7 mountains   8 presentation   9 research
10 conference   11 exciting   12 Dempsey
13 bought   14 policy

15 thinking   16 borrowing   17 of this   18 verify
19 I can   20 7 percent   21 from you
22 decision

IN LESSON 35

- Dictation speed building
- Transcription skill development
- Mailable production letter
- Semicolon in compound sentence

DICTATION SPEED BUILDING

The preview words below appear in the speed dictation practice which follows. Practice writing these words using the shorthand outlines. Then, using the key below, dictate the words to yourself.

Dictation Preview Words

Key: Rich, computer, insurance, quickly, persuade, consider, updated, software, appreciate, demonstrate, you have, you can, one of our, you will be able, we would be, of this

Speed Dictation Practice

35.1 Computer Sales

[86 words]

TRANSCRIPTION SKILL DEVELOPMENT

Transcribe the following words and phrases, noting spelling and capitalization. Then transcribe the transcription letter in unarranged format. A word count is provided to begin recording transcription speed.

Transcription Preview Words
35.2

Word Count

10

10

10

Transcription Practice

35.3 Credit Card

[shorthand outlines]   9

[shorthand outlines]   17

[shorthand outlines]   28

[shorthand outlines]   43

[shorthand outlines]   53

[shorthand outlines]   63

[shorthand outlines]   75

[shorthand outlines]   84

Mailable Production Letter

Transcribe the following mailable production letter in block style, assuring proper placement of the date, inside address, salutation, closing, writer's name, title, and reference initials. Insert punctuation prior to transcribing, and capitalize proper nouns in the address and closing lines.

35.4 Savings Plan

[shorthand outlines] 22 19--

[shorthand outlines]

75 *[shorthand outlines]*

[shorthand outlines] 58/04

[shorthand outlines]

[shorthand outlines]

[shorthand outlines] 20 *[shorthand outline]*

[shorthand outlines]

[84 words]

Semicolon in Compound Sentence

Two complete sentences that are closely related may be joined into one sentence without a conjunction to serve as a connecting word. In conversation this results in an abrupt pause. The pause is denoted by a semicolon in writing.

Since there is no conjunction between the two complete sentences, the abbreviation *nc* will be used for *no conjunction*.

The semicolon in a compound sentence is indicated by ⊙

[shorthand outlines]

His editing ability is not adequate; we need to discuss this matter.

[shorthand outlines]

Her novel was written with a real sense of humor; it will make anyone laugh.

[shorthand outlines]

The day is cold and windy; I enjoyed it immensely.

35.5 Outline for a Phone Message

[shorthand outline]

[44 words]

35.6 Insurance Renewal

[shorthand outline]

35.7 Recommendation for Appointment

[shorthand outline]

[112 words]

[81 words]

1 Rosen   2 difficult   3 insurance   4 effect
5 unless   6 premium   7 lose   8 Maybe
9 $180

10 at this time   11 as soon as possible   12 Higgins
13 Boston Banking Commission   14 professionalism

IN LESSON 36

- Dictation speed building
- Transcription skill development
- Mailable production letter
- Semicolon in a series

DICTATION SPEED BUILDING

The preview words below appear in the speed dictation practice which follows. Practice writing these words using the shorthand outlines. Then, using the key below, dictate the words to yourself.

Dictation Preview Words

(shorthand outlines)

Key: Evans, business, community, contributions, unfortunately, distributed, impossible, budget, attempt, as you, of course, we can, we have, it will be, we will, Sincerely yours

Speed Dictation Practice

36.1 Committee Contribution

(shorthand outlines)

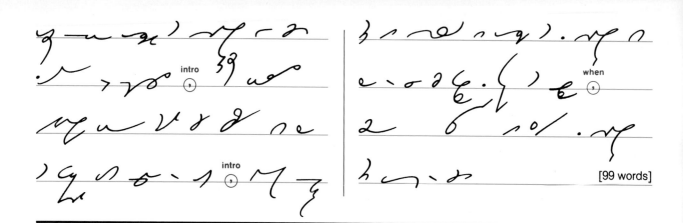

[99 words]

Transcribe the following words and phrases, noting spelling and capitalization. Then transcribe the transcription letter in unarranged format.

Transcription Preview Words
36.2

Word Count

10

10

10

Transcription Practice

36.3 Interview

Word Count

11

26

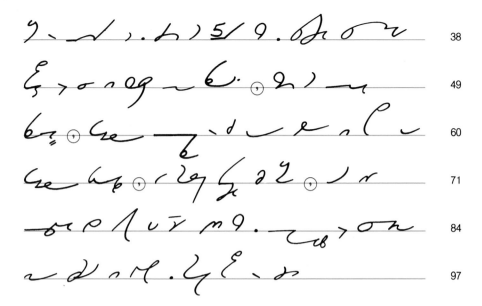

38

49

60

71

84

97

Mailable Production Letter

Transcribe the following mailable production letter in block style, assuring proper placement of the date, inside address, salutation, closing, writer's name, title, and reference initials. Insert punctuation prior to transcribing, and capitalize proper nouns in the address and closing lines.

36.4   Alumni Gift

Semicolon in a Series

When one or more of the items in a series already contains a comma, semicolons are used to separate the items in the series.

The series semicolon is indicated by (;)

The program will be presented on Thursday, November 6; Friday, November 7; and Monday, November 10.

Our officers for the coming year are Bob Davis, president; Amy Jones, vice president; and Daniel Strong, secretary/treasurer.

We have sales representatives in Boston, Massachusetts; Chicago, Illinois; and St. Louis, Missouri.

36.5 Phone Message

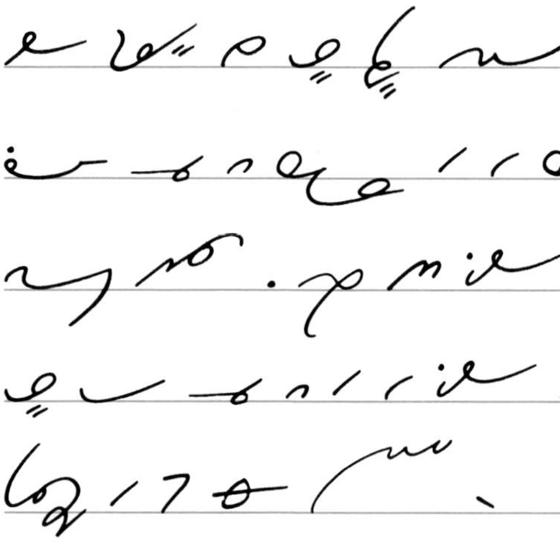

[35 words]

36.6 Request for Price List

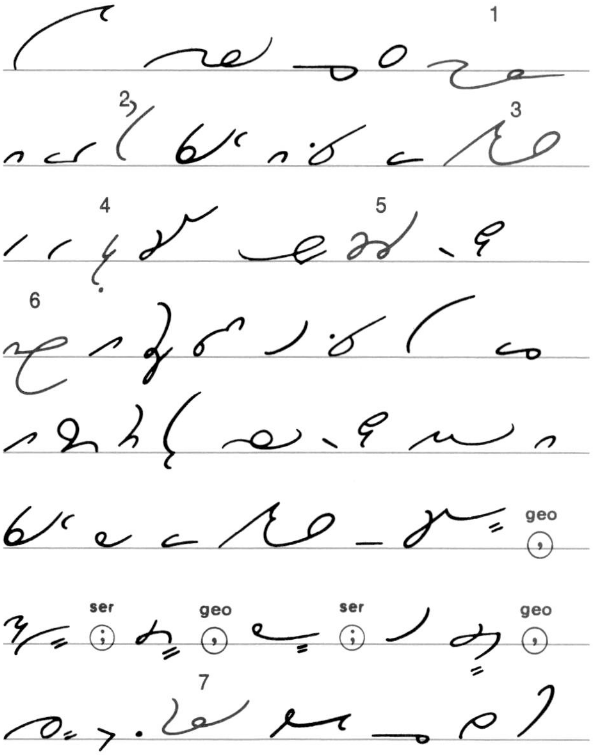

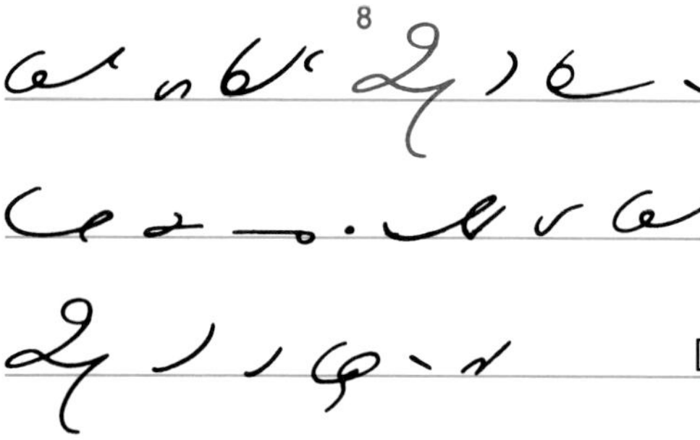

[89 words]

1 compliment 2 superb 3 display 4 shopping
5 weekend 6 unable 7 friend

36.7 Lawn Care

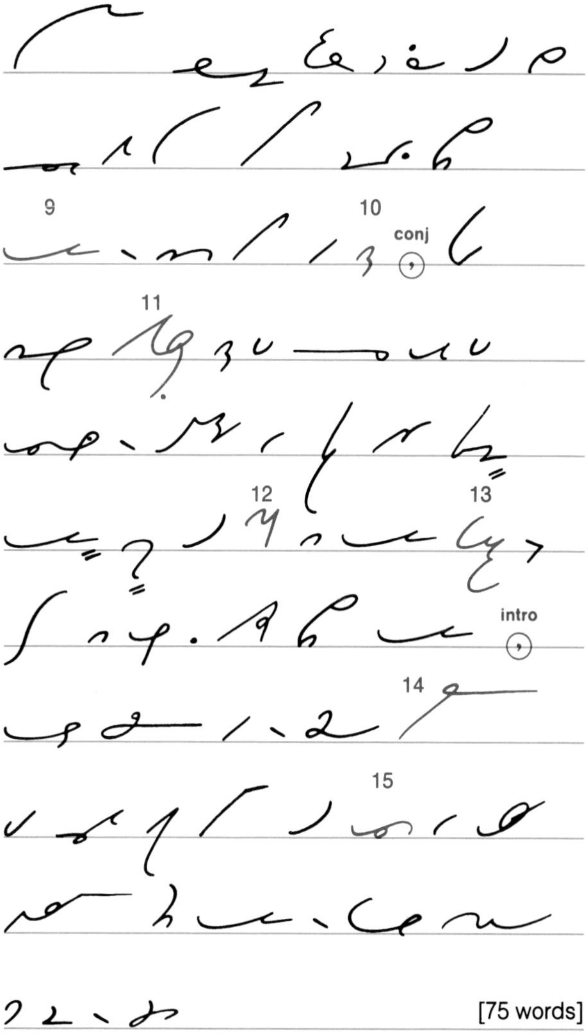

[75 words]

8 available 9 lawn 10 yourself 11 depriving
12 watch 13 prosper 14 determine
15 recommend

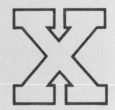

UNIT

X

IN LESSON 37

- Dictation speed building
- Transcription skill development
- Mailable production letter
- Enclosure notation

DICTATION SPEED BUILDING

The preview words below appear in the speed dictation practice which follows. Practice writing these words using the shorthand outlines. Then, using the key below, dictate the words to yourself.

Dictation Preview Words

Key: organization, annual, research, conference, schedule, hectic, speaker, discuss, details, will be, that the, of your, we would, to have, we can, of the

Speed Dictation Practice

37.1 Speaker Invitation

[shorthand text]

intro *[shorthand text]*

conj *[shorthand text]*

as *[shorthand text]*

[86 words]

TRANSCRIPTION SKILL DEVELOPMENT

Transcribe the following words and phrases, noting spelling and capitalization. Then transcribe the transcription letter in unarranged format.

Transcription Preview Words

37.2

Word Count

[shorthand text] — 10

[shorthand text] — 10

[shorthand text] — 10

Transcription Practice

37.3 Price Increase

[shorthand notation]   12

[shorthand notation]   26

[shorthand notation]   36

[shorthand notation]   47

[shorthand notation]   60

[shorthand notation]   75

[shorthand notation]   85

[shorthand notation]   97

Mailable Production Letter

Transcribe the following mailable production letter in block style, assuring proper placement of the date, inside address, salutation, closing, writer's name, title, and reference initials. Insert punctuation prior to transcribing, and capitalize proper nouns in the address and closing lines.

37.4 Market Survey

[shorthand notation]

[shorthand outlines]

[95 words]

Enclosure Notation

If one or more items are to be included in the envelope with the letter, indicate that fact by typing the word *Enclosure* or *Enclosures* at the left margin on the line below the reference initials.

If the letter states that the material will be sent "under separate cover," the material is not enclosed with the letter. Therefore, an *enclosure notation* is not used, and the material is to be sent in a separate envelope.

Dictation and Transcription Practice

37.5 Phone Message

[shorthand outlines]

1 Kelly

[shorthand outlines]

[30 words]

37.6 Scholarship Recommendation Letter

[Shorthand outlines]

[94 words]

2 recommend 3 Spencer 4 scholarship
5 Claire 6 highest

37.7 Insurance Solicitation

[Shorthand outlines]

[116 words]

7 Delgado 8 property 9 wondering
10 destroy 11 Almost 12 office 13 but
14 superficial 15 attention 16 protection
17 vital 18 convenient 19 I would
20 fireproof 21 systems

LESSON
38

IN LESSON 38

- Dictation speed building
- Transcription skill development
- Mailable production letter
- Punctuation at end of courteous request

DICTATION SPEED BUILDING

The preview words below appear in the speed dictation practice which follows. Practice writing these words using the shorthand outlines. Then, using the key below, dictate the words to yourself.

Dictation Preview Words

Key: Harper, interview, operation, executive, whom, introduced, convinced, qualifications, substantial, thank you for, I was, I would, it is

Speed Dictation Practice

38.1 Job Interview

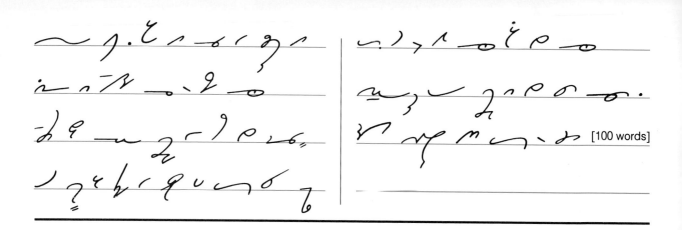

[100 words]

TRANSCRIPTION SKILL DEVELOPMENT

Transcribe the following words and phrases, noting spelling and capitalization. Then transcribe the transcription letter in unarranged format.

Transcription Preview Words

38.2

	Word Count
	10
	10
	10

Transcription Practice

38.3 Travel Plans

	Word Count
	11
	22
	33

[shorthand outline]　44

[shorthand outline]　54

[shorthand outline]　65

[shorthand outline]　76

[shorthand outline]　89

Mailable Production Letter

Transcribe the following mailable production letter in block style, assuring proper placement of the date, inside address, salutation, closing, writer's name, title, and reference initials. Insert punctuation prior to transcribing, and capitalize proper nouns in the address and closing lines. Note that an enclosure notation is needed. What is the enclosure?

38.4　Insurance Sales

[shorthand outline] 7 19--

[shorthand outline]

[shorthand outline]

[shorthand outline] 19952

[shorthand outline]

[shorthand outline]

[shorthand outline]

[shorthand outline]

[shorthand outline]

[shorthand outline]

[shorthand outline]

[shorthand outline]

[shorthand outline]

[shorthand outline]

[100 words]

Punctuation at End of Courteous Request

Often a request is phrased in the form of a question so that it will seem less severe. If you expect your reader to respond by acting rather than by giving you a yes-or-no answer, it is a courteous request and, therefore, the sentence ends with a period.

[shorthand]

Would you please sign your check.

[shorthand]

Will the meeting come to order.

[shorthand]

Can we have a moment of silence.

Dictation and Transcription Practice

38.5 Interoffice Note

[shorthand]

[29 words]

38.6 Ideas Under Consideration

[shorthand]

1 Linda   2 St. Louis   3 New York

(shorthand outlines with reference markers)

[91 words]

38.7 Fire Insurance Benefits

(shorthand outlines)

[99 words]

4 evaluation   5 studying   6 I will   7 progress
8 scheduled   9 Levine   10 successful
11 executive   12 protect

13 fire   14 contents   15 temporarily   16 that
will   17 of your   18 offices   19 built
20 If you

To work in today's office, secretaries need to know how to use printers with tractors that guide continuous-form paper.

IN LESSON 39

- Dictation speed building
- Transcription skill development
- Mailable production letter
- Capitalization of titles

DICTATION SPEED BUILDING

The preview words below appear in the speed dictation practice which follows. Practice writing these words using the shorthand outlines. Then, using the key below, dictate the words to yourself.

Dictation Preview Words

Key: Dear Mrs. Harrington, payment, television, pleasure, notice, deduct, discount, enclosed, opportunity, future, thank you for your, for the, we hope that, we may have

Speed Dictation Practice

39.1 Payment Allowance

[shorthand notations]

[92 words]

TRANSCRIPTION SKILL DEVELOPMENT

Transcribe the following words and phrases, noting spelling and capitalization. Then transcribe the transcription letter in unarranged format.

Transcription Preview Words

39.2

	Word Count
[shorthand]	10
[shorthand]	10
[shorthand]	10

Transcription Practice

39.3 Letter of Regret

Word Count

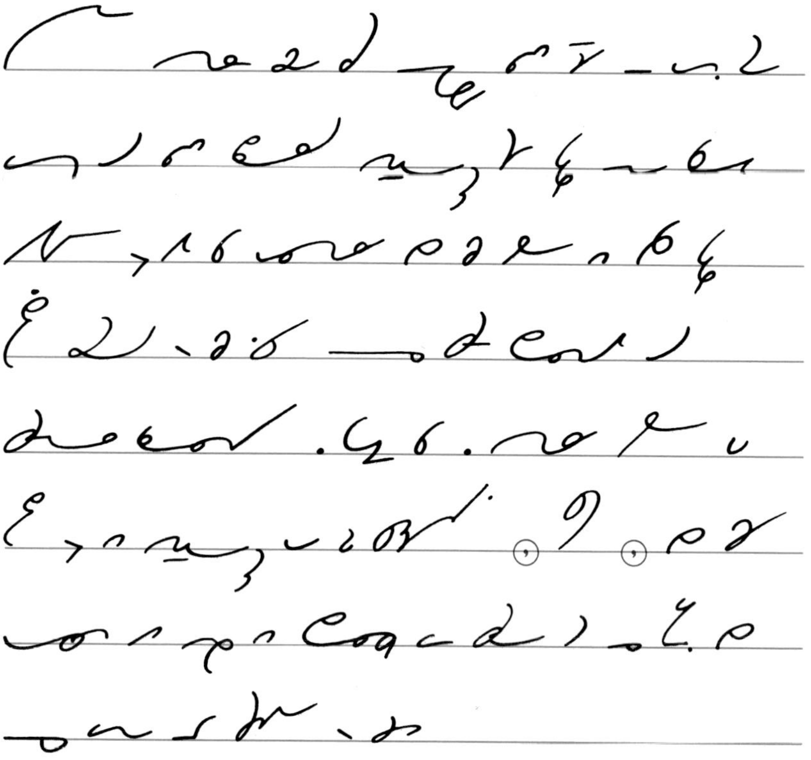

15
31
44
54
63
78
90
98

Mailable Production Letter

Transcribe the following mailable production letter in block style, assuring proper placement of the date, inside address, salutation, closing, writer's name, title, and reference initials. Insert punctuation prior to transcribing, and capitalize proper nouns in the address and closing lines. Note that an enclosure notation is needed. What is the enclosure?

39.4 School Material

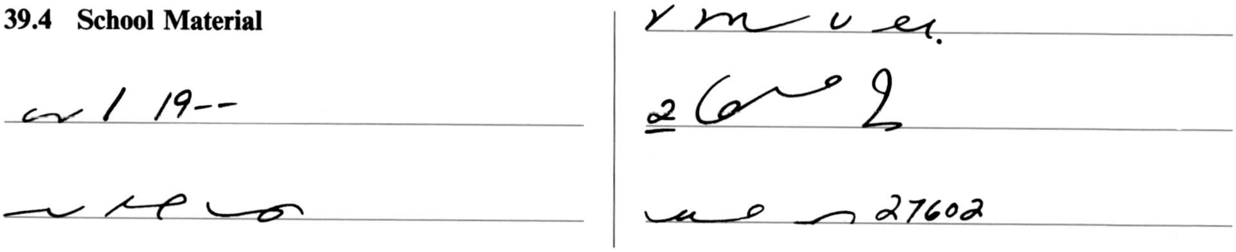

Acoustic couplers allow secretaries to transmit copy using a telephone handset held in a cushioned cradle.

Capitalization of Titles

Titles of company officials should not be capitalized when they follow or replace a personal name.

[shorthand]

I will send the report to Louis Stevens, *president*.

[shorthand]

The *manager* will not be at the meeting in California.

Do not capitalize such titles when the personal name that follows is in apposition and is set off by commas.

[shorthand]

Yesterday the *president*, William Woodward, issued a news release.

Capitalize all official titles of honor and respect when they replace the titles *Mr.*, *Ms.*, *Mrs.*, and *Dr.*

[shorthand]

President Elizabeth Billings

[shorthand]

Professor Steven Shea

[shorthand]

Governor Olson

Dictation and Transcription Practice

39.5 "To Do" List for the Boss

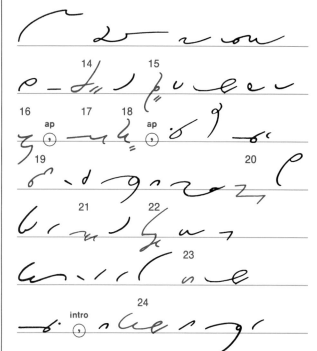

[33 words]

39.6 Security Procedures

1 Robert   2 Security   3 Procedures
4 increasing   5 avoid   6 problems   7 helpful
8 simple

[94 words]

39.7 Insurance Follow-Up

9 notify   10 intention   11 behind
12 cooperation   13 appreciated   14 January
15 February   16 representative   17 Mrs.
18 Fox   19 with you   20 information   21 costs
22 benefits   23 of your   24 promised

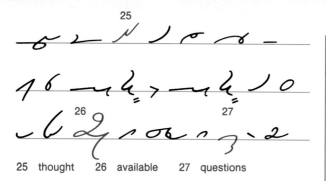

25 thought   26 available   27 questions

[100 words]

28 coverage   29 convenient   30 to do so

LESSON 40

IN LESSON 40

- Dictation speed building
- Transcription skill development
- Mailable production letter
- Compound adjectives

DICTATION SPEED BUILDING

The preview words below appear in the speed dictation practice that follows. Practice writing these words using the shorthand outlines. Then, using the key below, dictate the words to yourself.

Dictation Preview Words

Key: effective, collection, delinquent, retain, goodwill, assembled, binder, editorial, approval, enclosed, suit, you can, are not, we have, if you will

Speed Dictation Practice

40.1 Collection Letters

[shorthand notation]

[99 words]

TRANSCRIPTION SKILL DEVELOPMENT

Transcribe the following words and phrases, noting spelling and capitalization. Then transcribe the transcription letter in unarranged format.

Transcription Preview Words

40.2

	Word Count
[shorthand notation]	10
[shorthand notation]	10
[shorthand notation]	10

Transcription Practice

40.3 Education Specialist

Word
Count

[shorthand outlines]   11

[shorthand outlines]   22

[shorthand outlines]   35

[shorthand outlines]   44

[shorthand outlines]   59

[shorthand outlines]   72

[shorthand outlines]   86

[shorthand outlines]   88

Mailable Production Letter

Transcribe the following mailable production letter in block style, assuring proper placement of the date, inside address, salutation, closing, writer's name, title, and reference initials. Insert punctuation prior to transcribing, and capitalize proper nouns in the address and closing lines. Note that an enclosure notation is needed. What is the enclosure? The enclosure reminder will no longer appear. You must make the decision by reading the content of the letter.

40.4 Recreation Program

[shorthand outlines]   375 [shorthand outlines]

8 19--   [shorthand outlines] 66701

[shorthand outlines]   [shorthand outlines]

[105 words]

Compound Adjectives

A compound adjective is a one-thought modifier and is usually followed by a noun. It consists of two or more words that express a single meaning and is generally hyphenated.

We received the up-to-date report.

The compound adjective *up to date* expresses one thought and is followed by the noun *report*. In addition, the words *up to date* cannot be used separately to convey the intended meaning.

The report we received is up to date.

In this example *up to date* is a prepositional phrase instead of a compound adjective. Note that it is not hyphenated.

Dictation and Transcription Practice

40.5 Notes From the Library

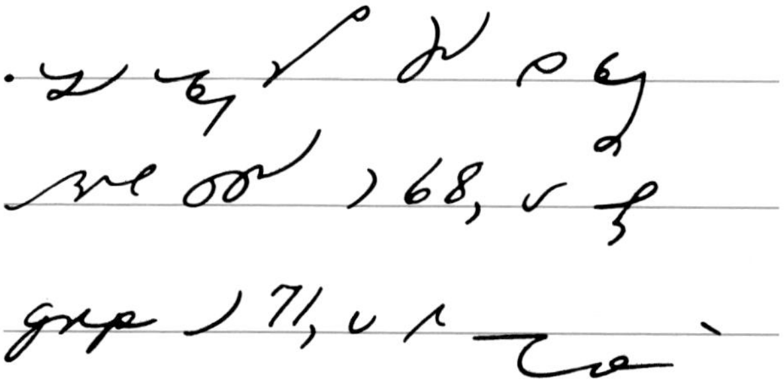

[34 words]

40.6 Information on Disability

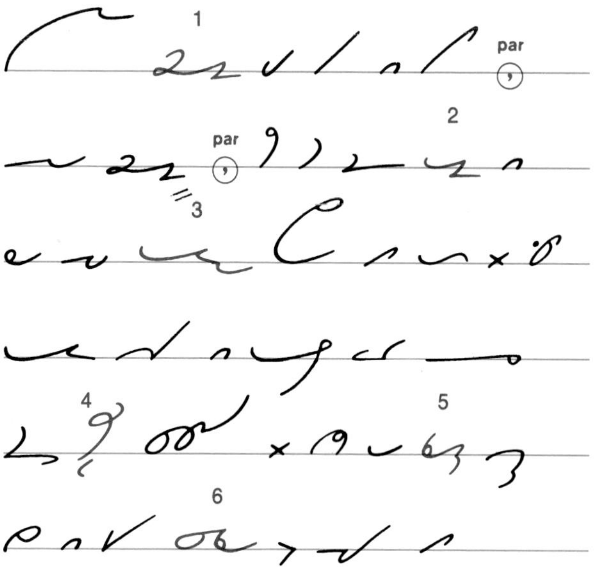

1 Wilson 2 reason 3 longer 4 savings
5 serious 6 answer

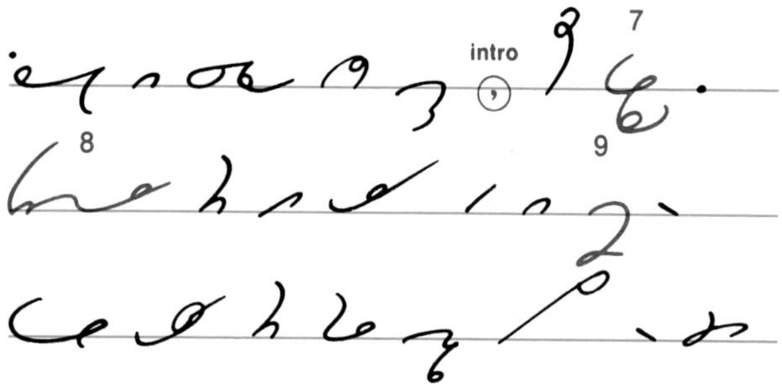

[66 words]

40.7 Congratulatory Note

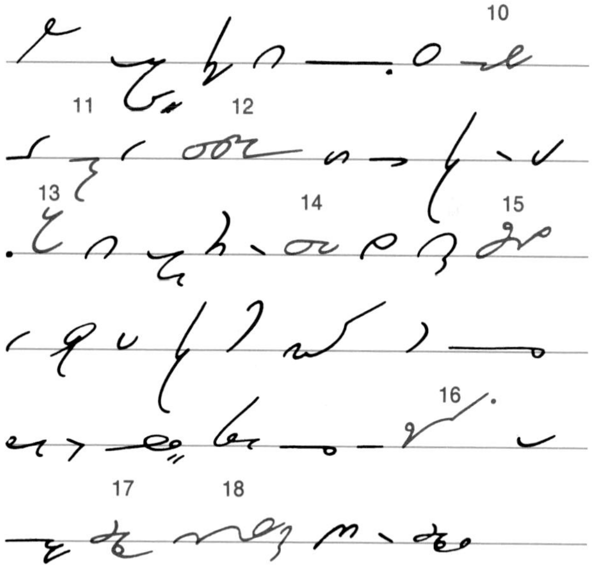

[56 words]

7 prepared 8 booklet 9 convenience
10 noticed 11 newspaper 12 announcement
13 opportunity 14 I know 15 exactly
16 extending 17 sincere 18 congratulations

IN LESSON 41

- ■ Dictation speed building
- ■ Transcription skill development
- ■ Mailable production letter
- ■ Capitalization of company names and other organizations

DICTATION SPEED BUILDING

The preview words below appear in the speed dictation practice which follows. Practice writing these words using the shorthand outlines. Then, using the key below, dictate the words to yourself.

Dictation Preview Words

Key: Henderson, considered, business, relationship, organization, quality, merchandise, wondering, trouble, anything, to be, with your, for the, we are

Speed Dictation Practice

41.1 Business Relationship

[Shorthand outlines]

conj

par

if

[96 words]

TRANSCRIPTION SKILL DEVELOPMENT

Transcribe the following words and phrases, noting spelling and capitalization. Then transcribe the transcription letter in unarranged format.

Transcription Preview Words

41.2

	Word Count
[Shorthand outline]	10
[Shorthand outline]	10
[Shorthand outline]	10

Transcription Practice

41.3 Letter of Appreciation

Word
Count

(shorthand outlines)

12

27

39

51

64

76

86

Mailable Production Letter

Transcribe the following mailable production letter in block style, assuring proper placement of the date, inside address, salutation, closing, writer's name, title, and reference initials. Insert punctuation prior to transcribing, and capitalize proper nouns in the address and closing lines.

41.4 Lawn Mower Purchase

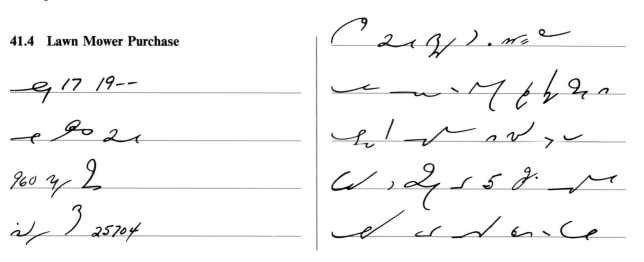

[shorthand symbols]

[80 words]

Capitalization of Company Names and Other Organizations

Capitalize the names of companies and other organizations. Follow the style established by the organization itself by referring to the company letterhead, if available. For example, an organization may use the *ampersand* (&) instead of the word *and*.

Prepositions like *of*, *for*, and *on* are not capitalized unless they have four or more letters like *from*. The articles *a* and *an* are not capitalized. The article *the* preceding the name of an organization is capitalized only when it is part of the legal name of the organization.

[shorthand outline]

World Manufacturing Company

[shorthand outline]

Gold & Franklin

[shorthand outline]

the Department of Education

[shorthand outline]

the Committee for Economic Development

[shorthand outline]

The New York Times

41.5 Organization Grant

(shorthand outlines)

[102 words]

41.6 Complaint

(shorthand outlines)

1 proposing 2 with the 3 heavy 4 specifies
5 outlined 6 valuable 7 financial

[106 words]

8 install 9 serious 10 explanation
11 excessive 12 trouble

LESSON 42

- Dictation speed building
- Transcription skill development
- Mailable production letter
- Capitalization of departments within companies

DICTATION SPEED BUILDING

The preview words below appear in the speed dictation practice which follows. Practice writing these words using the shorthand outlines. Then, using the key below, dictate the words to yourself.

Dictation Preview Words

Key: investment, greatest, clients, mentioned, potential, information, select, expect, has been, on the, you might be, we can, may be

Speed Dictation Practice

42.1 Investment Counsel

[shorthand notation]

[96 words]

TRANSCRIPTION SKILL DEVELOPMENT

Transcribe the following words and phrases, noting spelling and capitalization. Then transcribe the transcription letter in unarranged format.

Transcription Preview Words

42.2

	Word Count
[shorthand notation]	10
[shorthand notation]	10
[shorthand notation]	10

Transcription Practice

42.3 Computer Rental Agreement

Word Count

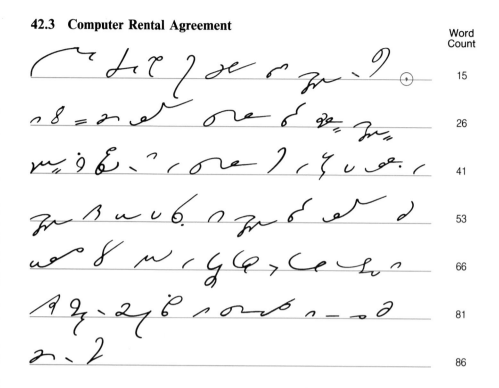

	15
	26
	41
	53
	66
	81
	86

Mailable Production Letter

Transcribe the following mailable production letter in block style, assuring proper placement of the date, inside address, salutation, closing, writer's name, title, and reference initials. Insert punctuation prior to transcribing, and capitalize proper nouns in the address and closing lines.

42.4 Textbook Selection

[shorthand outlines]

[105 words]

Capitalization of Departments Within Companies

Departments, such as the *Advertising Department*, are ordinarily capitalized when they are the actual names of units within the writer's organization or company. These terms are not capitalized when they refer to some other organization, unless the writer wishes to give these terms special emphasis.

[shorthand outline]

The *Accounting Department* will meet at 3 o'clock.

[shorthand outline]

The *accounting department* of Gold and Baker will review the order.

Dictation and Transcription Practice

42.5 Instructions for Mike

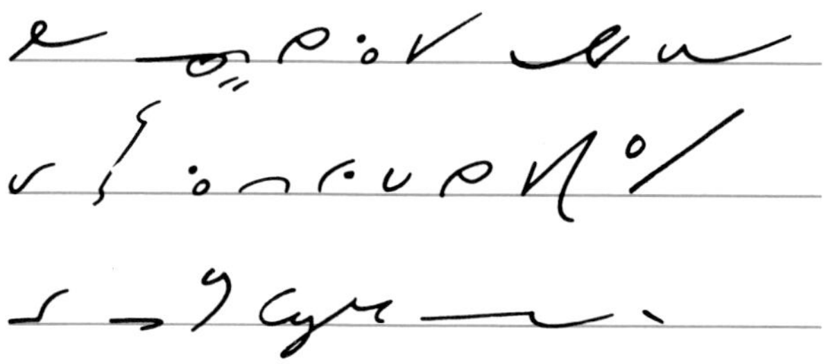

[shorthand notation]

[26 words]

42.6 Insurance Renewal

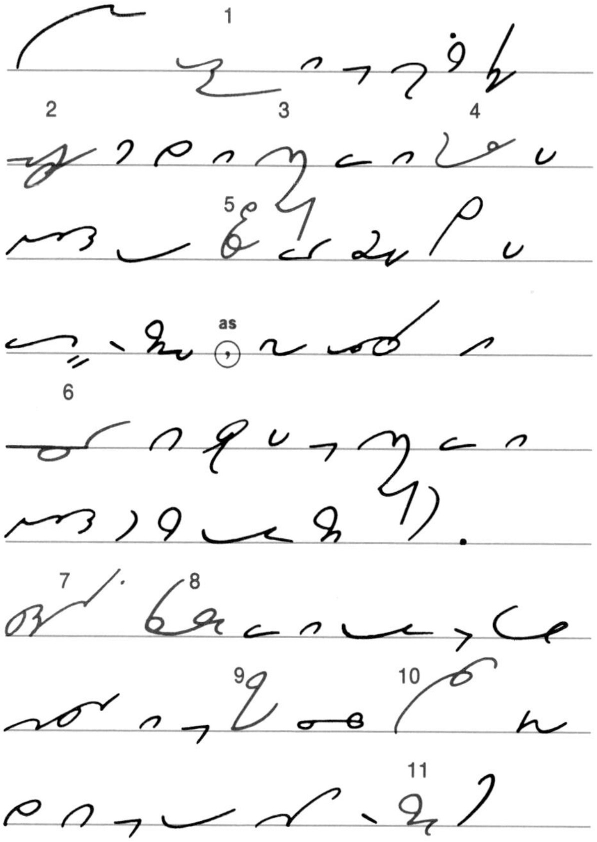

[shorthand notation with numbered markers 1-11]

[shorthand notation]

1 Russell   2 notified   3 coverage   4 fleet
5 expire   6 maintain   7 outstanding   8 balance
9 agent   10 to make   11 As soon as

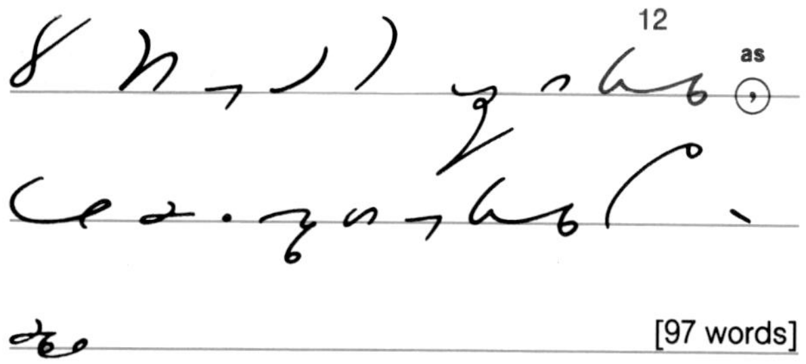

[shorthand notation with marker 12]

[97 words]

42.7 Business Conference

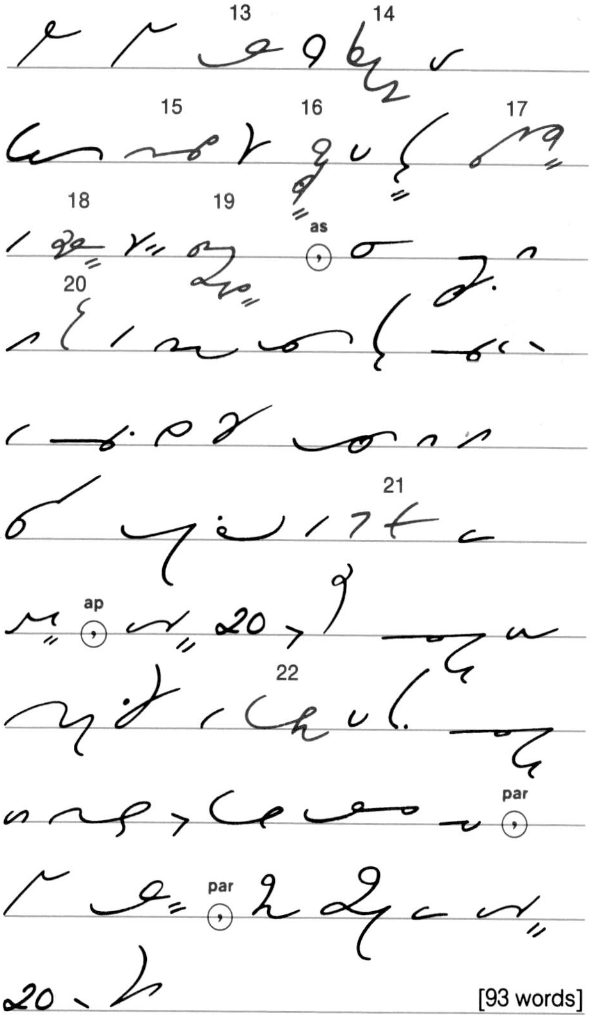

[shorthand notation with numbered markers 13-22]

[93 words]

12 policy   13 Lane   14 chairperson
15 committee   16 Association   17 Education
18 Western   19 University   20 speak
21 7 p.m.   22 pleasure

LESSON

IN LESSON 43

- ■ Dictation speed building
- ■ Transcription skill development
- ■ Mailable production letter
- ■ Titles of published works

DICTATION SPEED BUILDING

The preview words below appear in the speed dictation practice which follows. Practice writing these words using the shorthand outlines. Then, using the key below, dictate the words to yourself.

Dictation Preview Words

Key: Jackson, congratulations, purchase, ownership, furnace, expensive, inconvenient, fuel, available

Speed Dictation Practice

43.1 New Home

[shorthand symbols]

[122 words]

TRANSCRIPTION SKILL DEVELOPMENT

Transcribe the following words and phrases, noting spelling and capitalization. Then transcribe the transcription letter in unarranged format.

Transcription Preview Words

43.2

Word Count

[shorthand]   10

[shorthand]   10

[shorthand]   10

Transcription Practice

43.3 Hotel Reservations

[shorthand outlines] — 13

[shorthand outlines] — 24

[shorthand outlines] — 36

[shorthand outlines] — 45

[shorthand outlines] — 60

[shorthand outlines] — 72

[shorthand outlines] — 84

Mailable Production Letter

Transcribe the following mailable production letter in block style, assuring proper placement of the date, inside address, salutation, closing, writer's name, title, and reference initials. Insert punctuation prior to transcribing, and capitalize proper nouns in the address and closing lines.

43.4 Speaking Engagement

[shorthand outlines] 28 19--

[shorthand outlines]

69 *[shorthand outlines]*

[shorthand outlines] 70118

[shorthand outlines]

[shorthand outlines] 16 *[shorthand outlines]*

[shorthand outlines]

[shorthand outlines]

[Shorthand outlines at top of page, followed by] [90 words]

Titles of Published Works

Titles of major published works are typed with an underscore in business correspondence. A major work is a complete entity, such as a book, a play, or a regularly published magazine.

Titles of minor works are placed in quotation marks. Minor works are subdivisions of major works, such as a chapter within a book or an article within a magazine.

[Shorthand outline]

She is writing a book entitled America Today.

[Shorthand outline]

We subscribe to a magazine entitled The Business Review.

[Shorthand outline]

Tom's article, "Causes of Inflation," will be published in July.

43.5 Placement Service

[Shorthand outlines]

[93 words]

1 Jennings 2 individual 3 together
4 professional 5 We are 6 schedule
7 interviews

43.6 Magazine Subscription

[Shorthand outlines]

[97 words]

8 fleet 9 doubt 10 I am 11 publishing
12 Truck Driver Weekly 13 attractive 14 drivers

IN LESSON 44

- Dictation speed building
- Transcription skill development
- Mailable production letter
- Points of compass

DICTATION SPEED BUILDING

The preview words below appear in the speed dictation practice which follows. Practice writing these words using the shorthand outlines. Then, using the key below, dictate the words to yourself.

Dictation Preview Words

Key: Lynch, congratulations, factory, Chicago, boating, supplier, American, selection, marine, various, production, of your, I am sure, if you will

Speed Dictation Practice

44.1 Product Solicitation

[shorthand outlines]

[102 words]

TRANSCRIPTION SKILL DEVELOPMENT

Transcribe the following words and phrases, noting spelling and capitalization. Then transcribe the transcription letter in unarranged format.

Transcription Preview Words

44.2

	Word Count
[shorthand outline]	10
[shorthand outline]	10
[shorthand outline]	10

Transcription Practice

44.3 Price Increase

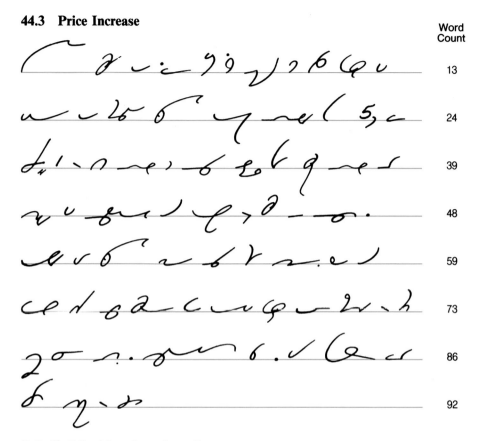

	Word Count
	13
	24
	39
	48
	59
	73
	86
	92

Mailable Production Letter

Transcribe the following mailable production letter in block style, assuring proper placement of the date, inside address, salutation, closing, writer's name, title, and reference initials. Insert punctuation prior to transcribing, and capitalize proper nouns in the address and closing lines.

44.4 Temporary Employment Agency

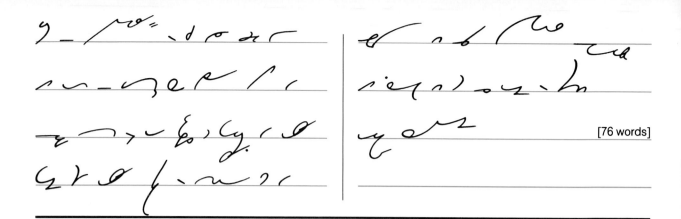

[76 words]

Points of Compass

Capitalize *north*, *south*, *east*, *west*, and derivative words, such as *northeast*, when they designate different regions or are part of a proper name.

She plans to be moving to the *North* in several months.

Most of our sales representatives are from the *West Coast*.

Do not capitalize these wor when they merely indicate general location.

They own a cottage on the *west* side of the bay.

To reach Florida you go *south* on Route 95.

44.5 Instructions From the Boss

[shorthand outlines]

[34 words]

44.6 Merchandise Sale

[shorthand outlines]

[99 words]

44.7 Student Loan

[shorthand outlines]

[80 words]

1 friend   2 recently   3 beautiful   4 limited
5 basis   6 variety   7 pictures   8 typical

9 sincerely   10 quality   11 myself   12 Parker
13 student   14 repayment   15 $54
16 assistance   17 further

U N I T

XII

LESSON 45

- **Dictation speed building**
- **Transcription skill development**
- **Mailable production letter**
- **Forming singular possessives**

DICTATION SPEED BUILDING

The preview words below appear in the speed dictation practice which follows. Practice writing these words using the shorthand outlines. Then, using the key below, dictate the words to yourself.

Dictation Preview Words

Key: Dailey, visited, privilege, philosophy, investments, Patterson, admit, somewhat, reluctant, watch, contact, to do so, Yours truly

Speed Dictation Practice

45.1 Stock Investments

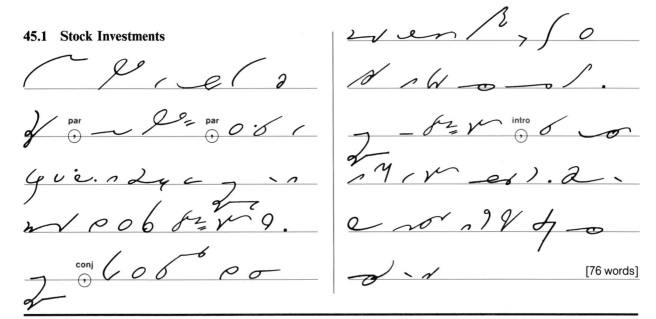

[76 words]

Transcribe the following words and phrases, noting spelling and capitalization. Then transcribe the transcription letter in unarranged format.

Transcription Preview Words

45.2

	Word Count
(shorthand)	10
(shorthand)	10
(shorthand)	10

Transcription Practice

45.3 Rug Order

Word Count

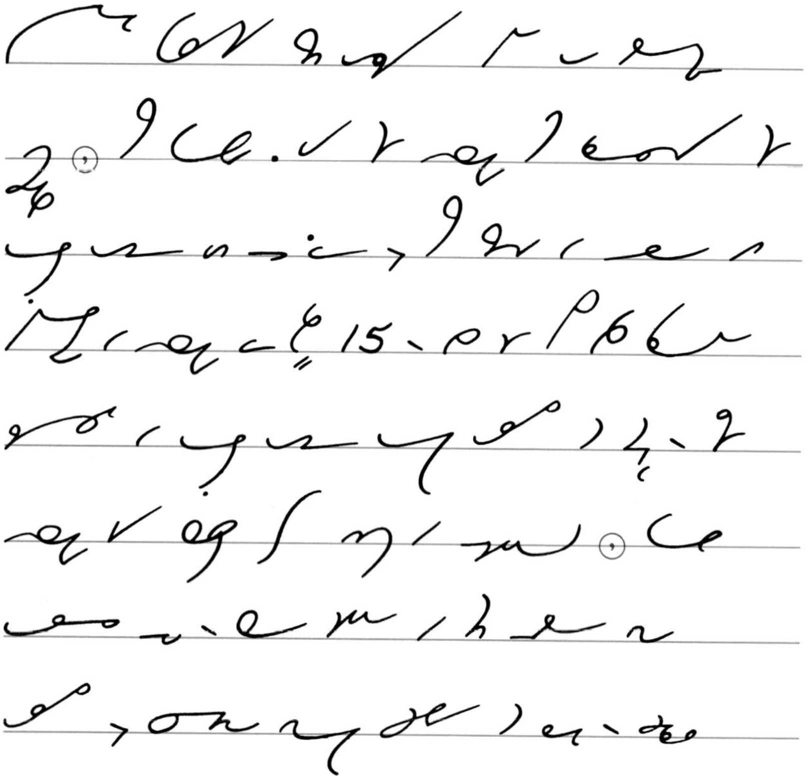

11
26
37
50
63
75
85
97

Mailable Production Letter

Transcribe the following mailable production letter in block style, assuring proper placement of the date, inside address, salutation, closing, writer's name, title, and reference initials. Insert punctuation prior to transcribing, and capitalize proper nouns in the address and closing lines.

45.4 Insurance Coverage

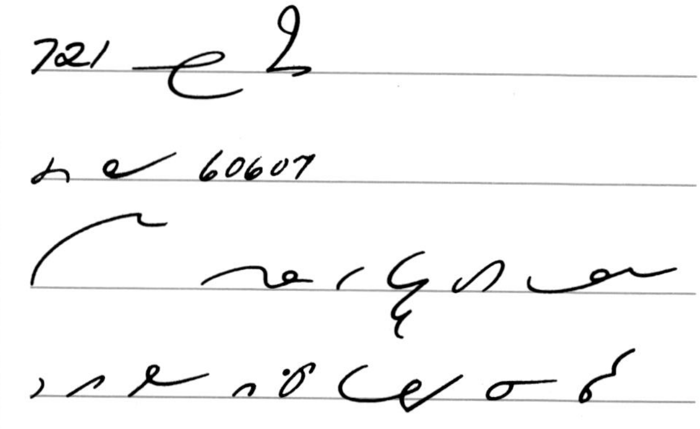

[107 words]

Forming Singular Possessives

When transcribing connected matter in shorthand, it is not always readily evident that a word is not in the possessive form as opposed to the plural form. Therefore, it is important to transcribe carefully and read for meaning.

A noun ending in the sound of *s* is usually in the possessive form if it is followed immediately by another noun. Try substituting an *of* phrase to determine if the possessive form should be used. If the substitution sounds correct, the possessive form should be used.

the company's circular
(the circular of the company)

the lawyer's advice
(the advice of the lawyer)

To form singular possessives, apply the following rules:

1 Add an *'s* to form the possessive of a singular noun not ending in an *s* sound.

the *company's* report

2 Add an *'s* to form the possessive of a singular noun that ends in an *s* sound if a new syllable is formed.

the *church's* account   your *business's* decision

3 Add only an apostrophe to a word ending in an *s* sound if the addition of an extra syllable would be hard to pronounce.

Los Angeles' restaurant   *Phillips'* project

Dictation and Transcription Practice

45.5   Office "To Do" List

517-555-1472

[25 words]

45.6   Contract Agreement

1 Add   2 Gordon   3 Jacobs   4 revision

[88 words]

5 collective   6 bargaining   7 Electronics
8 Incorporated   9 Workers   10 satisfactory
11 parties   12 effect

45.7 Vacation Arrangement

[Shorthand outlines]

par par

13 14

intro

15

16 intro

13 we have been   14 vacations   15 mentioned
16 July

17

18

19

20 21

22

23 conj

24

[129 words]

17 favorite   18 Colorado   19 deposit
20 middle   21 plenty   22 mountains
23 consider   24 decision

School placement offices can help you prepare a résumé and locate prospective employers. Shorthand is a skill that adds to your marketability.

IN LESSON 46

- Dictation speed building
- Transcription skill development
- Mailable production letter
- Forming plurals

DICTATION SPEED BUILDING

The preview words below appear in the speed dictation practice which follows. Practice writing these words using the shorthand outlines. Then, using the key below, dictate the words to yourself.

Dictation Preview Words

Key: Allen, sometimes, emergency, regular, advantage, national, apply, enclosed, application, approved, with the, of our, will be, as soon as

Speed Dictation Practice

46.1 Credit Information

[Shorthand outlines]

[110 words]

TRANSCRIPTION SKILL DEVELOPMENT

Transcribe the following words and phrases, noting spelling and capitalization. Then transcribe the transcription letter in unarranged format.

Transcription Preview Words
46.2

Word Count

[Shorthand outlines]   10

[Shorthand outlines]   10

[Shorthand outlines]   10

Transcription Practice

46.3 Income Tax Guide

Word Count

[shorthand outlines with word count markers]

9

19

32

41

53

66

75

87

96

Mailable Production Letter

Transcribe the following mailable production letter in block style, assuring proper placement of the date, inside address, salutation, closing, writer's name, title, and reference initials. Insert punctuation prior to transcribing, and capitalize proper nouns in the address and closing lines.

46.4 Insurance Policy

[shorthand outlines]

15 19--

436

36///

[Shorthand notation]

[108 words]

Forming Plurals

When transcribing words ending in *s*, there is no clue as to the spelling of these words. Therefore, it is important to apply the following rules when forming plurals.

1 Add *s* to the singular form.

committee	quota	conference	idea
committees	quotas	conferences	ideas

2 Add *es* when the singular form ends in *s*, *x*, *ch*, *sh*, or *z*.

business	tax	church	wish
businesses	taxes	churches	wishes

3 Change the *y* to *i* and add *es* when a singular noun ends in *y* preceded by a consonant.

copy	policy
copies	policies

4 Add *s* when a singular noun ends in *y* preceded by a vowel.

delay	attorney
delays	attorneys

Nouns Ending in O

1 Add *s* when a singular noun ends in *o* preceded by a vowel.

stereo   stereos

2 Singular nouns ending in *o* preceded by a consonant form their plurals in different ways.

photo	potato	zero	piano
photos	potatoes	zeros, zeroes	pianos

Dictation and Transcription Practice

46.5 Personal Note

[shorthand]

[30 words]

46.6 Staff Survey Memo

[shorthand]

1 Paula

[shorthand]

2 Perhaps   3 conducted   4 survey
5 determine   6 opinions   7 quality
8 management   9 important   10 everything
11 I think

[Shorthand text] [158 words]

46.7 Membership Application

[Shorthand text] [80 words]

12 questionnaire   13 form   14 summer
15 frequent

16 National   17 memberships   18 encouraged
19 magazine   20 impressed   21 application

When you go on a job interview, be sure to bring along a steno notepad because you may be asked to take a dictation and transcription test.

LESSON 47

IN LESSON 47

- Dictation speed building
- Transcription skill development
- Mailable production letter
- Transcription of plurals

DICTATION SPEED BUILDING

The preview words below appear in the speed dictation practice which
follows. Practice writing these words using the shorthand outlines.
Then, using the key below, dictate the words to yourself.

Dictation Preview Words

[shorthand outlines]

Key: Hastings, representative, Morris, perfume, marketing,
popular, sample, packages, opportunity, success, campaign,
of the, to know, that the

Speed Dictation Practice

47.1 Product Information

[shorthand outlines]

[shorthand notation] [90 words]

Transcribe the following words and phrases, noting spelling and capitalization. Then transcribe the transcription letter in unarranged format.

Transcription Preview Words

47.2

	Word Count
[shorthand notation]	10
[shorthand notation]	10
[shorthand notation]	10

Transcription Practice

47.3 Product Information

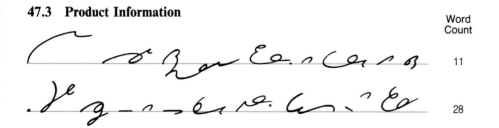

	Word Count
[shorthand notation]	11
[shorthand notation]	28

LESSON 47 ▰▰ **277**

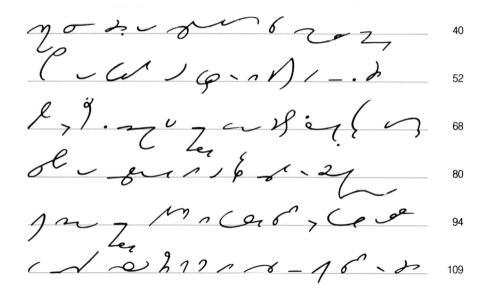

	40
	52
	68
	80
	94
	109

Mailable Production Letter

Transcribe the following mailable production letter in block style, assuring proper placement of the date, inside address, salutation, closing, writer's name, title, and reference initials. Insert punctuation prior to transcribing, and capitalize proper nouns in the address and closing lines.

47.4 Business Purchase

Transcription of Plurals

Nouns With Irregular Plurals

The plurals of some nouns are in a different form and do not end in *s*.

woman	man
women	men

child	foot
children	feet

Compound Nouns

When a compound noun is a solid word, pluralize the final element in the compound as if it stood alone.

printout	birthday
printouts	birthdays

The plurals of *hyphenated* or two-word compounds are formed by pluralizing the main element of the compound.

father-in-law	editor in chief
fathers-in-law	editors in chief

When a *hyphenated* compound does not contain a noun, simply pluralize the final element.

go-between	show-off
go-betweens	show-offs

47.5 Meetings Memo

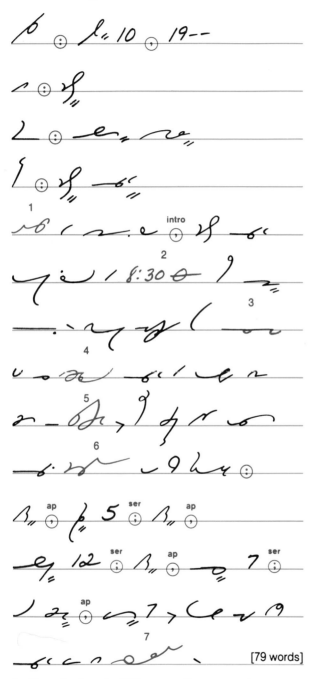

[79 words]

1 Throughout   2 8:30 a.m.   3 memorandum
4 canceled   5 advance   6 schedule   7 calendar

47.6 Price Quotations

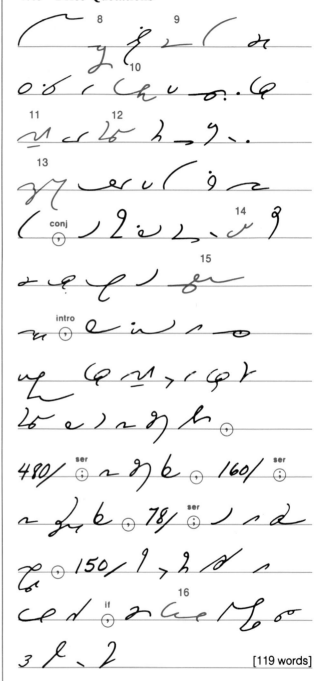

[119 words]

8 Novak   9 some time   10 pleasure
11 quotation   12 furniture   13 considerable
14 Although   15 material   16 promise

LESSON 48

IN LESSON 48

- Dictation speed building
- Transcription skill development
- Mailable production letter
- Forming plural possessives

DICTATION SPEED BUILDING

The preview words below appear in the speed dictation practice which follows. Practice writing these words using the shorthand outlines. Then, using the key below, dictate the words to yourself.

Dictation Preview Words

Key: Kate, famous, athlete, 100,000, copies, program, speeches, colors, special, handled, project, to be, we have, we can

Speed Dictation Practice

48.1 Job Opportunity

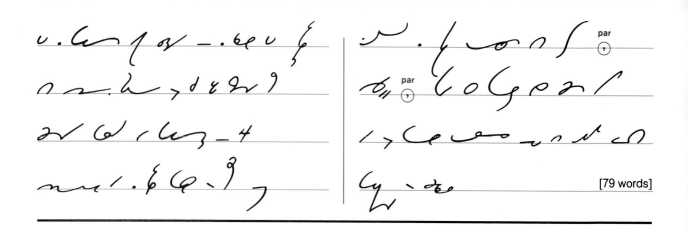

[79 words]

Transcribe the following words and phrases, noting spelling and capitalization. Then transcribe the transcription letter in unarranged format.

Transcription Preview Words

48.2

	Word Count
	10
	10
	10

Transcription Practice

48.3 Follow-Up Letter

	Word Count
	11
	25
	35

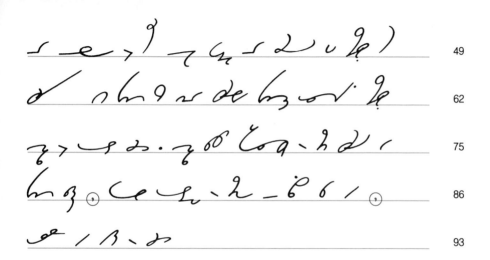

	49
	62
	75
	86
	93

Mailable Production Letter

Transcribe the following mailable production letter in block style, assuring proper placement of the date, inside address, salutation, closing, writer's name, title, and reference initials. Insert punctuation prior to transcribing, and capitalize proper nouns in the address and closing lines.

48.4 **Business Seminars**

[94 words]

Forming Plural Possessives

When transcribing connected shorthand material:

1 Add only an apostrophe to form the plural possessive of a plural noun that ends in *s*.

witnesses' tenacity   attorneys' advice

2 Add an *'s* to form the plural possessive of a plural noun that does not end in *s*.

women's organization   children's books

Note: It is important when forming the possessive of a plural noun that you first apply the rule for making the word plural; then apply the rule for forming the plural possessive.

Dictation and Transcription Practice

48.5   While You Were Out

[32 words]

1 Vega   2 form   3 microfilm

48.6   Complaint

4 Stevens   5 complaining   6 automobile
7 $200   8 According   9 records

[Shorthand outlines]

[131 words]

48.7 Insurance Request

[Shorthand outlines]

[105 words]

10 regular   11 owner's   12 manual   13 routine
14 procedures   15 customer   16 Bloom   17 As
the   18 draws

19 income   20 higher   21 financially
22 understand   23 retirement   24 teacher
25 deposited   26 information

UNIT XIII

LESSON 49

- Dictation speed building
- Transcription skill development
- Developing an address from a letterhead
- Mailable production practice

DICTATION SPEED BUILDING

The preview words below appear in the speed dictation practice which
follows. Practice writing these words using the shorthand outlines.
Then, using the key below, dictate the words to yourself.

Dictation Preview Words

Key: Nelson, appointed, committee, employee, industry,
consequently, details, personnel, with the, in our, we will be,
you will, of this, will be

288 ◼◼◼ LESSON 49

Speed Dictation Practice

49.1 Employee Insurance

[shorthand notation] intro *[shorthand notation]*

[89 words]

Transcribe the following words and phrases, noting spelling and capitalization. Then transcribe the transcription letter in unarranged format.

Transcription Preview Words

49.2

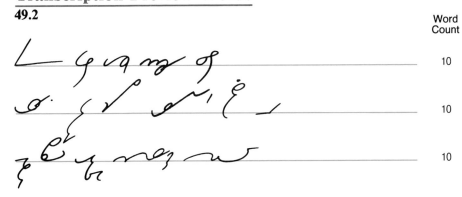

	Word Count
	10
	10
	10

Transcription Practice

49.3 Congratulatory Letter

Word
Count

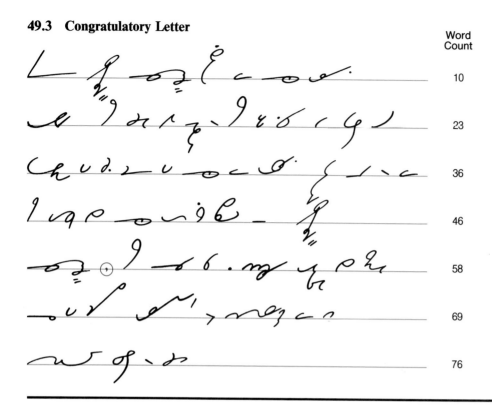

	10
	23
	36
	46
	58
	69
	76

Developing an Address From a Letterhead

The closing of a letter, along with the information contained in the letterhead, should provide all the facts that are needed in order to develop a letter address. For example, you would look at the writer's identification in the closing for the name and title of the addressee. You would look at the letterhead at the top of the letter for the company name and address.

Many letterheads also contain such information as lists of company officers or advertising slogans, which would not be used in addressing correspondence.

Peruse the letter at the top of page 291 and determine the letter address that would be used.

JUDD-KANE, INC.
1410 Glenarm Street, Denver, CO 80202

February 20, 19--

Mr. Wilson J. Baker, President
Parsons and Company, Inc.
316 West Street
Chicago, IL 60607

Dear Mr. Baker

Recently I wrote to John Smith about the possibility of his joining your staff as a sales representative. You will recall that I mentioned to you that he was going to change positions and that he might be interested in joining your organization as a sales representative in Florida.

Today I had a reply from him in which he thanked me for writing him about the position at Parsons and Company, but he had accepted a job with the National Products Company.

I am sorry that he obtained a new position so quickly. I know that he would have made a good addition to your staff.

Sincerely yours

John H. Graham
President

ee

Mailable Production Practice

Write the following mailable production letters in your shorthand notebook. Insert punctuation and check the spelling of any words that would give you difficulty when transcribing. You will then be asked to transcribe the letters from your shorthand notes in block style, assuring proper placement of the date, inside address, salutation, closing, writer's name, title, and reference initials. The word count begins with the salutation and ends with the closing lines.

49.4 Account Collection

33716

[shorthand content]

[115 words]

49.5 **Special Account**

19 19--

1965

9 85201

[82 words]

LESSON
50

IN LESSON 50

- Dictation speed building
- Transcription skill development
- Addressing an envelope
- Mailable production practice

DICTATION SPEED BUILDING

The preview words below appear in the speed dictation practice which follows. Practice writing these words using the shorthand outlines. Then, using the key below, dictate the words to yourself.

Dictation Preview Words

Key: Leslie, Tuesday, audit, reporting, offices, operations, December, forwarded, future, of your, to your, will be, as soon as, I hope, in the

Speed Dictation Practice

50.1 Audit Completion

[95 words]

TRANSCRIPTION SKILL DEVELOPMENT

Transcribe the following words and phrases, noting spelling and capitalization. Then transcribe the transcription letter in unarranged format.

Transcription Preview Words

50.2

Word Count

10

10

10

Transcription Practice

50.3 Family Move

Word Count

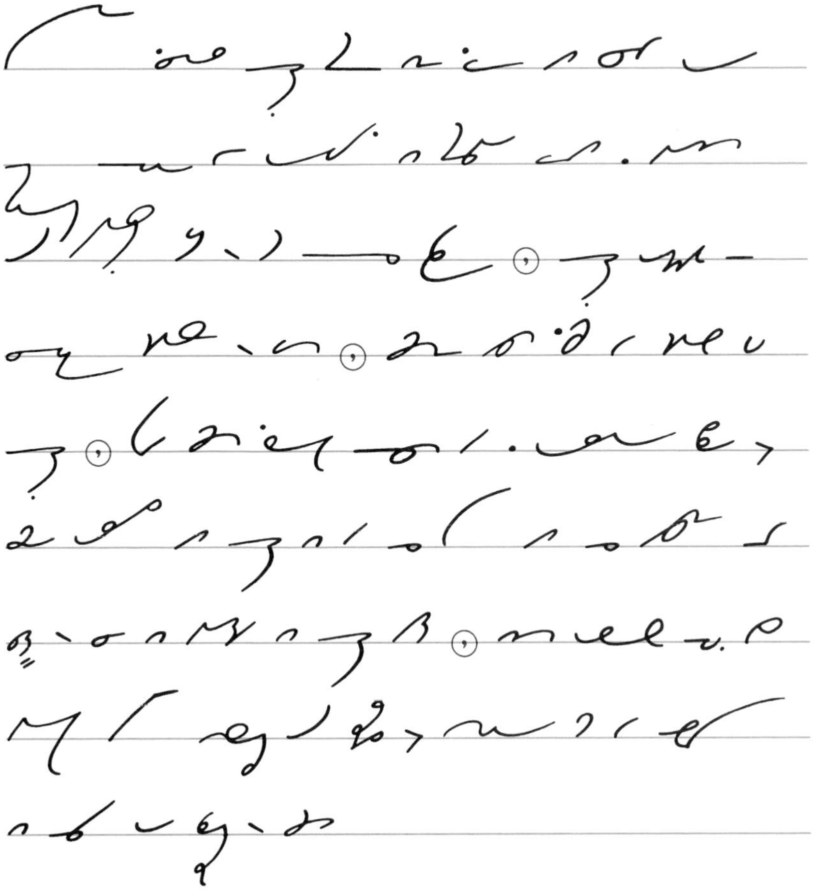

10
21
31
43
52
63
74
87
95

Addressing an Envelope

Return Address

When the envelope contains a printed return address, type the name of the writer above the printed return address. See the illustration at the bottom of page 296.

If a printed address does not appear on the envelope, type the return address in the upper left corner, beginning on line 3 about l/2 inch from the left edge. The return address should list the following information, arranged on separate lines:

1 Name of writer
2 Name of company
3 Street address or box number
4 City, state, and ZIP Code

Jonathan T. Brant
B. W. Witcomb
2178 Market Street
San Francisco, CA 94114

Letter Address

When typing a letter address on an envelope, use these guidelines:

1 Always use single spacing and block each line at the left.
2 Capitalize the first letter of each word except conjunctions, articles, and very short prepositions used within a name or title.
3 Type the city, state, and ZIP Code on the last line.
4 Use the two-letter state abbreviation.
5 Use a large envelope and start the address on line 14 at 50 for elite type and at 42 for pica type.

Special Notations—Personal and Confidential

Personal or *Confidential* should begin on line 9 or a triple space after the return address. Begin each word with a capital letter, use underscoring, and align at the left with the return address.

Attention Line

If an attention line was used within the letter, it should appear on the envelope. The attention line can be typed exactly like a *personal* or *confidential* notation.

Mailing Notations

If a special mailing notation is used, type the appropriate notation—such as *Special Delivery* or *Registered*—in capital letters in the upper right-hand corner of the envelope on line 9 or a triple space below the stamp. Begin backspacing the notation (one space for each letter) 1/2 inch from the right edge of the envelope.

It is important in an interview to be prepared to talk about your past work experiences and skills, as well as learn about the job and company.

Mailable Production Practice

Write the following mailable production letters in your shorthand notebook. Insert punctuation and check the spelling of any words that would give you difficulty when transcribing. You will then be asked to transcribe the letters from your shorthand notes in block style, assuring proper placement of the date, inside address, salutation, closing, writer's name, title, and reference initials. The word count begins with the salutation and ends with the closing lines.

50.4 Office Furniture

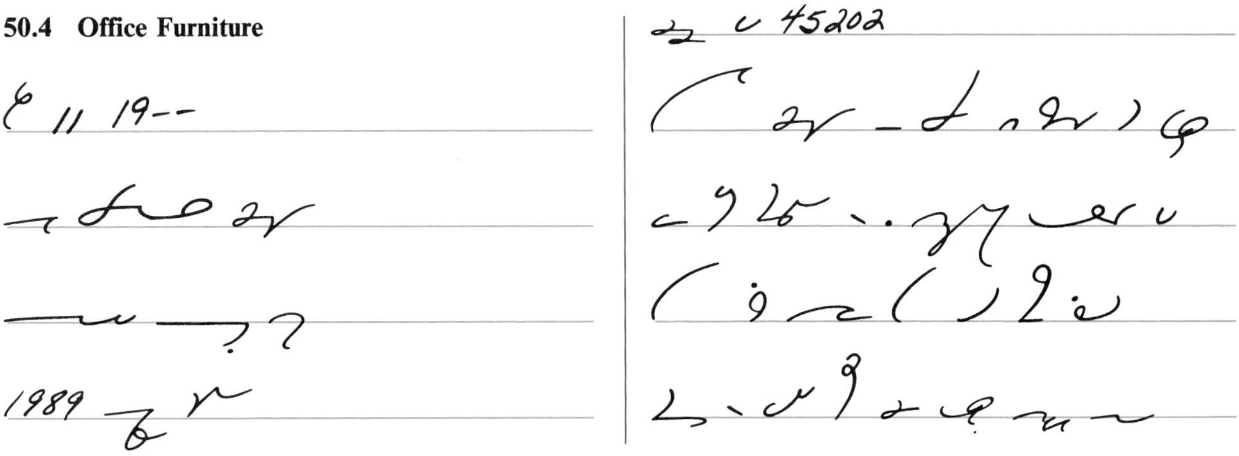

350/

3/ 3 =

150/

[108 words]

50.5   Price List

15 19--

14

62708

[98 words]

IN LESSON 51

- Dictation speed building
- Transcription skill development
- Copy notation
- Mailable production practice

DICTATION SPEED BUILDING

The preview words below appear in the speed dictation practice which follows. Practice writing these words using the shorthand outlines. Then, using the key below, dictate the words to yourself.

Dictation Preview Words

Key: invitation, Grant, stores, widely, valuable, hundreds, moment, requested, it is, in this, we will, you will be able, to make, United States, will you please

Speed Dictation Practice

51.1 Credit Consideration

[shorthand outlines]

[87 words]

TRANSCRIPTION SKILL DEVELOPMENT

Transcribe the following words and phrases, noting spelling and capitalization. Then transcribe the transcription letter in unarranged format.

Transcription Preview Words

51.2

	Word Count
[shorthand outline]	10
[shorthand outline]	10
[shorthand outline]	10

Transcription Practice

51.3 Bookstore Opening

[shorthand outlines] — 10

[shorthand outlines] 20 — 22

[shorthand outlines] — 36

[shorthand outlines] — 47

[shorthand outlines] 50, — 61

[shorthand outlines] 15 / 5t — 74

[shorthand outlines] — 85

[shorthand outlines] — 92

Copy Notation

A copy notation alerts the addressee that one or more persons will be sent a copy of the letter. Use these guidelines to type a copy notation:

1 Use the initials *cc* to denote the copy notation. See page 302.
2 Type *cc* at the left margin on the line below the last notation.
3 Type *cc* with or without a colon.
4 If more than one person is to receive a copy, list the names according to the rank of the persons or in alphabetic order.
5 Omit personal titles such as *Mr.*, *Mrs.*, or *Ms.*
6 The *cc* notation appears on the original and all the copies.

cc Janice Moses
   Peter Myers

```
              Very truly yours


              Elizabeth Arnold
              Assistant Vice President

              jtm
              cc:  Anne Jenkins
```

Write the following mailable production letters in your shorthand
notebook. Insert punctuation and check the spelling of any words that
would give you difficulty when transcribing. You will then be asked
to transcribe the letters from your shorthand notes in block style,
assuring proper placement of the date, inside address, salutation, closing, writer's name, title, and reference initials. The word count begins
with the salutation and ends with the closing lines.

51.4   Rifle Club

[shorthand outlines]

[104 words]

51.5 Advertising Appropriation

[Shorthand outlines]

LESSON 52

IN LESSON 52

- Dictation speed building
- Transcription skill development
- Blind copy notation
- Mailable production practice

DICTATION SPEED BUILDING

The preview words below appear in the speed dictation practice which follows. Practice writing these words using the shorthand outlines. Then, using the key below, dictate the words to yourself.

Dictation Preview Words

Key: July, merchandise, excellent, advantage, according, we will, do not have, to your, you will be able, of this

Speed Dictation Practice

52.1 Seasonal Sale

[shorthand notation] [97 words]

Transcribe the following words and phrases, noting spelling and capitalization. Then transcribe the transcription letter in unarranged format.

Transcription Preview Words
52.2

	Word Count
[shorthand notation]	10
[shorthand notation]	10
[shorthand notation]	10

Transcription Practice

52.3 Investments

	Word Count
	11
	23
	37
	48
	64
	74
	84
	94
	105

Blind Copy Notation

If the addressee is not to know that one or more persons are being sent a copy of the letter, a blind copy notation is used. To type a blind copy notation, follow these guidelines:

1 First remove the original letter and any copies on which the blind copy notation is not to appear.
2 On the remaining copies type the blind copy notation at the left margin on the second line below the last notation.
3 Use the initials *bcc* to denote the blind copy notation.
4 Type *bcc* with or without a colon.

5 If more than one person is to receive a copy, list the names according to the rank of the persons or in alphabetic order.

6 Omit personal titles such as *Mr.*, *Mrs.*, or *Ms.*

```
        Very truly yours


        Elizabeth A. Sinclair
        Accounting Department

        tma

        bcc:  Claire R. Harrington
```

Mailable Production Practice

Write the following mailable production letters in your shorthand notebook. Insert punctuation and check the spelling of any words that would give you difficulty when transcribing. You will then be asked to transcribe the letters from your shorthand notes in block style, assuring proper placement of the date, inside address, salutation, closing, writer's name, title, and reference initials. The word count begins with the salutation and ends with the closing lines.

52.4 Book Supplies

[shorthand outlines]

Applicants for secretarial positions who possess shorthand skills find it makes them more marketable.

[114 words]

52.5 Graduation Preparation

[111 words]

[111 words]

LESSON
53

IN LESSON 53

- Dictation speed building
- Transcription skill development
- Subject line
- Mailable production practice

DICTATION SPEED BUILDING

The preview words below appear in the speed dictation practice which follows. Practice writing these words using the shorthand outlines. Then, using the key below, dictate the words to yourself.

Dictation Preview Words

Key: uncommon, customers, complain, demand, compliment, outstanding, delighted, damaged, fender, terrific, it is, of your, do not, I was, you can be

Speed Dictation Practice

53.1 Car Service

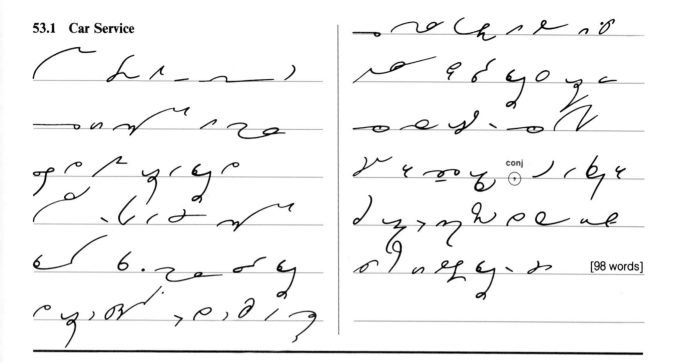

[98 words]

Transcribe the following words and phrases, noting spelling and capitalization. Then transcribe the transcription letter in unarranged format.

Transcription Preview Words

53.2

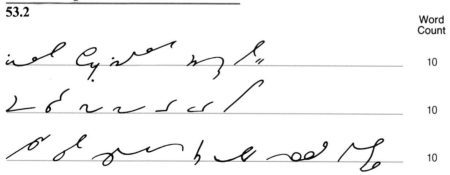

	Word Count
	10
	10
	10

Transcription Practice

53.3 Holiday Shopping

[Shorthand outlines] — 12

[Shorthand outlines] — 24

[Shorthand outlines] — 35

[Shorthand outlines] — 44

[Shorthand outlines] — 54

[Shorthand outlines] — 64

[Shorthand outlines] — 73

[Shorthand outlines] — 86

[Shorthand outlines] — 97

Subject Line

The subject line is used to introduce the topic or message set forth in the letter.

1 The subject line appears between the salutation and the body, with one blank line above and below. See the illustration on page 315.
2 The subject line is usually placed at the left margin.
3 The subject line can be typed in capital and small letters or entirely in capital letters.
4 The subject line is not usually underscored but can be underscored for special emphasis.
5 The term *Subject:* or *Re:* usually precedes the actual subject but may be omitted.

Subject: Subscription Renewal
Subject: Advertising Proposal
Re: Parker versus Baker

ALL-SEASON
SPORTING GOODS
1983 DURAND AVENUE, RACINE, WI 53403

September 18, 19--

Rossi Supply Company
328 Glenn Street
Denver, CO 80202

Ladies and Gentlemen

Subject: Winter Rates for Personnel

Write the following mailable production letters in your shorthand notebook. Insert punctuation and check the spelling of any words that would give you difficulty when transcribing. You will then be asked to transcribe the letters from your shorthand notes in block style, assuring proper placement of the date, inside address, salutation, closing, writer's name, title, and reference initials. The word count begins with the salutation and ends with the closing lines.

53.4   Potential Customer

[shorthand outlines]

42501

[99 words]

53.5 Car Purchase

19--

1940

2 73462

[97 words]

LESSON 54

- Dictation speed building
- Transcription skill development
- Attention line
- Mailable production practice

DICTATION SPEED BUILDING

The preview words below appear in the speed dictation practice which follows. Practice writing these words using the shorthand outlines. Then, using the key below, dictate the words to yourself.

Dictation Preview Words

Key: Vega, increasingly, account, overdue, opportunity, special, consideration, unfortunately, replied, situation, serious, for the, about your, we have, you have not

Speed Dictation Practice

54.1 Overdue Account

[shorthand notation]

[99 words]

TRANSCRIPTION SKILL DEVELOPMENT

Transcribe the following words and phrases, noting spelling and capitalization. Then transcribe the transcription letter in unarranged format.

Transcription Preview Words

54.2

	Word Count
[shorthand notation]	10
[shorthand notation]	10
[shorthand notation]	10

Transcription Practice

54.3 Car Rental

[shorthand outlines] 13

[shorthand outlines] 25

[shorthand outlines] 38

[shorthand outlines] 49

[shorthand outlines] 61

[shorthand outlines] 72

[shorthand outlines] 84

[shorthand outlines] 89

Attention Line

When a letter is addressed directly to a company, an attention line may be used to direct the letter to a particular title (name unknown) or to a particular department. Use the following guidelines for the attention line:

1 The attention line should be typed on the second line below the inside address at the left margin. The salutation follows the attention line. See the illustration on page 320.
2 The attention line may be typed in capital and small letters or entirely in capital letters.
3 Type a colon after the word *Attention*.
4 The word *Attention* should not be abbreviated.
5 Do not underscore the attention line unless additional emphasis is required.

Atlanta Manufacturing Company
907 Ryan Avenue
Atlanta, GA 30329

Attention: Sales Manager

Dear Sir or Madam

Worth Publishing Company
710 Armstrong Street
Kansas City, KS 66202

ATTENTION: ADVERTISING DEPARTMENT

Ladies and Gentlemen

Morgan-Eastern
School of Business
Student Government Association
(301) 555-8384 Extension 2202
Baltimore, Maryland 21239

March 4, 19--

Samuels Manufacturing Company
318 Elm Street
Baltimore, MD 21239

Attention: Accounting Manager

Dear Sir or Madam

Write the following mailable production letters in your shorthand notebook. Insert punctuation and check the spelling of any words that would give you difficulty when transcribing. You will then be asked to transcribe the letters from your shorthand notes in block style, assuring proper placement of the date, inside address, salutation, closing, writer's name, title, and reference initials. The word count begins with the salutation and ends with the closing lines.

54.4 Accounting Publication

[shorthand outlines]

19--

1985

48835

[106 words]

54.5 Request for Recommendation

(shorthand outline) 5 19--

[112 words]

IN LESSON 55

- Dictation speed building
- Transcription skill development
- Academic degrees
- Mailable production practice

DICTATION SPEED BUILDING

The preview words below appear in the speed dictation practice which follows. Practice writing these words using the shorthand outlines. Then, using the key below, dictate the words to yourself.

Dictation Preview Words

Key: Lowe, special, discount, Cunningham, furniture, Ames, arrangement, considering, concluded, appropriate, policy, thank you for your letter

Speed Dictation Practice

55.1 Employee Discount

[Shorthand outlines]

intro

[94 words]

Transcribe the following words and phrases, noting spelling and capitalization. Then transcribe the transcription letter in unarranged format.

Transcription Preview Words

55.2

	Word Count
[Shorthand outlines]	10
[Shorthand outlines]	10
[Shorthand outlines]	10

Transcription Practice

55.3 Clothing Shipment

[shorthand]   11

[shorthand]   22

[shorthand]   32

[shorthand] 35 *[shorthand]*   45

1940 *[shorthand]*   59

[shorthand]   71

[shorthand]   84

[shorthand]   97

[shorthand]   104

Academic Degrees

Use the following guidelines for academic degrees:

1 Academic degrees such as *Ph.D.* and *M.D.* require a period after each element but no internal space.
2 When academic degrees follow a person's name, do not use such titles as *Dr.*, *Mr.*, *Mrs.*, or *Ms.* before the name.

Dr. Grace March
Grace March, Ph.D.
(*Not*: Dr. Grace March, Ph.D.)

It is important for the office worker to read professional publications to keep aware of changes and advancements in his or her particular field.

Mailable Production Practice

Write the following mailable production letters in your shorthand notebook. Insert punctuation and check the spelling of any words that would give you difficulty when transcribing. You will then be asked to transcribe the lctters from your shorthand notes in block style, assuring proper placement of the date, inside address, salutation, closing, writer's name, title, and reference initials. The word count begins with the salutation and ends with the closing lines.

55.4 Speaking Invitation

[131 words]

55.5 Communications Seminar

21260

[125 words]

LESSON

56

IN LESSON 56

- Dictation speed building
- Transcription skill development
- Abbreviation of titles following personal names
- Mailable production practice

DICTATION SPEED BUILDING

The preview words below appear in the speed dictation practice which follows. Practice writing these words using the shorthand outlines. Then, using the key below, dictate the words to yourself.

Dictation Preview Words

Key: Brooks, travel, agent, unfortunate, Italy, minute, scheduled, engine, apologies, inconvenience, confident, for the, will be

Speed Dictation Practice

56.1 Flight Trouble

(shorthand outlines)

intro ,

[87 words]

TRANSCRIPTION SKILL DEVELOPMENT

Transcribe the following words and phrases, noting spelling and capitalization. Then transcribe the transcription letter in unarranged format.

Transcription Preview Words

56.2

Word Count

(shorthand outline)   10

(shorthand outline)   10

(shorthand outline)   10

Transcription Practice

56.3 Account Inquiry

[shorthand outlines]   10

[shorthand outlines]   23

[shorthand outlines]   37

[shorthand outlines]   49

[shorthand outlines]   62

[shorthand outlines]   76

[shorthand outlines]   89

[shorthand outlines]   104

Abbreviation of Titles Following Personal Names

Esq.

The title *Esquire*, abbreviated to *Esq.*, is used primarily by lawyers.

1 *Esq.* is used in the letter address and is not retained in the salutation.
2 No title such as *Mr.*, *Mrs.*, or *Ms.* should precede the name.
3 A comma separates the name from the title.

Philip Samuels, *Esq.*
621 West Pittsburgh Street
Greensburg, PA 15601

Dear Mr. Samuels

Jr. and *Sr.*

1 Always abbreviate *Jr.* and *Sr.* when they follow personal names.
2 Do not use commas to set off *Jr.* and *Sr.* unless the writer uses a comma.
3 A title such as *Mr.* and *Dr.* may precede the name.
4 *Jr.* and *Sr.* are not used in the salutation.

Mr. George Rosenberg Jr.
931 East Main Street
Philadelphia, PA 19104

Dear Mr. Rosenberg

Mailable Production Practice

Write the following mailable production memo and letter in your shorthand notebook. Insert punctuation and check the spelling of any words that would give you difficulty when transcribing. You will then be asked to transcribe the memo and letter from your shorthand notes, assuring proper placement of all memo and letter parts. In the letter the word count begins with the salutation and ends with the closing lines.

56.4 Problem Tires

[shorthand outlines]

[101 words]

56.5 Purchase Order

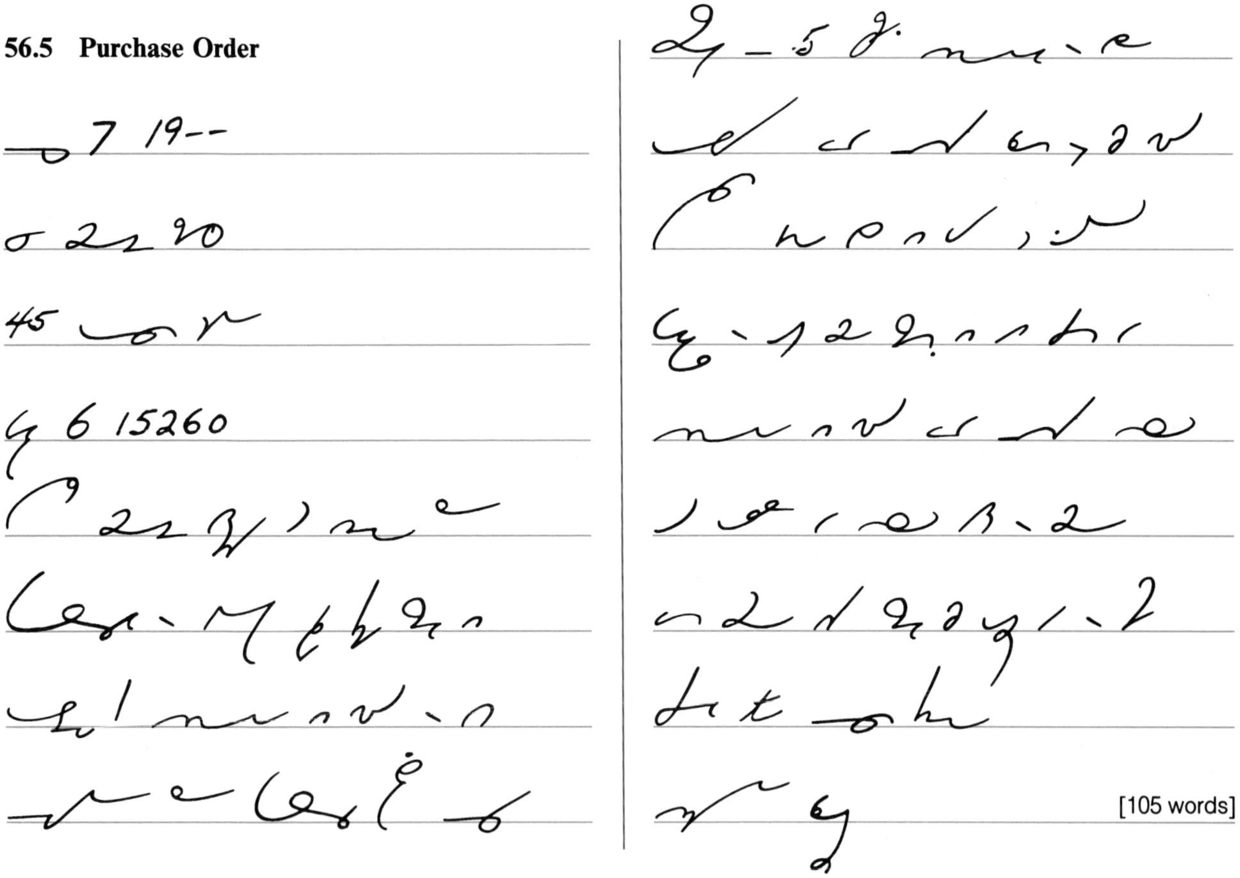

[105 words]

TRANSCRIPT

The material is counted in groups of 20 standard words or 28 syllables for convenience in timing the reading or dictation.

LESSON 1

1.1

1 The findings of the audit indicate that this has been a costly year.
2 We will credit your account accordingly.
3 We have several meetings scheduled early.
4 We readily furnished the needed details.
5 Mr. Johnson willingly collected the information and provided it to us.

¶ Charge Account

Dear Ms. Carter   We are aware that you are thinking of closing your charge account with us. Your account is extremely[1] important to us, Ms. Carter. If there is a service with which we have not provided you, we hope you will[2] let us know. We are sincerely interested in keeping you as a satisfied credit customer.[3] Sincerely yours   [62 words]

1.2

1 I will not be able to acknowledge your letter by June 15.
2 We will be able to print the advertisement in an hour.
3 Mrs. Brown was assisted in making the appropriate changes in the daily report.
4 It is not necessarily an advantage to deduct the interest in advance.
5 Our store will hold an anniversary sale early next month.

¶ Policy Changes

Dear Mr. Green   We have briefly reviewed the findings of the enclosed study, and we will be able to revise[1] our policies accordingly. Some of these changes will be quite costly and cannot be made very easily.[2] After these changes are made, however, the operations of our organization should be improved greatly.[3] Yours truly   [62 words]

1.3   Credit Cancellation

Dear Mr. Davis   Yesterday we received your letter canceling your membership in the National Credit[1] Association. We sincerely hope that your decision to cancel was not prompted by any failure on[2] our part to serve you properly.

We want to know if we have failed you in any way. We would appreciate your[3] giving us your reasons for discontinuing your membership. A stamped envelope is enclosed for your[4] convenience.

A National credit card is a valuable credential. We hope that you will reconsider[5] your request to cancel and that we may be able to serve you in the future. Sincerely yours   [115 words]

1.4   Urgent Request

Dear Mr. Blair   I am extremely upset by your discouraging telephone call on Tuesday, November 15,[1] in which you told me that you do not think you can complete my new house on schedule. I believed your promise[2] that the house would be finished on or before May 10 and sold my house in Dallas.

It is, therefore, essential that[3] you meet your original promise, even if your people have to work extra hours or you have to hire additional[4] help. Sincerely yours   [84 words]

1.5 Credit Approval

Dear Mrs. Wade   Your application for a credit account in the James Department Store has been approved.

Having[1] a credit account at the James Department Store will bring you many advantages. You will always be notified about[2] special sales before we announce them to the general public. You will also be able to use our personal[3] shopping service, which enables you to telephone your orders.

Please stop in to see me the next time you come to the[4] James Department Store. It will be a genuine pleasure to welcome you personally to our large family[5] of charge account customers. Sincerely yours   [108 words]

LESSON 2

2.1

1 Mr. Green will inform the former president of any modifications in the program.
2 It is doubtful that many men or women will meet these qualifications.
3 Miss Taylor is hopeful that the listed specifications will be altered.
4 We are fortunate to have Ms. Allen as our manager.
5 You may pay a minimum of $50 a month on your charge account.

¶ Furniture Sale

Dear Mr. Harvey   Our company will hold a formal furniture sale next month in our former warehouse on Main[1] Street. We will be very grateful if you would help to make this sale successful by promoting it in your circular.[2] Your efforts will be sincerely appreciated. Very truly yours   [53 words]

2.2

1 We will not be able to mail the 5,000 circulars for several days.
2 We hope you will be able to pay the minimum monthly fee as soon as possible.

3 Those managers who have been listed on the agenda will not be meeting until tomorrow.
4 We know that you have been having difficulty corresponding with the company executives.
5 I might have been able to review the specifications, but I did not receive them until yesterday.

¶ Supplies Request

Dear Sir   Our company received your correspondence several days ago, and we would like to thank you for[1] communicating so promptly. Under the circumstances, however, we cannot comply with your request for[2] additional supplies without some difficulty. We would like to discuss this matter with you at your earliest[3] convenience. Sincerely   [64 words]

2.3 Courtesy Thank-You

Dear Mr. West   Thank you for your thoughtfulness in writing us about the fine service extended to you by[1] one of our employees. I have shared your letter with Beth White, the young woman who took care of your order. She was[2] pleased.

She has been with us for five years and is one of our most valuable employees. On many occasions[3] she has gone out of her way to help our customers in an emergency.

We hope that you and your students are[4] enjoying our economics textbook. It is the latest one on the market and is used by more than 600[5] colleges. Sincerely yours   [106 words]

2.4 Magazine Subscription

Dear Miss Ames   Our Chicago office forwarded your letter of June 25 to us. Your name has been placed[1] on our mailing list to receive our magazine as you requested. You should receive your first copy soon.

We are sure[2] you will enjoy reading the material it contains. It has been prepared especially for secretaries[3] by secretaries.

We appreciate your interest in our publication and hope that you find it helpful. Please[4] let us know if we can be of any further assistance. Sincerely yours   [94 words]

2.5 Acknowledging Gift

Dear Mrs. Nelson   Thank you sincerely for the copy of the <u>World Atlas</u> that you so thoughtfully sent me[1] as a Christmas present. As usual, you chose something that was useful and practical.

The atlas is a[2] beautiful publication. It is an excellent example of what I regard as book publishing at its[3] best. To show you how much I think of the atlas, I have ordered five copies that I will give my children and[4] friends on special occasions.

Again, Mrs. Nelson, thank you for a most thoughtful and delightful Christmas present.[5] Sincerely yours   [103 words]

LESSON 3

3.1

1 J. B. Baker would like to develop a definite security plan for the immediate future.
2 Recent research indicates that our current policies need to be modified.
3 Frank Thomas has the authority to revise the annual sales report.
4 I hope you listed the different reasons for the failure of the plan.
5 This employee shows great loyalty and has the ability to perform quite well.

¶ Successful Businesses

Dear Mr. Lee   The success of any business enterprise relies on the quality, durability, and[1] dependability of its products. This is particularly true in the furniture business. The security[2] of your actual investment in furniture is determined by the reliability and[3] integrity of the company that makes it. Sincerely yours   [71 words]

3.2

1 The executives did not know about your electrical experience.
2 Roy Johnson is the director of security at this time.
3 Enclosed is a revised copy of the equipment specifications.
4 I would like to know if Dr. Underwood was present during the operation.
5 Every employee should try to do the job to the best of his or her ability.

¶ Sales Report

Dear Ms. Miller   Enclosed is a report of the proceedings of our annual management meeting.

While the year[1] was not exceedingly profitable, the executives in upper management are to be congratulated[2] at this time for a record year in terms of unit sales. During the year we made more shipments of equipment[3] than in any other year. Yours truly   [67 words]

3.3 Telephone Convenience

Dear Mr. Sims   Many people do not realize that the telephone can be a very efficient tool. It can[1] spare you the frustration of driving 20 miles to surprise your parents, only to find that they have gone away[2] for the day. It can spare you the impulse to call on your best customers and find that they are out. Your telephone[3] can save you a gallon of gas here and there.

So use your telephone frequently and efficiently. Sincerely yours[4]   [80 words]

3.4 Hotel Advertisement

Dear Mrs. Arnold   We have made many changes since your last visit to the Johnson Inn. These changes were[1] designed to make our guests even more comfortable.

You will find when you come again that we have added 15 deluxe[2] rooms. All of these rooms are equipped with the best of furnishings. We have also added a golf course and another[3] swimming pool.

While we have changed our accommodations, we have not changed our courteous and efficient service. Plan[4] now to spend a week or two with us this summer. We promise you a vacation that you will not soon forget.[5] Cordially yours   [102 words]

3.5 Business Note

Mr. Bates   I have devised a plan that should save our organization at least $500,000[1] over the next year or two. I would sincerely appreciate an opportunity to go over this plan with you.[2] Can you spare me about half an hour next week? James H. Temple   [51 words]

LESSON 4

4.1

1 Our entire account should be settled by the insurance agent promptly.

2 You were billed on July 15, and we would like to remind you that your payment is due.
3 We have been informed that Mr. Brandon has been named as the director of the billing department.
4 Our current insurance policy has been canceled, and it is urgent that a new one be prepared as soon as possible.
5 We have hired several new employees, and they should prove to be valuable assets to our firm.

¶ Plant Tour

Dear Mr. Jackson   Please indicate on the enclosed form whether you will be able to attend the tour of the[1] plant that will be held on the afternoon of December 3. Also indicate how many members of your[2] office staff will be able to take part in the program. Please return this form promptly to the public relations[3] department. Sincerely yours

[64 words]

4.2

1 I am not eligible for a promotion because of my lack of experience.
2 However, I will gladly credit your account if you return the damaged merchandise to us by August 1.
3 Generally, we are billed for goods before the end of the month.
4 I have not heard from you, and I hope that you did not forget about your account with us.
5 There will be some favorable changes made in some government regulations this year.

¶ Credit Card

Dear Mrs. Gray   I am pleased to inform you that we have approved your application for a credit card with our[1] company. Generally, we grant credit up to $1,000 for the first year for new customers, but[2] you have such an outstanding credit record that we are glad to extend additional credit privileges[3] to you. We have set an initial credit limit for you at $2,200. If I can be of any[4] further assistance to you, please let me know. Yours truly   [90 words]

4.3   Recycling Program

Dear Ms. Gray   You will be happy to know that our recycling program for newspapers is off to a fine start. The[1] Wilson Company collected many tons of newspapers and magazines on the date of the first pickup. This[2] has relieved us of the burden of burning these materials and made a significant saving in operating[3] costs. The ultimate success of this program depends on your continued cooperation.

Our recycling[4] program for cans will continue at the collection centers on Main Street and on Park Road. Sincerely yours[5]   [100 words]

4.4   Plant Control

Dear Mr. Black   Many industrial firms today are faced with the problem of controlling plant costs. I was[1] therefore interested when I read your letter announcing your new publication and sent for a copy.

After[2] reading the first few chapters, I was convinced that it contained the solution to many of our problems. I am[3] so impressed with the book that I am ordering six copies for our staff. Please convey my congratulations to the[4] author.

You may use this letter in an advertising issue for your publication if you wish.[5] Cordially yours

[101 words]

4.5   Dental Appointment

Dear Mr. Sanchez   At your last dental examination you will remember that we discussed the importance[1] of regular dental appointments.

A card indicating your appointment time and date is enclosed. Please let us know[2] if this appointment time is inconvenient for you.

We are looking forward to seeing you. Very truly yours[3]   [60 words]

LESSON 5

5.1

1 Offer some assistance to the customers.
2 The president is attending tomorrow.
3 Were either of the people able to identify the individual who damaged your car?
4 Mr. Davis is an outstanding, competent manager who does a thorough job.
5 Certainly those standards are temporary.

¶ Managers' Meeting

Date: January 16, 19--
To: Staff
From: Steven Simon
Subject: Staff Meeting

The president[1] is calling a meeting of managers and assistant managers tomorrow at 9 o'clock. He intends to[2] present his views on temporary promotions in certain departments. He also plans to review work schedules.[3] Please try to attend.

[64 words]

5.2

1 Mrs. Hastings purchased a morning newspaper at the store next door.
2 Please write a memorandum to the staff members in the personnel department.
3 Our company was incorporated in 1983.
4 I have never purchased life insurance before.
5 I would not recommend that you attend the demonstration.

¶ Policy Changes

Dear Ms. Wilson   I will be attending a meeting for all managers of local manufacturing[1] companies tomorrow. This meeting should include items of immediate importance to all managers. It is[2] my intention to discuss any important policy changes that have been proposed by Ms. Green and Mr. Frank[3] of the marketing department. I will be able to report to you on the events of this meeting in the[4] next several days. Very truly yours   [88 words]

5.3   Communications Services

Dear Mr. Willis   Our organization wants to provide the best possible service for American[1] businesses. We therefore have a standing offer to executives and managers to attend one of our monthly[2] conferences on the latest communications services and ideas.

Have some of your management personnel[3] attend one of these conferences. They will learn how other businesses are solving their communications problems.[4] They will also have an opportunity to exchange ideas with other managers.

Return the enclosed form[5] or call for complete information about our conferences. Sincerely yours

[114 words]

5.4   Opening-Day Celebration

Dear Dr. Brown   The Atlanta Leather Manufacturing Company is moving. After 30 years in our[1] present location at 14 South Street, we are moving because we are crowded in our present building. We have[2] signed a contract to lease the entire building at 12 West Street.

We are having an opening-day party on April[3] 10. There will be special gifts for all who visit us on that day. It is our hope, Dr. Brown, that we will[4] see you on this important occasion. Sincerely yours

[91 words]

5.5   Sales Seminar

Dear Mr. Harris   Give us a day with ten of your salespeople. We will give you back ten better salespeople.

On[1] that day we will conduct a seminar for your salespeople and show them how they can use their time more efficiently[2] by utilizing telemarketing. We will teach them how to use the telephone to your best advantage[3] in setting up appointments, finding the right person at the company they are calling, and bringing in new[4] business.

The net result will be that every salesperson will have more time to spend on selling. Why not give us a try?[5] Cordially yours   [103 words]

LESSON 6

6.1

1 It will not be necessary for your supervisor to examine the report.
2 With the exception of one page, that was an excellent analysis.
3 We insist that the tax is more than even we expected ourselves.
4 There was a substantial increase in our operating expenses.
5 Return the questionnaire in the self-addressed envelope.

¶ Report

Dear Mr. Evans   We are extremely pleased to submit to you a copy of our services report for your[1] examination. As you know, this report shows the processes our company followed, and expenses are now[2] approximately 5 percent below those of last year. The supervisors are to be commended for their[3] superb efforts. Sincerely yours   [66 words]

6.2

1 There are several employment opportunities in the Los Angeles area for an individual with your qualifications, and we would like to know whether you are interested.

2 The main objective of our newspaper article was to obtain the opinion of leading officers in our local businesses.

3 It will not be necessary for you to submit your order until August 20.

4 It was an outcome that we did not expect.

5 One of your district officers recently attended a meeting to discuss the possibility of building a new plant at the Philadelphia site.

¶ Ordering Procedures

Dear Mr. Dempsey   Our office is pleased to submit to you a revised article to be published in the next[1] edition of our newspaper. This article describes the processes customers should follow when placing[2] orders for our products. Our objective is to keep our customers satisfied with our low prices and superb[3] services while still maintaining low operating costs within the company. Yours very truly   [77 words]

6.3   Enrollment Solicitation

Dear Mr. Carter   The ability to keyboard is a very valuable asset to the business[1] person, the professional person, and the student. Why not spend some of your spare time learning to keyboard with our[2] new methods and techniques that develop keyboarding skill quickly and easily.

In our school we do not have[3] classes or fixed schedules. You come to school when it is convenient and learn at your own pace.

Come in soon for a free[4] demonstration lesson. Find out just how easy it is to learn the keyboard. You will be placing yourself under[5] no obligation. Very truly yours   [106 words]

6.4   Self-Improvement Course

Dear Ms. Billings   Do you want to get ahead in the business world, Ms. Billings? Of course you do, but you must have[1] such qualities as self-confidence, self-assurance, and self-reliance to attain your objective. Without these[2] qualities, your goal will be a difficult one.

You can acquire these qualities by enrolling in the National[3] Self-Improvement Course, a self-improvement course that has enabled thousands of people to obtain well-paying[4] jobs. If you would like our circular that describes our self-improvement courses, return the enclosed stamped,[5] self-addressed card. Under the circumstances, you will be making no mistake, Ms. Billings. Yours truly   [116 words]

6.5   Editorial Meeting

Date: January 2, 19--
To: All Editors
From: A. C. Baker
Subject: Editorial Meeting[1]
Congressman Charles Martin will be our speaker at our editorial meeting on January 15.[2]

Congressman Martin has agreed to spend the entire morning with us discussing ways in which we can make our buildings[3] more accessible to the needs of students who are disabled. Congressman Martin has also agreed to answer[4] any questions.

Please plan to attend this meeting. It promises to be one of the most interesting and[5] profitable meetings that we have held in recent months.

[109 words]

LESSON 7

7.1

1 Your donation has been quite beneficial to our relationship and partnership.

2 His proficiency in using the computer led to the promotion to his current position.

3 I would appreciate your cooperation in obtaining the additional stationery.

4 We would like to get your permission to advertise in our national magazine.

5 Please send an application form to our personnel department.

¶ Textbook Publication

Dear Mrs. Moore   The first edition of our textbook has been published, and it is already a financial success![1] Under present conditions, we feel assured that this success is due to the efficiency of the members[2] of the staff in handling the essential details of the publication. These individuals have a reputation[3] for working under conditions of hardship, and we are extremely grateful for their sincere cooperation.[4] Sincerely yours [84 words]

7.2

1 Presently there is a partial reduction in the production of these items at our Denver location.
2 They probably will alter the format of the initial program.
3 Your advertising account in particular is overdue in payment.
4 They will represent our corporation and advise the other members of any necessary changes.
5 This is the part of the plan which is being changed, and we would like your advice.

¶ Production Report

Dear Miss Allen We are privileged to announce that production has increased in our eastern division. As a[1] result, there is a need for additional employees in our St. Louis plant in particular. These staff[2] additions probably will be made by fall. In addition, there are some proposed changes in the scheduled program for[3] production. We hope that these changes will keep our corporation up to date with modern ideas. Very truly yours[4]
[80 words]

7.3 Job Offer

Dear Mr. Edwards Thank you for your letter telling me that I have been accepted as a management trainee[1] in the Edison Electric Company.

Unfortunately your offer arrived just two days too late. On July 15 I received[2] a telephone call from the Wilson Power Company offering me a position in[3] their sales department. I accepted their offer.

Thank you for considering my application and for the time[4] you spent with me during our interviews. I am sure that I would have enjoyed working for the Edison Electric[5] Company. Cordially yours
[106 words]

7.4 Membership in Association

Dear Mr. Hastings It gives me considerable pleasure to tell you that the application you submitted[1] for membership in the International Communications Association has been accepted by the[2] board of directors.

As soon as we receive your check for $150, the annual membership[3] fee, we will send you your membership card.

We are confident, Mr. Hastings, that your membership in our[4] association will be a source of new friendships and profitable relationships. Sincerely yours [97 words]

7.5 Education Offer

Dear Mr. Beck Perhaps you realize that you must continue to acquire knowledge to get ahead in business.[1] Many people cannot attend school in the evenings because of the demands of their job.

It is for people like[2] you that Reese Institute has started its weekend classes. Reese Institute offers many courses that meet on[3] Saturdays. In these weekend courses you can earn up to six college credits in six weeks.

Our fall semester begins[4] on November 11. Get full information about our weekend courses. All you have to do is sign and[5] mail the enclosed form. Very truly yours [108 words]

LESSON 8

8.1

1 The current price of our product has just been reduced by 25 percent, and you will be billed accordingly.
2 We calculate that our dividends have accumulated $2,000 for the last three years.
3 We were quite surprised to receive the manuscript so soon, and we are happy to offer our assistance.
4 The quote we received from you was more than generous, and we appreciate your trust in us.
5 We must wait for an increase in our sales before we will consider hiring more assistants.

¶ Promotion

Dear Miss Leonard Congratulations on your recent promotion to advertising consultant of your[1] firm. You have always put forth extra effort to bring desirable results in every task. We hope you will[2] continue to succeed in all of your endeavors and that your ultimate goals will indeed be reached. Cordially yours[3] [60 words]

8.2

1 We hope you will not be reluctant to build your new plant at this site.
2 A large quantity of these booklets are available to your assistants for checking.
3 We plan to move our main office to the eastern section of our community regardless of any extra cost.
4 You will be pleased to learn of the substantial progress we made in this area.
5 We would like to formulate a regular procedure that can be followed.

¶ Speech

Dear Ms. Trenton   Your speech at the December conference has received national[1] recognition. Consequently, the recommendations you gave will be published in the next issue of our national[2] magazine. If you have any questions regarding this matter, please contact us. Sincerely yours   [53 words]

8.3   Editorial Speech

Dear Mr. Brown   Thank you for taking time from your busy schedule at Wilson University to speak to the[1] editors of our newspaper.

The things you said will be helpful in forming our editorial policy[2] for the years ahead.

Please accept the enclosed check for $200 as a small token of our appreciation.[3] I hope we may enjoy the pleasure of having you speak again. Sincerely yours   [76 words]

8.4   Assembly Plant Project

Dear Mr. Johnson   Thank you for the opportunity you gave us to discuss the plans for building a new[1] assembly plant in the northern part of Birmingham. Thank you also for asking us to submit costs on the basis of the[2] plans and specifications you left with me.

Our staff is now at work on the preparation of these costs.[3] I will definitely be able to deliver them to you on July 18. Sincerely yours   [78 words]

8.5   Congratulatory Letter

Dear Mrs. Best   Congratulations, Mrs. Best, on a job well done! All of the members of our association[1] who heard your presentation last Friday in Chicago were as thrilled as I was. We accept the challenges[2] you outlined for us, and you can be sure that you have helped to make our retail association more effective.[3]

Thank you, Mrs. Best, for an entertaining presentation that was well done. Very truly yours
[77 words]

9.1

1 It will be impossible to complete the transaction until March 27.
2 We look forward to attending the meeting.
3 It was an enjoyable conference, and we are interested in returning again next year.
4 We do not want to interfere with this endeavor, but we feel you should emphasize the strong points in your future advertising.
5 Your international policies have remained stationary for years, and we hope you will try to improve them.

¶ Employee Promotions

Dear Mr. Jones   On Monday, February 12, we will be interviewing several employees who expressed[1] interest in the position of supervisor of transportation. This position offers many rewards,[2] and we are anxious to transfer one of our own employees. However, there is a great likelihood that[3] it will remain open until late spring. It seems that the interviewing process will undoubtedly be a long[4] one. Very truly yours   [83 words]

9.2

1 One of our representatives will be in your area as soon as he returns from San Francisco, and he will write you at that time.
2 We know, of course, that several other plans should be reviewed.
3 The proposed manuscript is shorter than was expected, and you have the right to review it at your own convenience.
4 The speaker stated that there is a greater likelihood for some transfers in the Philadelphia region.
5 Please send the completed application blank to us as soon as possible on your company stationery.

¶ Statement

Dear Mr. Nelson   We hope that the enclosed statement is satisfactory. Some of the significant changes[1] that you requested are outlined in the accompanying letter. If there are any other questions, we hope you will[2] let us know as soon as possible by completing and sending the enclosed form to our Pittsburgh branch office.[3] Sincerely

[62 words]

9.3   Approval of Credit Application

Dear Miss Baker   You will be pleased to know that your application for a charge account at our store has been approved.[1] We hope that you will use it frequently.

You will receive a statement of your purchases on the last day of each[2] month. Your payment is due within ten days.

Stop in and see me the next time you are out shopping. It will be a[3] pleasure to meet you personally. My office is on the second floor. Sincerely yours

[75 words]

9.4   Billing Error

Dear Mr. West   No business person fails to pay bills because of an oversight. I am no exception. I have not[1] paid my June 15 bill in the amount of $300 because I seem to be fighting a losing[2] battle with your computer.

In June I purchased a suit for $300. When it was delivered, I found[3] that it was not the suit I had purchased. I returned the suit and wrote to your adjustment department, asking them[4] to send me the correct suit. Since that time I have received three requests for payment but no response to my letter[5] asking for an adjustment.

I will gladly send you my check for $300 when I receive the suit that[6] I ordered. Yours very truly

[127 words]

LESSON 10

10.1

1 We will hire several new employees at our next board meeting at 10 a.m.
2 May we compliment you on living in such a beautiful city.

3 We have not yet received your bill and hope you will cooperate fully in settling this problem.
4 If you prefer to use your own judgment, please feel free to do so.
5 A variety of catalogs will be shipped to you this year at a 5 percent discount.

¶ Refund Policies

Dear Mrs. Mason   We have reviewed your refund policies, and we would like to call several principal points[1] to your attention. We believe that a copy of the policy should be provided to all customers who[2] take advantage of your services. In addition, if a refund is ever refused, it is in your best[3] interest to fully explain such a decision to that customer in writing. By following these suggestions,[4] your organization should overcome any of the prior difficulties you have had. Yours truly   [98 words]

10.2

1 Do you have any current statistics on the subject of "Principles of Economics"?
2 Thank you for your suggestions; we hope we can correct this situation.
3 I would like to have the meeting at our main office on Park Street at 3 o'clock.
4 Do you know whether a large variety of items would better complement the display?
5 If you are in the city this summer, I hope you will come in to visit us.

¶ Spring Conference

Dear Mr. Gray   Thank you for your invitation to the spring conference in Chicago. As you know, I have[1] attended this event for five years, and I have found it to be quite successful in improving employee performance[2] in my own corporation. I am anxious to participate again this year in the conference and am looking[3] forward to hearing your guest speakers present their views on the subject of improving employee performance.[4] Yours very truly   [84 words]

10.3   Employment Interview

Dear Mr. Parker   On June 15 I had lunch with your friend James Weston. After lunch I took him through our offices[1] and arranged brief interviews for him with several of our executives. All of them were very much impressed[2] with him personally as well as with his knowledge of computers.

The position in our research department[3] that I spoke to you about has not been filled. I think we can use Mr. Weston in that position. He has an[4] appointment to see our research director next week. Thanks for recommending him. Yours truly
[96 words]

10.4 Moving Arrangements

Dear Dr. Hugo In the business section of the Daily Tribune there was a notice yesterday that you have been[1] promoted to the position of head of the advertising department of the United Fuel Company.[2] This is a unique opportunity for you, and we are sure you will make the most of it.

Perhaps your immediate[3] problem is making arrangements to move. The Hughes Moving Company can take care of these arrangements for you. The[4] Hughes staff will pack your things for shipment and move them to your apartment. You simply move in.

May we recommend that[5] you make an appointment with a Hughes representative to review our service with you. Call Ms. Mary Baker at[6] 555-1796. Sincerely yours   [131 words]

10.5 Report Information

Dear Mrs. Burns Thanks for so promptly sending me that material requested in my letter of November[1] 15. I have read through the material and find that it gives me just the information I need to prepare[2] my report to the president. I will send you a copy when the report is ready.

Please let me know if at[3] any time you need a favor. I will be happy to accommodate you. Cordially yours   [76 words]

LESSON 11

11.1

1 Our quarterly report has been distributed to all of our council members.
2 The southern states showed a great deal of support for our products, while the eastern and western areas were not as supportive.
3 We have returned the portable typewriter to the

manufacturer and find that it requires an assortment of repairs.
4 The attorney determined that the contract will terminate on June 24.
5 Your magazine article was logical, practical, and quite useful to all homeowners in Atlanta.

¶ Charity Donations

Dear Mr. Bond As you may know, every organization sets aside a part of its budget for charitable[1] projects such as yours. You realize, of course, that we frequently receive requests for contributions.[2] Obviously, we cannot take care of them all. Unfortunately, we have already distributed all funds set[3] aside for projects of this nature this year. Consequently, it will be impossible for us to grant your[4] request for a contribution this year. When we prepare a subsequent budget, we will attempt to include a[5] contribution for your organization. Sincerely yours   [110 words]

11.2

1 He is a speaker who is well known throughout the world, and his counsel is well respected.
2 We will not be able to answer your inquiry without some additional research.
3 Mrs. Jackson met with your local representative yesterday, and he had several worthwhile comments to make.
4 Therefore, we can have these individuals meet with you next month to determine what can be done to offset the adverse effects of the new law.
5 He made a contribution worth nearly $5,500, and we wish to express our sincere gratitude.

¶ Plant Closing

Dear Mr. James As you know, we have determined that it will be necessary to close our Washington production[1] plant. The layoff will affect 200 workers in this area. This is not a pleasant thing for us[2] to do, and we wish there was something else we could do without taking such an extreme measure. If you have any[3] suggestions, we will be glad to discuss them with you at your earliest convenience. Yours truly   [77 words]

11.3 Sales Training Videotapes

Dear Mrs. Foster Thank you for your letter offering me the opportunity to prepare a videotape[1] to be used in your sales training program. Thank you also for the contract that you sent with your letter. I am[2] asking my lawyer to review it so I can return it to you.

I have already begun collecting[3] material for the videotape. I hope to be able to show you the copy when I am in Chicago[4] during the week of January 15.

Please send me a copy of your sales training manual. I misplaced the[5] copy you sent me. Sincerely yours   [106 words]

11.4   Court Case

Dear Mr. Porter   I want to report to you that last week our attorney, Mr. James Turner, advised me that[1] our case against the Western Export Company would be tried in the southern district of the New York Supreme Court[2] on Tuesday, August 17. That means that you may be called as a witness on that date. I suggest, therefore, that[3] you do not make any appointments for August 17.

If you want further information about the trial,[4] call Mr. Turner at 555-7102. I think we are extremely fortunate to have so competent[5] an attorney as Mr. Turner representing us. Sincerely yours
[114 words]

11.5   Manuscript Publication

Dear Mr. Thomas   Miss James and I appreciate the time you spent with us discussing our manuscript on[1] investments. We fully understand why your organization is not in a position to publish and market[2] a book of this type.

You will be interested to know that we followed your suggestion and showed the manuscript[3] to the National Publishing Company. We discussed the book with their business editor. She was so impressed[4] with it that she gave us a contract on the spot. The book will be on the market by July 1. Sincerely yours[5]   [100 words]

LESSON 12

12.1

1 Were you able to discuss this issue with your client prior to the trial?
2 The personnel manager will appoint Mrs. James to the permanent position, and we hope she will accept it.

3 Our associates will complete the project by Tuesday; then they will be able to begin working for you.
4 We hope to negotiate a new contract promptly this summer.
5 We will be pleased to accommodate you by sending the invoice to you separately.

¶ Computers

Dear Mr. Davis   We know, Mr. Davis, that you purchased a computer from us and that[1] you have found it allows you to handle claims quickly. May we persuade you to consider purchasing one of our[2] updated personal computers? Perhaps you will be surprised by how much more this up-to-date model can[3] do, but we feel sure you will appreciate the speed of processing data even more. We would be proud to[4] demonstrate the features of this new model any time at your convenience. Sincerely yours   [91 words]

12.2

1 We have discussed this matter throughout the year, and we might have to make some major changes.
2 Under the circumstances I might be delayed in making my return trip to Boston.
3 This time they were able to act on the problem themselves rather than request our assistance.
4 I would like to take some unusually drastic steps in handling this issue.
5 All of the items except one were shipped yesterday, and you should have them in a short period of time.

¶ Life Insurance Policy

Dear Mrs. Andrews   Enclosed is your copy of your life insurance policy you recently purchased from our[1] agent. As you may have some additional questions regarding your policy, we hope you will take some time[2] to review it closely. This is a very valuable investment for you, and we think you will be pleased that[3] you selected the American Life Insurance Company to represent your needs. Very truly yours   [79 words]

12.3   Personal Note

Dear Mr. Davis   You will be interested to know that we now have an opening on our sales staff in

Wisconsin[1] and Minnesota. Our representative resigned last week to accept a position with another company.

The[2] information you gave us on your application form convinces us that you have the training and the aptitude[3] to handle the position successfully. Call me collect if you are interested, and I will arrange[4] an interview for you with our sales manager. Sincerely yours   [91 words]

12.4 Piano Recital

Dear Lydia   The piano recital you gave at the Peoria Theater was brilliant. I do not[1] play the piano or any other instrument, but I can appreciate an outstanding recital when[2] I attend one.

My associate Maria Garcia is an accomplished pianist, and she[3] was definitely thrilled by your piano technique. Her comment to me was, "It is plain to see that she devoted[4] years to the development of that piano technique." Lydia, all I can say is "Keep up the good work."[5] Sincerely yours

[101 words]

12.5 Newspaper Advertisement

Dear Mr. Ames   We were very pleased to receive the report on the results that you obtained from your advertisement[1] in the April 10 issue of our newspaper. It is a source of pleasure to us to hear that you received[2] so fine a return from such a small investment. You may be surprised to learn that returns like these are not unusual[3] for our advertisers.

We hope that the results of your first advertisement in our newspaper will encourage[4] you to place more of your advertising with us.

Thank you for writing us. Sincerely yours

[97 words]

LESSON 13

13.1 Blood Drive

Dear Miss Grant   Thank you for your help in recruiting donors for the blood bank. As of yesterday we collected[1] 400 units. We have met our goal with the contribution from your[2] company. This is a very successful performance.

Please tell your staff how important their contributions were. We will let you know when we will have our[3] next drive. Sincerely yours   [64 words]

13.2

Harvey referred salespeople causing personnel Charlotte suggestions morale opportunity whether convenient of the   of your   about the   if you can

13.3

1 I referred your letter about the three salespeople to Mrs. Smith.
2 She has several suggestions that may help you solve the problem.
3 Morale will not be affected.
4 She would like to have dinner with you on June 15.
5 Please let her know whether this date is convenient.

13.4 Personnel Problem

Dear Mr. Harvey   I referred your letter about the three salespeople who are causing you a serious[1] personnel problem to the personnel manager. Her name is Mrs. Charlotte Smith. She has several suggestions that[2] may help you solve the problem without affecting the morale of the rest of your staff.

Mrs. Smith would like an[3] opportunity to tell you about the suggestions if you can have dinner with her on the evening of June 15.[4] Please let her know whether this date is convenient. Sincerely yours

[92 words]

13.5 "To Do" List for the Boss

Today I should remind Mr. Martin to:
1. Acknowledge receipt of the letter from Sarah[1] Hughes.
2. Reply to the memo from the director of marketing.
3. Prepare a recommendation for[2] job promotion for Mary.   [45 words]

13.6 Insurance Questions

Dear Mrs. Clark   About five years ago I bought an insurance policy from you. I am now thinking about[1] borrowing money on my insurance policy because present interest rates at the banks are high. Will you[2] therefore give me some information.

Please tell me the exact cash value of this policy, whether I can still[3] borrow the cash value of the policy, and what the interest rate of the policy is.

I will make a[4] decision as soon as I hear from you. I will then get in touch with you again. Very truly yours   [98 words]

13.7 Publication Correction

Dear Mr. Collins   I know that your magazine is not responsible for the opinions expressed by your writers.[1] I am sure that the policy of your magazine is to print articles that are technically correct. One[2] of your authors states on page 15 of your May issue that it is not possible for an electrical[3] circuit to carry more than one electrical frequency at a time. This is not quite accurate. It is[4] possible to have a very high radio frequency in the same circuit as a low direct current.[5]

I hope this information is helpful. I did feel that you should know that you published information that was not quite[6] accurate. Yours truly
                                          [124 words]

LESSON 14

14.1 Sales Letter

Dear Mr. Smith   All music lovers know that the Connelley compact disc is the finest on the market. But what[1] many of them do not know is that you can purchase a Connelley disc for only a few dollars more than[2] you would have to pay for an ordinary tape.

Come in and check out the several Connelley discs we have in[3] stock. You will be glad you did. Yours very truly   [69 words]

14.2

to the staff pleasure announce appointed Toronto responsibility operations eastern export India distinction   has been   will be   I know   you will

14.3

1 Ann Evans has been appointed general manager of our Toronto branch.
2 Ann has been sales manager for our Eastern region.
3 She was in charge of export sales to India.

4 She has served with distinction in a number of positions.
5 Wish Ann the best of success.

14.4 Career Move

To the Staff   It gives me pleasure to announce that Ann Evans has been appointed general manager of our[1] Toronto branch. Next week she will be moving to Toronto to assume responsibility for our operations[2] in Canada.

For several years Ann has been sales manager for our Eastern region in charge of export sales[3] to India. She has served with distinction in a number of other positions prior to this appointment.[4]

I know you will want to wish Ann the best of success in her new assignment.   [94 words]

14.5 Purchase Information

Dear Ms. Wong   Thank you for your order for our electrical materials. The materials are being shipped[1] promptly from our Phoenix factory.

This order represents your first purchase of these materials. We are therefore[2] enclosing a folder that suggests the best ways to use them. Our representative in your city will[3] also be glad to answer your questions.

We are sure that you will be happy with our service.[4] Yours very truly   [82 words]

14.6 Catalogs

Dear Mrs. Weeks   I have a suggestion that may make the operation of our business easier.

Your office[1] sends each of our branch stores a new edition of our catalog every three weeks. There are 75 stores that[2] receive this new catalog. The cost of printing and mailing these catalogs must be increasing.

Why not purchase a[3] microfilm reader for each store? That way the catalog could be published as film instead of paper. Both publishing[4] and mailing costs would be much less. Yours truly [88 words]

LESSON 15

15.1 Investment Program

Dear Mr. Harris   It was a pleasure to have the opportunity to discuss with you my future investment[1] plans. Thank you for sending me the information you prepared about investments.

I am reviewing the[2] investment program and will be in contact with you shortly to discuss the proposal in detail. Very truly yours[3]   [60 words]

15.2

impressed difficult customers reprint forthcoming manual solely beginning enclosed we are with your   we would   we will   it is

15.3

1 We are so impressed with your suggestions.
2 We would like to reprint them.
3 Our training manual will be distributed solely to our sales staff.
4 We will indicate that the reprint is taken from your book.
5 Please sign the enclosed form.

15.4   Publication Material

Dear Mr. James   We are so impressed with your suggestions on how to handle difficult customers that we would[1] like to reprint them in our forthcoming sales training manual.

We would be happy to pay you $100[2] for permission to reprint them. Rest assured that our training manual will be distributed solely to our[3] sales staff and that we will indicate at the beginning of the reprint that it is taken from your book.

Please[4] sign the enclosed form and return it to us after you have reviewed the terms. Sincerely yours   [96 words]

15.5   Instructions

Be sure to tell Karen that we need to have 200 copies of our advertising circular run[1] on an offset press. We need to be able to pick them up from the printer by June 18.   [36 words]

15.6   Response to Request

Dear Miss Santos   Your note of congratulations is most sincerely appreciated. It was very exciting[1] for us to receive the award for publishing. Thank you for your interest in our company publication.[2]

As you requested, I am enclosing three copies.

Our editor does an excellent job. The enclosed copies[3] are typical of the content and quality.

If there is any additional way in which I can help you,[4] please let me know. Yours very sincerely   [87 words]

15.7   Speaker Request

Dear Ms. Allen   As you may remember, I attended the seminar that you conducted in Seattle. You[1] spoke on statistics in the advertising industry. Your presentation was superb!

This year I am a[2] member of the program committee for the National Association of Advertising Executives. Would[3] you be able to be a speaker at this convention?

If you accept, your presentation will be given at[4] 9 a.m. on December 19. Our association will pay all of your expenses and an additional[5] $250.

Please let me know if you will be able to take part in our program.[6] Very truly yours   [123 words]

LESSON 16

16.1   Purchase Order

Dear Mr. Goldman   Thank you for the order you phoned in this morning. As you requested immediate service,[1] your shipment of 1,500 business envelopes is on its way to you.

I am also sending along a[2] purchase order that I have already completed for you. Will you please sign it and return it to me. Please[3] accept my apology for any inconvenience this may cause you. I feel it is necessary to[4] follow these procedures.

Thank you for your help. Sincerely yours   [90 words]

16.2

education   seriously   Wilson College   campus facilities   talk   faculty   information   if you are let us   with the   of our   some of our   in the

16.3

1 Wilson College would like to have you visit.
2 Let us show you our facilities.
3 Talk with students and faculty.

4 Sit in on some of our classes.

5 Fill out the enclosed card and return it in the business reply envelope.

16.4 Campus Information

Dear Miss Green   If you are a high school senior who takes education seriously, Wilson College would like to have[1] you visit its campus. Come let us show you our facilities. Talk with the students and with the members of our faculty.[2] Sit in on some of our classes.

If you would like more information about Wilson College, fill out the[3] enclosed card and return it in the business reply envelope. Sincerely yours
[74 words]

16.5 Instructions

Draft a letter of congratulations to the sales representatives who have sold more[1] than their sales quotas. Give the rough draft to Mrs. Dean for her approval. She needs it by August 3.   [38 words]

16.6 Employee Vacations

Dear Ms. Gleason   Eight years ago we first discussed giving all the employees of our printing shop their vacations[1] at the same time. This year we are finally going to do so.

Closing the plant entirely will avoid the[2] problems of having someone to cover the jobs of those people who are on vacation. If you have any[3] questions about the scheduling of your printing jobs, please get in touch with me before July 15. Very truly yours[4]
[80 words]

16.7 Banking Services

Dear Mr. Solomon   You may be interested to know that Mr. Robert Smith has purchased the Southern Manufacturing Company[1] here in Atlanta. Mr. Smith is a successful business executive and will no doubt make the Southern[2] Manufacturing Company very profitable.

I think that it would be a good idea for you to contact him.[3] Tell him about the services that our bank provides. Seven local companies take advantage of our services.[4] If we can get him to do his banking with us, we will be acquiring a very important account.[5] Very truly yours   [102 words]

17.1 Direct Deposit

Dear Mrs. Hayes   If you receive government benefits, do you realize that you can have your checks directly[1] deposited in your bank? As a result, you will never again have to worry about having your checks lost,[2] stolen, or mislaid.

When you are in our neighborhood, stop in to see what our bank can do for you. Just fill out[3] a short form authorizing the government to transmit your checks directly to our bank each month and we will do[4] the rest. Yours very truly   [85 words]

17.2

organized   consisting   responsibility   one million
efficient   energy   conserve   we have

17.3

1 We have recently organized a new department.
2 They are responsible for efficient use of energy.
3 They have already met with customers.
4 What can you do to conserve energy?
5 Send for our energy conservation booklet today.

17.4 Energy Conservation

Dear Mr. Drake   We have recently organized a new customer service department consisting of 15[1] people. Their responsibility is to help our more than one million customers make wise and efficient use[2] of all forms of energy.

This new department has already met with many customers to help them improve[3] their use of energy. What can you do to conserve energy? Send for our energy conservation[4] booklet today and find out. Yours truly   [87 words]

17.5 "To Do" List

1. Select a place to have lunch. Make a reservation for four people for 12 p.m.
2. Call Helen Green's office to[1] ask when they will send us the research progress report.
3. Request a service call for the typewriter in Room 5.[2]   [40 words]

17.6 Home Building

Dear Mr. Roman   As I promised you a week ago, I have discussed the completion of your home with our crew.[1] They tell me that they can easily complete your home by April 10.

You will be pleased to know that the members of the[2] crew are working late to finish your home. I am sure you will find the quality of workmanship to be superior.[3]

If you have any questions or comments, please let us know. Yours truly   [74 words]

17.7 Grand Opening

Dear Mr. Franks   You will be pleased to know that the new branch office of our bank will be opening on Madison[1] Avenue on Monday, May 5.

You will find that we have excellent facilities for both your personal and[2] your business accounts. We have no service charge on checking accounts. Our interest rates on business loans are as low as[3] those of any other bank in the city.

We will be glad to tell you how we can serve your banking needs both[4] today and in the future. Sincerely yours   [88 words]

LESSON 18

18.1 Job Placement

Dear Mrs. Green   During the past two years we have employed several of your students as secretaries[1] in our organization. We are highly pleased with their performance. We also think that they are pleased with us and[2] find our organization a good place to work.

If you have any students who will complete their training in your[3] school this month and who might be interested in joining our organization, please ask them to come in soon to see[4] us. Our personnel department will be happy to interview them Monday through Friday during regular working[5] hours. Sincerely   [104 words]

18.2

fitness center employees advantage programs theft belongings stolen essential assurance executive committee security of the   will not be

18.3

1 Our fitness center is a great success.
2 The one problem we have is theft.
3 Employees have reported their belongings have been stolen.
4 It is essential that they be given some assurance.
5 We must provide some form of security protection.

18.4 Fitness Center

Date: August 15, 19--
To: Robert Green
From: Joe Hamilton
Subject: Fitness Center
Our fitness[1] center is a great success. Many of our employees have taken advantage of the different programs[2] that are offered.

The one problem we have is theft. Five employees have reported that belongings have been[3] stolen from their desks. I am sure you will agree it is essential that they be given some assurance that their belongings[4] will not be stolen.

I suggest that we take up this matter at our next executive committee meeting. We must[5] provide some form of security protection.   [109 words]

18.5 Meeting Schedule

The staff meeting that was scheduled for April 9 at 10 a.m. has been canceled. The meeting will be held on[1] April 11 at 10 a.m. in the conference room.   [31 words]

18.6 Thank-You Letter

Dear Andrew   Thank you for sending me the first edition of your wonderful new publication, Investment[1] Management. Over the years I have subscribed to four of your publications and your newsletter.

Enclosed[2] is my check for a subscription to your new publication. I will be looking forward to receiving it in the[3] coming years. It is expected to be one of my best sources of information about finance.

You have my[4] best wishes for success in the area of financial publishing. Sincerely yours

[96 words]

18.7 Incomplete Order

Ladies and Gentlemen Just this morning our school received the box of books that you sent us on December 12. When[1] I opened it, I found that there were 10 economics textbooks instead of 20.

The packing slip that came with the[2] books indicates that 20 copies were to be sent. The package would have been large enough to hold 20 books.[3] Of course there is the possibility that your shipping department made an error. Please look into this to see[4] if you can determine what happened to the additional 10 copies.

We would appreciate receiving the[5] remaining 10 books since we have already paid for 20 copies. Please send them to us immediately.[6] Sincerely

[122 words]

LESSON 19

19.1 Speech Acceptance

Dear Mr. Cooper   It is a pleasure for me to accept your invitation to speak to the managers in your[1] region. I am glad to have the opportunity to work with you in the development of your[2] business communications program.

Please let me know the exact time and place of the meeting. I have a good idea[3] of the subjects that I will cover in my program. Yours truly

[73 words]

19.2

subscription magazine expire authorization renew weekly reports guide simply length you will it is for you   we will   Sincerely yours

19.3

1 Your subscription to our magazine will soon expire.
2 We must have your authorization to renew it.
3 You will continue to receive weekly reports.
4 Simply check the enclosed card and drop it in the mail.
5 We will renew your subscription and bill you later.

19.4 Subscription Renewal

Dear Ms. Morris   Your subscription to our magazine will soon expire. We must have your authorization to[1] renew it.

If you renew now, you will continue to receive weekly reports of significant news affecting[2] business and the people who guide its course.

It is easy for you to renew. Simply check on the enclosed card the[3] length of time you want your subscription to run and drop the card in the mail. We will renew your subscription and bill[4] you later. Sincerely yours

[85 words]

19.5 Personal Shopping List

On the way home from work I should pick up:
1. Train ticket.
2. Newspaper.
3. Dry cleaning.   [16 words]

19.6 Insurance Claim

Dear Mrs. Boyd   As you know, the recent blizzard has caused problems for many people in our city. Last night an[1] ice storm did some damage to my property. An icy electrical line snapped, and the result was an[2] electrical fire in my home.

The fire was quickly brought under control, and the damage was not extensive. I[3] estimate that the repairs can be made for about $1,000.

Please let me know if you need to inspect[4] my home before I have a building contractor make the repairs. Yours sincerely   [93 words]

19.7 Banking Services

Dear Miss Benjamin   Next month we will be moving the home of our computer software company to Chicago.[1] We will also be moving our banking business to Chicago. Your bank has been recommended to us by[2] several people who have been happy with your service during the past several years.

I will be in Chicago[3] in June, and I would like to talk to someone at your bank about our special banking needs. Will you please have someone[4] write to me in order to tell me the time and day that will be most convenient for you. Very truly yours

[98 words]

LESSON 20

20.1 Conference Registration

Dear Ms. Rich   It has been one month since I sent you my registration form to attend your conference. With the form I enclosed[1] my check for $50. I received my canceled check from the bank on July 24.

It is now August[2] 3, and I have not yet received information on the conference. As you know, the conference is in two weeks. Will you please[3] send me the information immediately. Sincerely yours   [74 words]

20.2

Weber   congratulations   admitted   licensed   New York   concerns   accumulation   library   publisher   carefully   select   promptly   you have been   we have been

20.3

1 We read you have been admitted to the bar.
2 You are licensed to practice law in the state of New York.
3 We have been the leading publisher of law books since 1950.
4 Enclosed is our latest price list.
5 Look through it carefully and select the books that you want.

20.4 Law Publication

Dear Mrs. Weber   Congratulations! We read that you have been admitted to the bar and that you are licensed[1] to practice law in the state of New York.

No doubt one of your first concerns will be the accumulation[2] of a good law library. We have been the leading publisher of law books since 1950.

Enclosed is[3] our latest price list. Look through it carefully, select the books that you want, and fill out the order blank on the back[4] cover of the catalog. Your order will be sent promptly. Sincerely yours   [92 words]

20.5 Office "To Do" List

1. Write a letter to Sue Adams. Ask her when she will send us the contract which was due on[1] October 29.
2. Proofread the original copy of the new office procedures manual.
3. Take[2] dictation from Mrs. Brady.   [47 words]

20.6 Job Placement

Dear Mr. Cunningham   Thank you very much for your letter of Tuesday, April 18, in which you make some[1] very flattering comments about the work of the students we sent to you. We make every effort to give our[2] students the most thorough training possible, and we are glad that we seem to be succeeding in our efforts.[3]

We have several students graduating in June who expressed interest when I announced that there were secretarial[4] openings in your organization. I am sure you will hear from some of them.

Once again thank you for your kind comments.[5] Sincerely yours   [103 words]

20.7 Relocation

Dear Mr. Martinez   Recently I joined the staff of Adams Manufacturing in Los Angeles as an[1] electrical engineer.

I have been looking at several homes that are for sale. The next day that I have[2] available for looking at homes is February 9. Would it be possible for you to show me some property[3] that you have for sale for approximately $100,000?

Please let me know whether you or some member[4] of your staff will be able to meet me at 9 a.m. Very truly yours   [93 words]

LESSON 21

21.1 Life Insurance

Dear Mr. Graham   As you may realize, ordinary life insurance is insufficient to protect[1] you and your family. You need the coverage offered by the Merit Insurance Company.

The enclosed[2] materials will tell you how we can save money for you no matter how much insurance you now carry.

Let[3] our representative go over your current policy with you. There is no obligation attached for this[4] service. Sincerely yours   [84 words]

21.2

check $250 account excellent realized something happened payment importance spotless reputation thank you for your   you have been   did not   it is

21.3

1 Thank you for your check for $250.
2 Your record of payment has been excellent.
3 We were not concerned when your payment did not arrive.
4 Something must have happened to delay your payment.
5 It is a pleasure to deal with people like you.

21.4 Customer Payment

Dear Mr. Kane   Thank you for your check for $250 to bring your account up to date.

Your record of[1] payments during the ten years you have been buying from us is excellent. As a result, we were not concerned when[2] your payment did not arrive on the due date. We realized that something must have happened to delay your payment.[3]

It is a pleasure to deal with people like you who realize the importance of a spotless credit reputation.[4] Sincerely yours   [82 words]

21.5 Luggage Order

Dear Ms. O'Hara   Thank you for your order for leather luggage. According to your description of the luggage[1] set that you saw on display at the travel show, we have taken a set from our inventory and are[2] sending it to you through an air express company.

We usually have an employee of the express company[3] collect for the amount of the goods upon delivery. Since we already have your personal check for[4] $150, your account with us is paid in full.

If you have any problems with your luggage,[5] contact me. Yours truly   [104 words]

21.6 Annual Convention

Dear James   Once again the National Education Association will be holding its annual convention[1] in Jacksonville. The date of the meeting will be Friday, January 10. As you probably noticed, this is[2] a departure from our usual practice of holding the convention during the last week of June. To provide[3] you with the details of the meeting, we have enclosed a brochure for your information.

Please plan to attend[4] any of the sessions that may be of interest to you. If you will be able to join us, please let me know.[5] Very truly yours

[103 words]

LESSON 22

22.1 Employee Manual

Dear Kate   As we discussed at our meeting yesterday, our employee manual is out of date. I appreciate[1] your willingness to help us update it again.

It is very important that we keep our employees aware[2] of our procedures, benefits, and services. You could begin by deciding which sections are no longer[3] needed.

I enjoyed talking with you this morning, and I look forward to this opportunity to work with you.[4] Yours truly   [83 words]

22.2

Madison   inquiring   possibility   manufacturing   Washington   flattered   college   consider   utilize   thank you for your letter   with the   we are   should be able

22.3

1 Thank you for your letter inquiring about employment.
2 We are flattered you would like to work for us.
3 We are glad you feel the General Manufacturing Company is a nice place to work.
4 When you complete your education, please come see us.
5 We should be able to utilize your special training.

22.4 Employment Opportunities

Dear Ms. Madison   Thank you for your letter of April 25 inquiring about the possibility[1] of obtaining employment with the General Manufacturing Company of Washington. We are[2] flattered by your statement that you feel the General Manufacturing Company is a nice place to work.[3]

When you complete your college education and are ready to consider employment, please come to see us.[4] We should be able to utilize your special training when you graduate. Sincerely yours

[96 words]

22.5 Suggestion About Dictation

Tell him that it would be more efficient for him to dictate changes to rough drafts to me so that I may make the[1] corrections at the word processor. It is a waste of time for him to keyboard.   [34 words]

22.6 Telephone Confirmation

Dear Mr. Williams   This letter confirms our telephone conversation of 2 o'clock yesterday afternoon.[1]

We have agreed to manufacture your new business briefcase. We have already received your sample[2] briefcase and have begun selecting the special leather that will be required for manufacturing[3] your products.

As we have agreed, we will send you 20 briefcases from our plant for your approval. We will[4] manufacture the entire order of 5,000 briefcases when we receive your approval.[5]

You can expect to receive the shipment of the first 20 briefcases by the first day of September.[6] Very truly yours   [122 words]

22.7 New Home

Dear Mr. Steinberg   Recently I wrote to you to inquire if it would be possible for my wife and me[1] to obtain a loan from your bank for the purchase of a new home. After we filled out an information card, you[2] told us that our credit was acceptable and that we should notify you when we found a home.

Just two weeks ago[3] we heard of a house that was for sale in our own neighborhood. We would like to make an offer of[4] $200,000 for the purchase of the home. This means that we will need to borrow $100,000[5] from you.

If it would be convenient, I would like to meet with you at 3 o'clock on Thursday. Yours very truly[6]   [120 words]

LESSON 23

23.1 Invitation Acceptance

Dear Ed   After reading your kind comments about my talk to your group last year, I accept your invitation[1] to take part in your annual conference on humor.

I am planning to arrive in Los Angeles the afternoon[2] of November 11. If your schedule is free for that evening, I would be delighted to have dinner[3] with you.

I look forward to hearing from you. Sincerely yours   [71 words]

23.2

spare   minutes   representative   demonstration computer   greatly   simplify   time   instruction convenient   of your   let us know   it will be

23.3

1 Could you spare a few minutes of your busy day for a demonstration?
2 Our representative will show you how this computer can greatly simplify your work.
3 It can save money.
4 A person can learn to run it after 15 minutes of instruction.
5 Please let us know when it will be convenient for you to see our representative.

23.4 Computer Demonstration

Dear Mrs. Jones   Could you spare a few minutes of your busy day to see our representative give a[1] demonstration of our computer? In those few minutes our representative will show you how this computer can[2] greatly simplify your work and at the same time save you money. It is so simple that a person can learn to run[3] it after 15 minutes of instruction.

Please let us know when it will be convenient for you to see our[4] representative. Sincerely yours

[86 words]

23.5 Outline for a Letter

1. Thank Eleanor for her letter of April 7.
2. Tell her that I[1] already have a commitment on May 16.
3. Suggest that she ask Mary Browning to attend the meeting[2] in place of me.
4. Wish her good luck in the election of officers at the meeting. [56 words]

23.6 Book Order

Dear Mr. Pierce   Tuesday I had a very short, but important, visit with Mrs. Grace Ford. She teaches at the[1] Dale School of Business, and I have been trying to sell her business communications books for many years.

Mrs.[2] Ford finally realizes that we have the best book on the market and has placed an order with us for[3] 25 copies of the Nelson text. Please place her name on the list of those customers who receive our magazine.[4]

There is always a feeling of accomplishment when you receive an order from a new customer. Therefore, make[5] sure that she receives her first copy of the magazine without delay. Very truly yours [116 words]

23.7 Closing of Bank Account

Ladies and Gentlemen   Recently I heard of an insurance agency that was for sale in San Francisco.[1] Three weeks ago I offered to buy the company, and my offer was accepted.

I am now completely[2] settled in my new office in San Francisco. As a matter of business convenience, I will be moving my[3] bank accounts to San Francisco shortly. I will, therefore, be closing my accounts with you next week. During the time[4] that I have been your customer, I have valued your banking services. Yours truly [94 words]

LESSON 24

24.1 Retirement

Dear Mr. Gray   Thank you for the gift you and the staff of Northern Bank gave me when I retired last month. It is one[1] that I will always remember.

My 30 years at Northern Bank were very special to me. During[2] those years I made many lasting friendships.

Thank you for making my retirement party so lovely. I am looking[3] forward to retirement. Sincerely yours [68 words]

24.2

Edwards sponsoring devoted design offices speakers subjects equipping reception utilizing we are that will be to the we have will be in our

24.3

1 We are sponsoring a conference devoted to the design of business offices.
2 We have invited speakers to discuss many subjects.
3 The conference will be held in our conference room.
4 Would you like to attend this conference?
5 Please fill out and return the enclosed card.

24.4 Design Conference

Dear Ms. Edwards   On June 18 we are sponsoring a conference that will be devoted to the design[1] of business offices.

We have invited speakers to discuss such subjects as furnishing an executive[2] office, equipping a reception room, and utilizing general office space. The conference will be held in our[3] conference room.

If you would like to attend this conference, please fill out and return the enclosed card at your convenience. Cordially yours[4] [80 words]

24.5 Phone Message

Claire Hall called to say that she is in town on a business trip. She did not have any message in[1] particular. She just called for a friendly visit. She will call again when she is in town on business in a[2] few months. [41 words]

24.6 Account Closing

Dear Ms. Chase   Recently I heard of a travel agency that was for sale in Chicago. I was an agent[1] there years ago and knew of the outstanding record of that company.

One month ago I bought the company.[2] I am now completely settled in my new office in Chicago.

As a matter of business convenience,[3] I will be moving my bank accounts to Chicago. Therefore, I will be closing all my accounts with you next week.[4] During the time I have been your customer, I have valued your banking services. Yours truly
[96 words]

24.7 Sale of Books

Dear Mr. Washington   On February 7 I had a very successful visit with Mrs. Mary[1] White. She teaches at the Nashville Technical College, and I have been trying to sell her accounting books for[2] many years. I think that she finally realizes that we have the best book on the market. I expect Mrs. White[3] to transfer her business to me the next time I call.

It would, therefore, be very helpful if you would place her name[4] on the list of those customers who receive our magazine, Accounting Today. Make sure that she receives her first[5] copy of the magazine without delay. Very truly yours   [112 words]

LESSON 25

25.1 Carpeting Purchase

Dear Mr. Owens   When homeowners pay $5,000 for carpeting, they expect it to look good and wear[1] well for many years. However, what you expect and what you get are two different matters. It is not that way when[2] you purchase carpeting from us.

We have a worldwide reputation as a reliable carpeting manufacturer.[3] Come to our store the next time you need carpeting. You will get exactly what you wish. Sincerely yours[4]   [80 words]

25.2

indicates   technical   requirements   programming necessary   Springfield   interview   appointment you have   one of the   we have   on our   let us know will be   for you   with our

25.3

1 Your personal data sheet indicates that you have the technical requirements for the job.

2 We have a position open on our Springfield staff.
3 You are invited to come for an interview in Springfield.
4 Please let us know which day will be most convenient for you.
5 We can set up an appointment with our personnel manager.

25.4 Interview

Dear Ms. Smith   Your personal data sheet indicates that you have the technical requirements and the[1] experience in programming and data processing necessary to handle one of the positions we have[2] open on our Springfield staff.

You are invited, therefore, to come for an interview in Springfield any day during[3] the week of January 15. Please let us know which day will be most convenient for you so that we can[4] set up an appointment with our personnel manager. Sincerely yours   [93 words]

25.5 Personal "To Do" List

1. Send an anniversary card to Brian and Sue.
2. Study for the business statistics[1] test.
3. Keep working on the introduction to the history report until it is satisfactory.[2]
4. Ask Lee to go to the basketball game on Friday.
[49 words]

25.6 Notes From a Visitor

Tell Barbara that a sales representative from an office supply company stopped to see her. He left his business[1] card. He will try reaching her by telephone tomorrow morning in order to set up an appointment.[2]   [40 words]

25.7 Transportation Needs

Dear Mr. Larson   Sometime in May or early June my family and I will be moving from Seattle,[1] Washington, to St. Paul, Minnesota. We are looking for a transportation company that will handle our move.[2] We need a company that will load our furniture on a truck, drive the truck to St. Paul without delay, and safely[3] deliver the furniture.

If you want to come out to our home to take an inventory of our furniture,[4] you should find someone home every day.

Please let us know if you are interested in the job. Yours truly   [98 words]

25.8 Student Loan

Dear Mr. Nash   Recently I wrote to you to inquire if it would be possible for me to obtain a student[1] loan from your bank. After I filled out an information card, you told me that you would notify me if my[2] loan was accepted.

Just one week ago you called to let me know that I had a loan. However, I just received[3] a scholarship that will take care of my finances. This means that I will no longer need to borrow $7,000[4] from you. Sincerely yours   [86 words]

LESSON 26

26.1 Graduation

Dear Aunt Helen   You will be happy to learn that I have passed all my courses. Would you believe I had a perfect[1] score in math? It took a lot of hard work to achieve these grades, but it means that you will have the pleasure of seeing[2] me receive my diploma on June 4.

Thank you for the trip to California as a graduation gift. It was[3] the perfect incentive for the investment of time and effort. Love   Amy   [74 words]

26.2

Bates cabinets according credit explanation arrangements business difficulties your order it is we have not we will be glad to make to take

26.3

1 You placed your order for six filing cabinets on June 15.
2 We filled your order promptly.
3 We expected you to pay our bill for $600.
4 We have not had a payment or an explanation.
5 We will be glad to make special arrangements for you to take care of your account.

26.4 Late Payment

Dear Mr. Bates   When you placed your order for six filing cabinets with us on June 15, we filled your order[1] promptly. We also expected you to pay our bill for $600 according to our[2] regular credit terms.

It is now September 15, and we have not had a payment or an explanation.[3]

We will be glad to make special arrangements for you to take care of your account if your business is having financial difficulties.[4] Sincerely yours
                [82 words]

26.5 Outline for a Business Letter

1. Thank Mrs. Black for the invitation to attend the meeting.
2. Explain that I will be out of town on[1] that day.
3. Suggest that she ask Helen Miller to attend.
                [32 words]

26.6 Convention Invitation

Dear Tim   Once again the National Doctors Association will be holding its annual convention in[1] Portland. The meeting this year will be held the weekend of January 8. As you probably notice, this is a[2] departure from our usual practice of holding the convention during the last week of May.

The enclosed brochure[3] provides the details of the meeting. Please plan to attend any of the sessions that may be of interest to you.[4] Very truly yours   [84 words]

26.7 Quartz Watch

Dear Mr. Oliver   Thank you for your order for a quartz watch. According to your description of the watch,[1] we have taken a watch from our inventory, and we are sending it to you under separate cover through[2] first-class mail.

We usually ship our goods with an express company and have an employee of the express[3] company collect for the amount of the goods upon delivery. Since we already have your personal check for[4] $160, your account with us is paid in full.

If you have any problems with your new watch, please[5] call me. Yours truly   [104 words]

LESSON 27

27.1 College Position

Dear Mr. Wayne   Would you welcome an opportunity to work in a growth area of business? We are now[1] inviting eager college people to apply for positions in many areas of business.

We have many[2] openings in our Denver office. If you are accepted, you will be paid a fine salary with increases[3] as you demonstrate what you can do. Fill out and mail the enclosed card if this interests you. Yours very truly[4]   [80 words]

27.2

Klein western familiar privileges international medical directory countries phone you are with the   with our

27.3

1 As a holder of a Western credit card, you are familiar with the privileges.
2 Are you familiar with our international medical directory service?
3 The directory provides a list of doctors.
4 The doctors are in 150 cities.
5 Help is a phone call away.

27.4   Credit Card

Dear Mr. Klein   As a holder of a Western credit card, you are no doubt familiar with the many privileges[1] the card provides. However, are you familiar with our new international medical directory service?[2]

The international medical directory provides a list of doctors in 150[3] cities in 75 countries who speak English. Medical help is only a phone call away wherever[4] you are.

If you would like a copy of this directory, simply fill out and return the enclosed card. Sincerely yours[5]   [100 words]

27.5   House Hunting

Dear Mrs. Martin   Recently I joined the staff of Phillips Incorporated in Providence as a business[1] consultant. As a result, I will soon be moving my family to your city.

I would like to enlist your[2] help in finding a home. The next day that I have available for looking at homes is July 8. Would it be[3] possible for you to show me some of your homes? I know that the interest rates are somewhat high, but I think we could[4] get a mortgage at 9 percent.

Please let me know whether you or someone on your staff will be able to meet me[5] at your office on that date. Very truly yours   [109 words]

27.6   Publication of Book

Dear Mrs. Hartman   Thank you for meeting with me on Friday, May 20. I enjoyed discussing the publication[1] of my new book. After considering the matter carefully, I have decided not to accept the terms[2] of your offer.

I feel that your contract will not allow me a very good rate of return for my efforts.[3] According to your contract, you would have to sell 50,000 copies in order for me to make $3,000.[4] I am looking for at least a 15 percent return on my book. Please return my manuscript as soon as possible.[5] Very truly yours   [104 words]

LESSON 28

28.1   Fitness Center

Dear Mr. Scott   What is one of the most worthwhile things you can do for your employees to keep them happy? Provide[1] them with a fitness center on your premises.

Let the Smith Company do it. We plan and build 500[2] centers a year in business and industry. We have the ability to provide all types of centers.

Give[3] us a call and find out what we can do for you. Sincerely yours   [71 words]

28.2

special obtain companies advertised constantly advantage   you are   about the   in the   this is we hope you will

28.3

1 Here is a special invitation to our readers.
2 You are invited to obtain more information about the companies that are advertised.
3 Simply check the names of the advertisers listed on the enclosed form.
4 We keep you better informed about the constantly changing business scene.
5 We hope you will take advantage of it.

28.4   Invitation

Dear Mr. Green   Here is a special invitation to our readers. You are invited to obtain more[1] informa-

355

tion about the companies that advertised their products in the January issue of our[2] magazine.

Simply place a check next to the names of the advertisers listed on the enclosed form and return[3] it to us. We will then process the information. This is just another way to keep our readers informed about the[4] constantly changing business scene.

We hope you will take advantage of it. Cordially yours [95 words]

28.5 Satisfied Customer

Dear Ms. Grant   Yesterday I had lunch with Arnold Jones. The purpose of our luncheon meeting was for me to inquire[1] if he is happy with the fleet of trucks that your company built for him.

He told me he has operated trucks[2] that have come from a variety of manufacturers. Of all the trucks he has ever owned, he rates yours as[3] being the best.

With this kind of recognition of the quality of your products, I am interested in[4] having you build a fleet of trucks for my company. When can we visit? Very truly yours [96 words]

28.6 Banking Needs

Dear Mr. Baker   Next year we will be moving the home office of our manufacturing company to Birmingham.[1] We will also be moving our investment firm to Birmingham. Your company has been recommended to us[2] by several of our business contacts in Birmingham.

I will be in your city during the first week of October.[3] During that week I would like to talk to someone at your firm about our requirements. Please get in touch with me[4] to let me know when we can get together for a consultation. Very truly yours [96 words]

LESSON 29

29.1 Typing Class

Dear Mrs. Blake   For the past three months I have been teaching typing to a group of senior citizens. It has been[1] an extraordinary experience, and I look forward to each class. All of my students have the ability[2] to type 50 words a minute.

This fine achievement is proof that your book is a winner! After examining[3] many typing books, I

chose yours. Congratulations on this fine book. Sincerely yours [76 words]

29.2

tennis winter Saturdays several slopes ski summer thank you for   I would   I have been   to do so

29.3

1 Thank you for offering me a place in your tennis group.
2 I would enjoy playing tennis during the winter.
3 I have been driving to the slopes on Saturdays during the winter to ski.
4 We plan to do so again this coming winter.
5 I suggest that you invite Bob Mason to join your group.

29.4 Tennis Group

Dear Jack   Thank you for offering me a place in your tennis group. I would enjoy playing tennis during the[1] winter, but I cannot play on Saturdays. For several years my daughter and I have been driving to the slopes on[2] Saturdays during the winter to ski. We plan to do so again this coming winter.

May I suggest that you[3] invite Bob Mason to join your group. I played with Bob several times last summer, and I know that he plays a fine game.[4] Sincerely yours [83 words]

29.5 Reminder

Mrs. Goldman has requested your attendance at a luncheon meeting on Wednesday,[1] December 3. It is very important. Do not forget to attend!

[32 words]

29.6 Investment Inquiry

Dear Mrs. Klein   Thank you for your letter inquiring about investments. We certainly will be glad to work with you,[1] Mrs. Klein.

First, you will have to provide us with some information. We will need a complete financial statement[2] from you that lists all of your assets and all of your debts. We need this information in order to have an accurate[3] picture of your current financial position.

As soon as we receive this information, we will make an[4] appointment with you. Cordially yours [87 words]

29.7 Textbook Shipment

Ladies and Gentlemen Just this morning the shipping room of our school received the package of books that you sent us[1] on January 15. When I opened the package, I found that it contained 30 books instead of 45[2] books.

The invoice slip indicates that 45 copies of <u>American History</u> were to be sent. There is,[3] of course, the possibility that your shipping department made an error. Please check into the matter.

Since we have[4] already paid for 45 copies, we would appreciate receiving the remaining 15 books. Sincerely[5]   [100 words]

LESSON 30

30.1 Job Applicant

Dear Mr. Larson A week ago a young man by the name of David Knapp inquired about the possibility[1] of joining my staff. He had all the qualifications of a good programmer. I was impressed by his attitude,[2] dedication, and ability.

I offered him a job as an assistant programmer. However, he[3] asked if we would increase our salary offer. Since we require a competent programmer, I highly recommend[4] raising his salary offer. Sincerely yours   [89 words]

30.2

Lawrence permission article magazine pleasure appreciate issue thank you for it is

30.3

1 Thank you for giving us permission to reprint your article.
2 It is a pleasure to find such a well-written article.
3 When we print the article, we will give you credit.
4 Would you appreciate receiving a copy of the issue?
5 Just return the enclosed card.

30.4 Article Reprint

Dear Miss Lawrence Thank you for giving us permission to reprint your article in our magazine. It is a[1] pleasure to find such a well-written article. When we reprint the article, we will give you credit.

Would you[2] appreciate receiving a copy of the issue of our magazine in which the article is[3] reprinted? Just return the enclosed card and you will receive a copy of the issue by the end of the month.[4] Very truly yours   [84 words]

30.5 Notes From Staff Meeting

Our weekly meeting of the Research Department was held on Friday, January 23.[1] At that meeting I agreed to develop an outline for a new research proposal. The purpose of this[2] research study will be to determine the types of electronic filing systems which are used in business today.[3] I agreed to have the proposal completed in three weeks.

[71 words]

30.6 Grand Opening

Dear Mr. Reed You will be pleased to know that our new store will be opening on Black Avenue on Tuesday, June[1] 14. On that date we will officially be open for business and ready for your first visit.

We are glad[2] to be located in your neighborhood because it gives us an opportunity to provide you with the most[3] convenient shopping service. You will find that we have name brands of your favorite foods. We welcome personal checks, and[4] our prices are lower than any other store in the city.

Please stop in and see us soon. You will be glad[5] you did. Sincerely yours   [105 words]

30.7 Book Publication

Dear Mr. Roman As I promised you a week ago, I have discussed the printing of your book with our[1] manufacturing staff. They tell me that our manufacturing facilities are not very busy at this time.[2] Consequently, we can easily produce your book by June 1.

You will be pleased to know that the members of our sales[3] staff are receiving many advance orders for your book. Therefore, the first edition will be printed in a[4] quantity of 25,000 copies.

If you have any questions or comments, please let us have them. Yours truly[5]   [100 words]

LESSON 31

31.1 Request

Dear Mrs. Taylor Several weeks ago the Johnson Institute asked me to give an aptitude test to their business[1] students on May 3. However, on that date I must be out of town and cannot keep my appointment.

I have[2] recommended you as a substitute. I would be interested to know, Mrs. Taylor, if you are available[3] on that date. If you can substitute for me, I would be grateful.

Please let me hear from you as soon as possible.[4]
Sincerely yours   [83 words]

31.2

kindnesses   college   computerized   electrical
engineering   methods   forthcoming   magazine
instruction   thank you   to me   I can   I would
of our   of the

31.3

1 Thank you so much for your many kindnesses.
2 Your computerized programs in electrical engineering represent a great advance.
3 Would you be willing to prepare an article?
4 I would like to publish it in a forthcoming issue of our magazine.
5 You have made great advances in engineering instruction.

31.4 Article Publication

Dear Dr. Smith Thank you so much for your many kindnesses to me during my visit to Green College on May[1] 15. Your computerized programs in electrical engineering represent a great advance in teaching[2] methods, and I can well understand why they are so popular at Green College.

Would you be willing to prepare[3] an article describing your programs? I would like to publish it in a forthcoming issue of our magazine.[4] I know that our readers would like to learn of the great advances you have made in engineering instruction.[5] Cordially yours   [103 words]

31.5 Important Reminder

We need to have a slide projector delivered to the conference room today. Mr. Kelly needs to use it[1] during our meeting at 8:30 a.m. tomorrow.
                                              [29 words]

31.6 Building of House

Dear Mr. Powers I have given a great deal of thought to the six bids we have received for the building of a[1] house on the south side of Baker Lake. I now recommend that we give the job to Harris Brothers. The lowest bid[2] is $73,000. The other bids were higher. They promise to finish the job by the first of the[3] year if they have reasonably good weather. How do you feel about my recommendation? Very truly yours[4]   [80 words]

31.7 Banking

Dear Mr. Rosen You may be interested to know that Ms. Ann Smith has purchased the Western Data Company[1] here in Seattle. Ms. Smith is a successful business executive and will no doubt make the Western Data[2] Company very profitable.

You should contact her and tell her about the services that our bank provides.[3] If we can get her to do her banking with us, we will be obtaining a very large account. Very truly yours[4]   [80 words]

LESSON 32

32.1 Employment

Dear Mr. Brown If you are looking for employment, our newspaper is the first place to look. Employers depend[1] on these ads to find competent employees, and employees depend on these ads to find excellent job[2] opportunities.

Employment agencies also depend on us to recruit job applicants. Turn to the ads[3] in our newspaper if you want to find a job that will make the most of your abilities. Pick up a copy[4] today. Yours very truly   [85 words]

32.2

successful   country   common   program   require
administered   specifically   adapted   information
enclosed   form   can be   for you

32.3

1 The leading successful companies in our country have one common factor.
2 They all use our training program.
3 It might require years for people to learn this on their own.
4 Each course can be specifically adapted to your needs.
5 Fill out and mail the enclosed form for more information.

32.4 Training Program

Dear Mr. Day   The leading successful companies in our country have one major factor in common. They all[1] use our training program. This program does in a few days what might require years for people to learn on their own.

The[2] program can be administered by either your staff or ours. Each course can be specifically adapted to your[3] particular needs and business.

For more information on how you can put us to work for you, fill out and mail[4] the enclosed form. Cordially yours   [86 words]

32.5 Outline for a Letter

1. Thank Mr. Simon for his invitation to have members of our staff tour his manufacturing[1] facilities.
2. Tell him we gladly accept the invitation.
3. Tell him[2] that there will be three of us joining him on the tour of his facility.
4. Ask if there is any way in which[3] we might repay his courtesy.   [66 words]

32.6 Order Information

Dear Ms. Raymond   I am sorry to tell you that we will not be able to deliver the office supplies you[1] ordered on March 17. The reason is that several of our suppliers have failed to send us the items that are[2] necessary to complete your order. I have also learned that the majority of the items were[3] being supplied by a company that has just gone out of business.

The best advice I can give you is to[4] either revise your order so that you may purchase merchandise that we have on hand or place your order with another[5] company. I am sorry for any inconvenience this may cause you.

If there is any way that I can be[6] of service to you, please get in touch with me. Sincerely
                    [131 words]

32.7 Convention Invitation

Dear Ms. Allen   Two years ago it was my privilege to attend the seminar that you conducted in Chicago.[1] Your presentation was superb!

This year I am a member of the program committee for the National[2] Association of Insurance Representatives. I am inviting you to be a speaker at this[3] convention. If you accept, your presentation would be given at 10 a.m. on Saturday, October[4] 18.

I hope that you will be able to take part in our program. Very truly yours   [94 words]

LESSON 33

33.1 Positive Response

Dear Mr. Bond   Last March I enrolled in your business relations course with the objective to become a better[1] sales representative for the Armstrong Insurance Company.

At the end of the course I achieved this objective[2] but also gained many other benefits. I learned how to earn the respect of people and how to persuade[3] people to accept my point of view.

Your course was well worth my time. I highly recommend it for anyone who[4] wants success in the insurance business. Sincerely yours   [90 words]

33.2

Barnes education publication written reading ahead

significant articles reports research subscription

today condensed regularly enable school form to do

33.3 Magazine Subscription

Dear Mrs. Barnes   Our monthly education publication brings you the best of what is being written, said, and done in education today. Each issue brings you the most significant articles, reports, and research in condensed form. Reading our publication regularly will enable you to do a better job in your school and will help you to move ahead.

A subscription costs only $20 a year. Use the enclosed form to send for our magazine today. Very truly yours

33.4 Catalog Advertising

July 24, 19--
Mrs. Susan Gaines
300 Grove Street
Milford, CT 06460
Dear Mrs. Gaines   I have a suggestion that may make the operation of our business easier.

Your office[1] sends our branch stores a new edition of our catalog monthly. There are 57 stores that receive this[2] catalog. The cost of printing and mailing these catalogs has grown significantly.

I would like to meet with you[3] sometime in the near future to discuss my ideas for reducing catalog costs. Please let me know when we can[4] get together. Yours truly
John Mason   [87 words]

33.5 Phone Message

Mr. Graham called while you were out. He said that the laboratory reports[1] will not be ready to leave his office until Friday. He extends his apology. He hopes that it will not[2] cause you any inconvenience.
[47 words]

33.6 Personnel Performance Review

Dear Mr. Simmons   Congratulations on the excellent job you did with your recent review of our departmental[1] personnel.

A personnel performance review is typically a difficult process. I am sure the work[2] you did in reviewing the performance of the members of our staff was no easy task. It required a[3] tremendous amount of objectivity and professional judgment. Your willingness to accept this challenge[4] is sincerely appreciated. Sincerely yours   [89 words]

33.7 New Customer

Dear Ms. Cruz   Thank you for your order for our flooring materials. The materials are being shipped promptly[1] from our factory.

Because this order represents your first purchase of this material, we are enclosing[2] a folder that suggests the best ways to use the material. As you can see, the suggestions are quite easy[3] to follow. You may hire an expert to do the work, or you may do it yourself.

We are sure that you will be[4] happy with your new purchase. Yours very truly   [88 words]

LESSON 34

34.1 Heating System

Dear Mrs. Kirk   Are you satisfied with your electric heating system? Why not look into heating your home with[1] natural gas. It is warm, clean, and economical. Natural gas has no emission so your walls never[2] need cleaning.

It is simple to find out how your present heating unit can be altered. Our representative[3] will be glad to demonstrate how easy the alteration can be made. Give us a call soon. Sincerely yours
[79 words]

34.2

begins Christmas management December plenty season

Tuesday   committee   decided   transmitting as you know

news   please   close   office   though   I am you will have

34.3 Office Closing

Date: February 16, 19--
To: Staff
From: Robert Cox
Subject: Store Closing
Here is some news that will please you. As you know, the new year begins on a Tuesday and so does Christmas. The management committee has decided to close the office on both December 24 and December 31.

Even though this is only November 15, I am transmitting this good news to you so that you will have plenty of time to make your Christmas season plans.

I hope that you all enjoy the happiest holiday season.

34.4 Company Meeting

June 11, 19--
Ms. Kathleen Matthew

2500 Fox Avenue
Minneapolis, MN 55410
Dear Kathleen   I am sorry you will not be able to join us for the annual company meeting on[1] January 5 in Dallas. I did contact Mr. Worth, and he agreed to attend the meeting in your place.[2] I will see that the minutes from this meeting are sent to you.

Do you have any ideas for the development[3] of research projects? If you do, it is important that I receive them before the company meeting.

I look[4] forward to seeing you in February. Very truly yours
Mary Preston   [95 words]

34.5   Party Arrangements

The band we wanted for our party is not available. We need to get together[1] to decide on another band to ask to play. It is very important that we meet this week!   [37 words]

34.6   Research Conference

Dear Dr. Evans   The month of June is here! As the date for our research conference approaches, our enthusiasm[1] grows and grows.

When you arrive at the airport in Denver, you will be met by one of our sales representatives.[2] He or she will drive you to our hotel located in the mountains west of Denver.

All arrangements[3] for your presentation at our research conference have been made.

Our planning has been completed.[4] All we need to do now is wait for the exciting, eventful day to arrive. Sincerely yours   [92 words]

34.7   Insurance Policy

Dear Ms. Dempsey   About ten years ago I bought an insurance policy from you. Because present interest rates[1] are high at the banks, I am thinking about borrowing money on my insurance policy. Will you please,[2] therefore, give me some information.

First of all, will you please tell me the exact cash value of this policy[3] at the present time. Second, will you please verify that I can still borrow the cash value of my policy[4] at 7 percent interest.

As soon as I hear from you, I will make a decision as to how much money[5] I will borrow. Very truly yours   [105 words]

35.1   Computer Sales

Dear Mr. Rich   We know, Mr. Rich, that you purchased a computer from us in 1985 and that you have[1] found you can handle insurance claims quickly.

May we persuade you to consider purchasing one of our[2] updated software packages. You will be surprised by how much more you will be able to do. You will appreciate[3] the speed at which you can process data.

We would be proud to demonstrate the features of this new package at your[4] convenience. Sincerely yours   [86 words]

35.2

Foster welcome family merit credit statement it is

holders   valuable   property   always   returned   purchase

charged   misplace   immediately   questions
if you have

35.3   Credit Card

Dear Ms. Foster   Welcome to our large family of Merit credit card holders.

Your Merit credit card is a very valuable piece of property. Always be sure it is returned to you after you have charged a purchase. Should you lose or misplace it, get in touch with us immediately by calling the number on the back of your monthly statement.

If you have any questions about your credit card, please do not hesitate to write or call us. Cordially yours

35.4   Savings Plan

August 22, 19--
Mr. Frank Lamb
75 Ford Road
Fargo, ND 58104
Dear Mr. Lamb   You will be interested to know that I have devised a plan that should save our investment[1] organization at least $20,000 over the next two months. This plan has been specifically

361

compiled[2] to deliver instant dividends to the company.

I would sincerely appreciate an opportunity[3] to go over this plan with you. I am sure you will not be disappointed. Can you spare about half an hour next[4] week? Sincerely
James Warren   [84 words]

35.5 Outline for a Phone Message

1. Call Adam Riley at extension 1903.
2. The cost[1] of the printing is $250.
3. We should charge it to account number 102.
4. We need[2] it by December 5.   [44 words]

35.6 Insurance Renewal

Dear Ms. Rosen This letter is a difficult one for me to write. I am sorry to tell you that your life[1] insurance policy will no longer be in effect unless we receive your premium by October 15.[2] It would be a sad thing for you to lose this insurance after paying for it for so many years.

Maybe[3] you cannot pay the entire premium of $180 at this time. If this is the case,[4] let us know soon. I am sure we can suggest a payment plan that you will find helpful.

Please let me hear from you[5] as soon as possible; we want to help you. Yours sincerely
                                    [112 words]

35.7 Recommendation for Appointment

Dear Mr. Higgins It is a pleasure for me to give my recommendation for the appointment of Mrs.[1] Brown to the Boston Banking Commission.

Although I do not know her very well, I have had the opportunity to[2] review her work. Several financial reports she has completed have been done with a great amount of[3] professionalism.

I think you would be making a good decision if you appoint her. Yours very truly[4]   [80 words]

LESSON 36

36.1 Committee Contribution

Dear Mr. Evans As you may know, every business sets aside a part of its budget for community projects.[1] You realize, of course, that we often receive more requests for contributions than we can handle.

Unfortunately,[2] we have already distributed all funds set aside this year for projects of this nature. Therefore,[3] it will be impossible for us to grant your request for a contribution this year. When we prepare a budget[4] for next year, we will attempt to include a contribution for your organization. Sincerely yours   [99 words]

36.2

Casey happy interview position December experience

Chicago office enclosed advance expenses personnel

against arrive Barnes about we are would be to you

36.3 Interview

Dear Mr. Casey We are happy to learn that you can come for an interview for our open sales position on December 15 in our Chicago office. Enclosed is a check for $500 as an advance against expenses.

When you arrive in our building, ask for Mrs. Barnes, personnel manager. She will tell you about our personnel policies, the fringe benefits we offer, and other matters that would be of interest to you as an employee.

I am sure you will find your trip a valuable experience. Sincerely yours

36.4 Alumni Gift

February 11, 19--
Ms. Kelly Pierce
1000 Driscoll Avenue
Colorado Springs, CO 80902
Dear Ms. Pierce Recently James Garcia, an alumnus of the Washington Institute, presented us with[1] a framed picture of the founder of the school. When it arrived, the frame was broken in several places. It will require[2] some minor repairs that I hope you can take care of.

The frame is presently in my office. I must leave today[3] for a series of meetings and cannot take care of this matter myself. Therefore, I will be grateful if you will[4] take the picture to the repair shop for me. Yours very truly
Ron Chase
Assistant Chancellor   [97 words]

36.5   Phone Message

Tell Fred that Ray Best called. He will not meet your airplane at the airport. You will have to take a cab to your hotel.[1] Ray will meet you at the hotel for breakfast at 7 a.m. tomorrow.   [34 words]

36.6   Request for Price List

Dear Ms. Grant   May I compliment you on the superb paintings you had on display at the shopping center last weekend.[1] I was unable to visit with you and had time only to ask for your business card. I was told your paintings[2] were on display in Seattle, Washington; Chicago, Illinois; and San Francisco, California.

A friend tells[3] me that you have prints of your paintings available for sale. Please send me a list of the prints you have available[4] and their prices. Yours truly   [89 words]

36.7   Lawn Care

Dear Mr. Nelson   Spring is here and that means it is time to do something about your lawn. You can do it yourself,[1] but you may be depriving yourself of many hours of recreation. Entrust the job to the Johnson Lawn[2] Company and watch your lawn prosper.

Before you reach a decision about your lawn, let us examine it.[3] We will determine what needs to be done and recommend the right treatment for your lawn. Please call us soon. Sincerely yours[4]   [80 words]

LESSON 37

37.1   Speaker Invitation

Dear Ray   Next April our organization will be holding its annual research conference. I realize that the[1] meeting is nearly a year from now, but I know that your schedule may be hectic.

Because of your vast experience[2] in research, we would like to have you as a speaker at our meeting on April 19. As soon as you know[3] whether you will be available, please get in touch with me. We can discuss all the details of the program[4] at a much later time. Sincerely   [86 words]

37.2

Sims memo announcing increase business third press

schools   rising   ourselves   market   very much when the

complained   production   cost   catalog   off we will not

37.3   Price Increase

Dear Mr. Sims   I have seen your memo announcing the July 1 price increase of our business books. This is the third increase, and it disturbs me very much.

In the past three months at least 15 schools have complained about our high prices. Rising production costs seem to be the reason for these increased prices. I hope we will not price ourselves out of the market by increasing the cost of our books.

When the new catalog comes off the press, please send this office 200 copies. Yours truly

37.4   Market Survey

May 15, 19--
Ms. Ann Welch
10 West Carpenter Street
Irving, TX 75061
Dear Ms. Welch   Many successful companies have found that a survey is the best way to obtain current information[1] about market conditions. Conducting market surveys is our specialty. Last year we conducted more[2] than 500 surveys for companies of all types.

Our staff will first study the requirements of your markets. Then[3] they will tell you which of your products are meeting these requirements and which are not.

Please sign and return the[4] enclosed card and we will get in touch with you. Very truly yours
James Brown
President   [95 words]

37.5   Phone Message

Jack Kelly called to remind you that there will be a meeting of research project leaders[1] in his office at 9:30 a.m. on Friday.   [30 words]

37.6 Scholarship Recommendation Letter

Dear Mr. King It is my pleasure to recommend Miss Claire Spencer as a student who is deserving of the[1] scholarship your organization offers.

I have known Claire for the past two years. She worked ten hours a week as a[2] secretary in my office while she was in high school. In addition, she worked at a[3] local department store last summer. The purpose for her employment was to save money for college.

Claire is a[4] very dependable person, and she has my highest recommendation. Sincerely yours

[94 words]

37.7 Insurance Solicitation

Dear Ms. Delgado As an insurance agent, it is my job to help other people to protect their property.[1]

I am wondering if you have the proper insurance on your paperwork. If a fire were to destroy your[2] offices, the loss of your important papers might very well cause your business more harm than the loss of your building.[3] Almost everyone recognizes the need to insure homes and office buildings, but many people give only[4] superficial attention to the protection of vital records.

If there is a time that is convenient to[5] talk, I would like to show you our line of fireproof filing systems. Yours very truly   [116 words]

LESSON 38

38.1 Job Interview

Dear Mrs. Harper Thank you for granting me an interview and for explaining to me in detail the[1] operation of your executive training program. I was glad to have an opportunity to meet the[2] executives to whom you introduced me. After my interview, I was more convinced than ever that Smith and[3] Company was just the type of organization I would enjoy working for.

It is my hope that my qualifications[4] will convince you that I can make a substantial contribution to your organization. Sincerely yours[5]

[100 words]

38.2

pleased visit Craig College manager arrive airport

coast office computer electrical engineers be able

program training interest compliment busy schedule

38.3 Travel Plans

Dear Mr. Brown We were pleased to learn that you will soon be able to visit Craig College. The manager of your West Coast office tells us that you will arrive May 3. I will meet you at the airport and drive you to the Range Inn.

We are sure you will find our computer program in training electrical engineers of great interest. We consider it a great compliment that you will take time from your busy schedule to spend a day with us. Very truly yours

38.4 Insurance Sales

May 7, 19--
Mr. Walter Dawson
12 Franklin Street
Harrington, DE 19952
Dear Mr. Dawson Perhaps you know Lee Green. His residence is in your neighborhood. Last year Lee sold more than $2 million[1] of insurance. He had the best record in the country among all our first-year representatives.

We are now[2] looking for a person to join Lee and our other representatives in Chicago. If you are that person,[3] we will put you on the payroll, train you, and devote considerable time to getting you started.

If you think[4] you are the person for this opening, return the enclosed card for an appointment. Cordially yours
Betty Evans[5]   [100 words]

38.5 Interoffice Note

We have an offer to buy the property that we have for sale on South Broadway. The client will[1] stop in on Wednesday to complete the agreement.

[29 words]

38.6 Ideas Under Consideration

Dear Linda Thank you for your note of April 10. It was good to see you in St. Louis and to hear some of your[1] ideas.

Upon my return to my office in New York, I gave your list of suggestions to Dave for his[2] evaluation. Dave has spent several hours studying your list, and he will send you a letter soon.

I will[3] keep you up to date on our progress. We have scheduled a meeting for next Thursday, and Dave and I will discuss[4] your ideas. You can expect to receive a letter by May 5. Sincerely yours

[91 words]

38.7 Fire Insurance Benefits

Dear Mrs. Levine As a successful executive, you have no doubt taken steps to protect your business against[1] fire. Do you realize, however, that an ordinary fire insurance policy covers only your building[2] and its contents? Your regular insurance does not cover a loss of income while your business is[3] temporarily closed.

We now offer you an insurance policy that will take the place of your lost income[4] while your offices are being built. If you think this insurance would interest you, please write to me. Cordially yours

[99 words]

LESSON 39

39.1 Payment Allowance

Dear Mrs. Harrington Thank you for your check for $150 in payment for the television[1] set you bought from us. We hope that you and your family are deriving a great deal of pleasure from it.

We[2] notice that you did not deduct the discount that we allow customers who send us their payment within ten days[3] after they have been billed. Our check for $5 is enclosed.

I certainly hope that we may have the opportunity[4] to serve you again in the near future. Very sincerely yours

[92 words]

39.2

impressed   interest   working   organization department

excellent qualifications position regret with your

applicants   finally   selected   future   we are we would

39.3 Letter of Regret

Dear Mr. Green We are very impressed with your interest in working for our organization and with your excellent qualifications for the position in our sales department.

It is with regret that we tell you that the position has been filled. We had many fine applicants and finally selected a person with a great deal of experience.

Your qualifications are so outstanding, however, that we would like to keep your application on file for any opening that may occur in the future. Sincerely yours

39.4 School Material

October 1, 19--
Mr. Thomas Lake
State School of Nursing
200 Bradley Avenue
Raleigh, NC 27602
Dear Mr. Lake It is our pleasure to provide material that will be helpful in your nursing program.[1] Unfortunately, we cannot supply copies of this material for all your classes.

We have made many[2] of our tapes available to schools offering instruction in nursing. If you would like to show any of these[3] tapes to your students, we can lend them to you. Please indicate on the enclosed form which tapes you would prefer.

If we[4] can be of any further service to you, please let us know. Cordially yours
Mary Garcia
Community Service[5] Director

[101 words]

39.5 "To Do" List for the Boss

1. Travel expense reports are due Friday.
2. The annual performance review of[1] department personnel needs to be completed by the end of November.

[33 words]

39.6 Security Procedures

Date: December 10, 19--
To: Staff
From: Robert Brown
Subject: Building Security Procedures
An increasing number of people have been[1] coming back to the office after hours. In order to avoid any problems, it would be helpful if everyone[2] would follow some simple procedures:

1. Please notify the security office of your intention to[3] return to the building after hours.

2. Turn off all lights in your area, and make sure the outside door locks behind[4] you when you leave.

Your cooperation will be greatly appreciated.

[94 words]

39.7 Insurance Follow-Up

Dear Mr. Feldman   You will recall that in January and February of last year our representative,[1] Mrs. Fox, had several meetings with you. She gave you complete information about both the costs and benefits[2] of our insurance program. At the time of your last meeting, you promised to give the matter some thought and then get[3] in touch with Mrs. Fox.

Mrs. Fox and I are both available to answer your questions. We are eager[4] to talk with you about your insurance coverage just as soon as it is convenient for you to do so. Cordially yours[5]

[100 words]

LESSON 40

40.1   Collection Letters

Dear Mr. Gray   Are you looking for effective collection letters that you can use right now to bring in checks from[1] delinquent accounts? Letters that bring in payments and retain customer goodwill are not easy to find.

We have[2] assembled for our customers a binder of 200 of the best collection and credit letters[3] selected by our editorial staff. I will send you the binder on approval if you will return the[4] enclosed card to me.

If you feel the letters suit your needs, just send us your check for $12. Sincerely   [99 words]

40.2

recall   March   informed   management   decided   advantage

expand   department   growing   demand   business   complete

education   materials   almost   desire   you will   to take

40.3   Education Specialist

To the Sales Staff   You will recall that on March 18 I informed you that management has decided to expand our department to take advantage of the growing demand for business education materials.

This expansion is now almost complete, but we still need a competent shorthand authority.

Perhaps in your territory you have run across someone who might be interested. If you can refer someone to us with the background we desire, we would be grateful.

40.4   Recreation Program

May 8, 19--
Mr. Glenn Worth
375 Peterson Drive
Fort Scott, KS 66701
Dear Mr. Worth   Enclosed is a copy of a brochure which describes the recreational courses offered by[1] our company. It lists all the courses that will be offered through the personnel department beginning in[2] September.

As you look through the brochure, you will notice many interesting courses that should help to fill your[3] recreational needs. It is our hope that you will encourage your personnel to take advantage of the[4] opportunities available to them through this fine program.

Please call if you have any questions about the[5] program. Sincerely yours
Janet Smith
Coordinator   [110 words]

40.5   Notes From the Library

A recent research study found that service industries account for 68 percent[1] of the nation's GNP and 71 percent of its employment.   [34 words]

40.6   Information on Disability

Dear Mr. Wilson   What would you do, Mr. Wilson, if for some reason you were no longer able to work? How[1] long could you live on the money from your savings account? These are serious questions that you should answer.

In order[2] to help you answer these questions, we have prepared a booklet for you to read at your convenience. Please write for your[3] free copy today. Sincerely yours   [66 words]

40.7   Congratulatory Note

Dear Robert   Just this morning I noticed in the newspaper the announcement of your new job. What an opportunity[1] this represents for you. I know that this is exactly the type of job you have wanted for many years.[2]

Mary joins me in extending our most sincere congratulations to you. Sincerely   [56 words]

LESSON 41

41.1 Business Relationship

Dear Ms. Henderson For five years our Smith Office Supply Company had what we considered to be a good[1] business relationship with your organization. You sent us an order for the office supplies you needed[2] every few months, and we sent you the quality merchandise you wanted.

Now it has been over a year since we have[3] heard from you, and we are wondering what the trouble could be. Have we done anything to offend you, Ms.[4] Henderson? If we have let you down in some way, please let us know about it. Very truly yours   [96 words]

41.2

explaining   decided   circumstances
thank you for the

openings   available   interview   opportunity
education

national   accept   scholarship   understand
I have been

41.3 Letter of Appreciation

Dear Ms. Frank   Thank you for the time you spent with me on May 10 explaining the openings available in the National Insurance Company. I enjoyed both my interview and the opportunity to learn more about your company.

I have decided, however, to continue my education and to accept a scholarship that I have been offered by Clark College in Dallas. Under the circumstances I am sure you can understand my decision. Sincerely yours

41.4 Lawn Mower Purchase

March 17, 19--
Miss Diana Wells
960 Washington Avenue
Huntington, WV 25704
Dear Miss Wells   Thank you for your order for a Worth electric lawn mower. It will be shipped just as soon as you[1] let us know which model you want.

Our product is available in the five exciting models listed on the[2] enclosed circular. Please check off the model you want on the enclosed card and return the card to us. We will, of course,[3] fill your order as soon as we receive it. Yours very truly
John Larson
Customer Service Manager[4]   [80 words]

41.5 Organization Grant

Dear Mr. Stone   Your letter proposing that our company provide your organization with a grant has been[1] referred to me.

I certainly agree with the purpose of the program which your letter has described. However,[2] requests for grants are very heavy this year. We have had to adopt a new policy which specifies[3] that we provide gifts only to organizations within our immediate service area.

I know that the[4] program you have outlined is valuable, and I hope you find good sources of financial support for it.[5] Sincerely yours   [102 words]

41.6 Complaint

Ladies and Gentlemen   On Monday, December 12, I bought four new tires from you. At the time I bought the tires,[1] I had you install them on my car. Your sales representative assured me that the tires would last 20,000[2] miles.

The tires began to show signs of serious wear after only 7,000 miles. I can find no possible[3] explanation for this excessive wear.

I would like to make an appointment to leave my car with you someday[4] in the very near future. At that time you can determine the trouble with my tires and tell me what adjustment[5] you plan to make. Very truly yours   [106 words]

LESSON 42

42.1 Investment Counsel

Dear Mr. Brown   For many years our investment firm has been helping people receive the greatest rate of return[1] on the money they have to invest. Some of our clients have mentioned that you might be a potential investor.[2]

We can provide you with information to help you select stocks and bonds for purchase and we can advise you on the[3] best time to buy and sell. Finally, we can help you to determine what rate of return to expect.

If you think[4] that our services may be helpful to you, please let us hear from you soon. Yours very truly   [96 words]

42.2

satisfied   expired   we hope   you have been we will be

however   rental   agreement   western   purchase with the

option   accommodate   let us know as soon as possible

42.3   Computer Rental Agreement

Dear Mrs. James We hope you have been satisfied with your computer. However, your eight-week rental agreement with the Western Computer Store has expired. Under the agreement you have the option of returning the computer to us or of buying this computer with the rental fee already paid toward the purchase price.

Please let us know your decision as soon as possible. We will be happy to accommodate you in any way we can. Yours very truly

42.4   Textbook Selection

July 24, 19--
Ms. Karen Black
District Manager
Nottingham Publishing Company
1539 Medford Road
Madison, WI 53703
Dear Ms. Black Since your company publishes a variety of books, you may be able to help me. I have been[1] asked to teach advanced computer subjects at West High School in Madison. Over the years I have taught many[2] computer courses but never at an advanced level.

This particular course is new at the school. Therefore,[3] it is up to me to choose a book for the class. Do you have a book that covers advanced computer languages[4] for the high school student? If you do, I would appreciate receiving a sample copy in the near future.[5] Very truly yours
James Martin   [105 words]

42.5   Instructions for Mike

Tell Mike that he should list all of the subjects he can think of that should be included in the[1] new office procedures manual.   [26 words]

42.6   Insurance Renewal

Dear Mr. Russell Your insurance company has just notified us that your coverage on your fleet of trucks[1] will expire on the first day of August. As you know, you are required to maintain this type of insurance coverage[2] on your trucks for as long as you have an outstanding balance on your loan.

Please contact your insurance agent[3] immediately to make sure that this insurance will continue. As soon as you have paid for this insurance and have[4] received your policy, please send a copy of your insurance policy to me. Sincerely [97 words]

42.7   Business Conference

Dear Dr. Lane As chairperson of the program committee for the Association of Business Education[1] at Western State University, I am inviting you to speak at one of our regular business meetings.[2] The meeting that we would like you to attend will be held at 7 p.m. on Thursday, October 20.[3]

Several members of our group have had the pleasure of being members of your classes.

Please let me know, Dr. Lane,[4] if you are available on October 20. Very truly yours   [93 words]

LESSON 43

43.1   New Home

Dear Ms. Jackson Congratulations on the purchase of your new home. Home ownership can be exciting. But[1] along with the excitement of owning a home comes responsibility.

It is easy to forget about[2] something like a furnace. Having your furnace checked seems to be a task you never get around to doing. Yet lack of[3] proper care can be expensive and inconvenient.

The Smith Fuel Company has several service contracts available[4] to assure that your furnace is safe to operate. Each type of contract is described in the enclosed[5] brochure.

After you have reviewed the enclosed information, please let us hear from you if we can assist you.[6] Yours truly [122 words]

43.2

Winston asking reserve however thank you for it is

education convention Milwaukee possible we will be

postpone visit suite March enclosed there is to do

43.3 Hotel Reservations

Dear Mr. Winston   Thank you for asking us to reserve a suite of rooms at our hotel for the week of March 6. However, there is an education convention in Milwaukee during that week, and all rooms were reserved many months ago.

If it is possible for you to postpone your visit to Milwaukee for a week, we will be happy to reserve a suite for you beginning March 13. Please return the enclosed card if you wish us to do this. Sincerely

43.4 Speaking Engagement

October 28, 19--
Mr. Sam Baker
6900 Cooper Street
New Orleans, LA 70118
Dear Mr. Baker   Thank you for your most welcome letter accepting my invitation to speak at one of the[1] meetings on April 16. I am sure that you will have a large and appreciative audience.

The details[2] of the program have not yet been worked out, but I will see that you receive the information you requested just[3] as soon as it is available.

I suggest that you stay at the Sanford Hotel in Phoenix. This is a new hotel,[4] and I am sure you will be comfortable there. Sincerely yours
Frank Temple [90 words]

43.5 Placement Service

Dear Ms. Jennings   Bringing the right individual and the right job together is what our placement service is[1] all about. When you hire one of our students, you hire a highly skilled, professional secretary.

We are delighted[2] that you called our placement service. Enclosed is our contract that explains in detail our services and our fee[3] schedule. After we

receive your signed contract, we will call you to set up interviews.

Whatever your needs may be,[4] we believe we can help you find the right secretary. Cordially yours [93 words]

43.6 Magazine Subscription

Dear Mr. Jones   As the owner of a fleet of trucks, you are no doubt concerned that your drivers take a professional[1] interest in their work.

I am the editor for a small publishing house that is just beginning to publish[2] a big new magazine called Truck Driver Weekly. The magazine is attractive, but it is not at all expensive.[3]

You will be pleased to know that you can obtain a group rate. By completing the enclosed order form, each week you will be[4] sending our magazine to the home of each of your drivers. Sincerely yours [94 words]

LESSON 44

44.1 Product Solicitation

Dear Mr. Lynch   Congratulations on the opening of your new factory in Chicago. I am sure that[1] your new line of boating products will be a success.

Have you made a contract with a supplier of paint yet? The[2] American Paint Company has a large selection of marine paints. Enclosed is a copy of our catalog[3] listing the various paints available along with prices.

If you will tell me how much paint you will need[4] during your first month of production, I will send you a price estimate. I look forward to hearing from you soon.[5] Sincerely [102 words]

44.2

informed furniture items increased 5 percent labor

January necessary sizable materials enclosing I am

convenience catalog order that the will be for the

44.3 Price Increase

Dear Mr. White   Our home office has informed us that the price of all our furniture items will be increased by 5 percent on January 1. This increase is made necessary by the sizable increase in the cost of materials and labor.

Why not make a list of the items you will need for the coming year and place your order now while present low prices are in effect. For your convenience I am enclosing a catalog with an order blank on the back cover. Sincerely yours

44.4 Temporary Employment Agency

November 21, 19--
Mr. Michael Scott
8 South Capitol Street
Palmer, WA 98048
Dear Mr. Scott   Helen Jones is one of the supervisors of the James Temporary Services Company.[1] She personally tests many applicants at her office in Detroit. She then sends them to work in[2] organizations where they will do the most good.

Our specialty is providing the right person for the right job.[3] Call us the next time you need temporary employees to help you for any reason. Very cordially yours
Robert Anderson   [76 words]

44.5 Instructions From the Boss

Within the next two weeks I should determine a tentative plan for changing our present[1] paper filing system into a computer-assisted retrieval system.   [34 words]

44.6 Merchandise Sale

Dear Mr. Miller   A friend of mine recently showed me a beautiful print that you had made. She told me that your[1] prints are available on a very limited basis. The purpose of this letter is to find out how wide[2] a variety of pictures you have available. Also, I am interested in knowing how much a[3] typical print might cost.

Please send me this information at your convenience. I am sincerely impressed with the[4] quality of your work, and I hope to be able to own one of your pictures myself. Yours truly   [99 words]

44.7 Student Loan

Dear Mr. Parker   Thank you for calling me this morning. I believe I answered all of your questions about your[1] student loan.

Enclosed is your loan repayment schedule. As you will notice, you should begin making payments on[2] January 1. Your payments will be $54 a month for 60 months.

I hope this information[3] has been of assistance to you. Should you have any further questions, please feel free to call me. Very truly yours[4]
                                          [80 words]

LESSON 45

45.1 Stock Investments

Dear Mr. Dailey   The last time we visited, Mr. Dailey, I had the privilege of hearing your philosophy[1] on investments. You suggested that I buy Patterson stock as an investment, but I admit that I am somewhat[2] reluctant to do so.

Before I decide to put my money into an investment in Patterson stock, I would like to[3] watch the stock market for a while. I will contact you if I should change my mind. Yours truly   [76 words]

45.2

Bradford   requested   during   telephone   placed   deliver

conversation   selected   builder   furnishings   you have

estimates   arrive   satisfied   as you   I have   I am sure

45.3 Rug Order

Dear Mrs. Bradford   As you requested during our telephone conversation, I have placed an order for the carpet you have selected for the living room of your new home.

I have asked the mill to deliver the carpet on September 15. That is the day that the builder estimates the living room will be ready for furnishings. If the carpet should arrive before you can have it installed, please let me know. I will store it for you until you are ready.

I am sure you will be satisfied for years. Sincerely

45.4 Insurance Coverage

July 30, 19--
Mr. Peter Green
Providence Financial
721 Maple Avenue
Chicago, IL 60607

Dear Mr. Green The purpose of this letter is to tell you how pleased I am with the business advice given to me[1] by your representative, Ms. Goodman. Ms. Goodman reviewed my entire insurance program with me and asked[2] many questions about my insurance needs.

Ms. Goodman ended our meeting by promising to get back to me[3] with her recommendations. When I received her recommendations, I had to admit that she had determined[4] my insurance needs perfectly.

I have enjoyed working with her, and I will be glad to entertain future[5] suggestions. Very truly yours
Ann Sims   [107 words]

45.5 Office "To Do" List

Add the phone number of Lewis Gordon to my list of speed-call numbers. It is[1] 517-555-1472.
[25 words]

45.6 Contract Agreement

Dear Mrs. Jacobs   I am pleased to tell you that our work has been completed on the revision of the contract.[1] Enclosed you will find a copy of the collective bargaining agreement between Eastern Electronics[2] Incorporated and the Electronics Workers Union.

This contract represents collective bargaining at its[3] best. It should prove to be satisfactory to all parties. The contract will go into effect on June 1, and[4] it will run for four years. Very truly yours
[88 words]

45.7 Vacation Arrangement

Dear John   For many years, John, we have been talking about the possibility of planning our vacations at the[1] same time. Since this talk could go on for years, I have decided that it is time for me to take action.

You[2] mentioned in one of your earlier letters that you might be able to take your vacation in July. Therefore,[3] I have gone ahead and rented two rooms at your favorite hotel in Colorado. I do not have to send the[4] deposit money to the hotel until the middle of June. You have plenty of time to decide whether you will be able[5] to join me for a vacation in the mountains.

Please consider my offer, and let me hear from you[6] when you have made a decision. Sincerely
[129 words]

46.1 Credit Information

Dear Miss Allen All of us are sometimes faced with the problem of paying emergency expenses. We cannot[1] always be ready to meet any emergency. But anyone with a regular job and a good credit[2] standing can take advantage of our new service in the form of a letter of credit. The letter of credit[3] assures you that money will be available when you need it from the First National Bank.

To apply for your letter[4] of credit, fill out and mail the enclosed application form. As soon as your application is approved, we will[5] mail your letter of credit to you. Sincerely yours   [110 words]

46.2

west   income   ahead   substantially   copy you will have

explains   various   payment   minimum   enclosed for your

months little sending guide things booklet company

46.3 Income Tax Guide

Dear Mr. West Income tax time is some months ahead, but with a little planning you may be able to save substantially on your taxes.

You can begin by sending for our income tax guide. This guide lists many things that may affect the amount of tax you will have to pay and explains the various steps you can take to keep your tax payment to a minimum.

The booklet is free from Smith and Company. Send for your copy today by simply filling out and returning the enclosed card. Sincerely yours

46.4 Insurance Policy

August 15, 19--
Ms. Gloria Pace
436 Center Hill Road
Montgomery, AL 36111

Dear Ms. Pace   As I am sure you know, the quarterly premium on your health insurance policy was due on[1] July 15. The amount of the premium is $200.

It is now August 15, and[2] we still have not received your check. We must receive either your check or a letter of explanation immediately[3] if your policy is to remain in effect. If we do not receive a letter from you by August[4] 16, we will have to discontinue your insurance policy.

Please get in touch with us at once. Sincerely yours[5]

Frank Sexton
Accounts Receivable   [108 words]

46.5   Personal Note

It would be a good idea to place the name of Paula Bates on the computerized address[1] list of people who receive our holiday greeting cards.

[30 words]

46.6   Staff Survey Memo

Date: October 17, 19--
To: David Larson
From: Warren Wright
Subject: Staff Survey

Perhaps you will recall, David, that three years ago[1] we conducted a survey of the members of our staff. The purpose of that survey was to determine their[2] opinions about the quality of management within our organization.

Such a study should be done[3] every few years. It is important that we do everything we can in order to determine what we are[4] doing right and in order to determine where we can improve our performance. I think it is time for us to do[5] a new study.

Would you please find a copy of the first study in your files. Review it and make any changes[6] that you think are necessary to bring it up to date. Once you have the questionnaire in a form you like, let us get[7] together to discuss it.

I would like to meet with you about this before the end of the summer.   [158 words]

46.7   Membership Application

Dear Ms. Lynn   For several years I have had frequent visits with some friends of mine who are members of the National[1] Ski Club. They seemed very pleased with their memberships and have often encouraged me to join. Also, I have seen[2] sev-

eral issues of the magazine that comes with membership in the club, and I am very impressed with it.[3]

Would you please send me an application form so that I may become a member of your club? Very truly yours[4]   [80 words]

LESSON 47

47.1   Product Information

Dear Miss Hastings   As a sales representative of the Morris Company, you will be happy to know that the[1] new line of perfume is now ready for marketing. We expect this new product to be one of our most popular[2] items.

Sample packages for your customers will be sent to you this week. We are sure they will buy the[3] product once they have the opportunity to try it.

All of us wish you the very best[4] success as you begin the most active sales campaign of the year. Sincerely yours   [90 words]

47.2

explaining video training program prices engineers

separate   complete   number
thank you for your letter

cover   information   adapt   we will be glad
one of our

47.3   Product Information

Dear Mr. Gates   Thank you for your letter explaining your plans to use a video cassette in your new sales training program. Under separate cover I am sending you our catalog with complete information about our products and prices. You should have it in a few days.

We have a number of engineers on our staff helping business organizations adapt our materials to their special needs. We will be glad to have one of our engineers discuss your plans with you.

Please return the enclosed card if you wish us to get in touch with you. Sincerely yours

47.4   Business Purchase

October 30, 19--
Ms. Sally Wade
1926 Kings Court
Chester, MA 01011

Dear Ms. Wade Your advertisement in the May issue of <u>Business Today</u> came to my attention at the best[1] possible time. In your advertisement you state that you wish to buy a retail store in the Boston area.[2]

After many years of work, I have decided that it is time for me to retire. Therefore, my business is for[3] sale. The Smith Clothing Store was started by my father many years ago and is presently maintained by me.

Since[4] you do not live far from our store, please stop in to see if our store is what you are looking for. Very truly yours[5]
Andrew Nelson
Marketing Manager   [107 words]

47.5 Meetings Memo

Date: December 10, 19--
To: Staff
From: Mark Green
Subject: Staff Meetings
Throughout the coming year, staff meetings will be held at 8:30 a.m.[1] every Monday morning. You will be notified by memorandum of any canceled meetings at least[2] one week in advance.

Several changes to the regular meeting schedule are as follows: Tuesday, February[3] 5; Tuesday, March 12; Tuesday, May 7; and Wednesday, August 7.

Please note these meetings on your calendar.
[79 words]

47.6 Price Quotations

Dear Mr. Novak It has been some time since I had the pleasure of making a price quotation on the furniture[1] for your new office. A considerable length of time has gone by, and I have not heard from you. Although we have[2] seen rising labor and material costs, I will hold to my original price quotation.

The prices[3] for the furniture were for one executive desk, $480; one executive chair,[4] $160; one visitor's chair, $78; and two file cabinets, $150[5] each.

If you decide to place your order, we can promise delivery within three days. Yours very truly
[119 words]

48.1 Job Opportunity

Dear Kate Today the press agent for a famous athlete stopped in at our office. She wanted to know if we could[1] print 100,000 copies of a program to be used in a series of speeches this coming fall.

She also[2] asked if we could print the programs in four colors at a special price. We have never handled a job like this[3] before, Kate, but I believe that we can do it.

Please let me know your thoughts on this project.
Sincerely   [79 words]

48.2

several   offered   complimentary   wondering   obligation

advertising   heard   whether   finest   books   let us know

important   persons   field   cited   regarding   I have not

48.3 Follow-Up Letter

Dear Mr. West Several weeks ago I offered to send you a complimentary copy of our book <u>Advertising Facts</u>. As I have not heard from you, I am wondering whether my letter was lost in the mail.

Several important persons in the field of advertising have cited this book as one of the finest books regarding advertising copy.

Let us send you a copy without obligation. If you find the book useful, please let us know. If you are not happy with it, return it to us. Sincerely yours

48.4 Business Seminars

April 28, 19--
Miss Kathy Lane
Regional Manager
Consolidated Electric
1927 Pierce Place
San Francisco, CA 94101
Dear Miss Lane Last spring our organization offered a series of business communications conferences[1] across the United States. This series of meetings was so successful that we are consider-

ing the[2] possibility of conducting the seminar in Canada this year. One of the places that we are considering[3] is Toronto.

Enclosed is an outline of our program. If you think some of the members of your staff might benefit[4] from this program, please send me a list of their names. Cordially yours

Nathan Rich   [94 words]

48.5 While You Were Out

Mrs. Vega stopped by to visit for a moment. She mentioned that you will be receiving a form next week.[1] It will ask us to identify which of our records in the filing area can be put on microfilm.

[39 words]

48.6 Complaint

Dear Mr. Stevens   I was sorry to receive your letter complaining about our charges for service on your[1] automobile. I can understand that anyone hates to receive a bill for over $200.[2] According to our records, however, this is the first time you have brought your car to us for service since you bought it[3] two years ago.

Every item on our bill was for parts which need to be replaced on a regular basis.[4] If you will check your owner's manual, you will see that we followed the recommended routine maintenance procedures.[5]

We would like to keep you as a satisfied customer. We hope you will view routine automobile maintenance[6] as a good way to save money in the long run. Yours truly   [131 words]

48.7 Insurance Request

Dear Ms. Bloom   As the month of April draws near, my thoughts are turning to the subject of income tax. Every year I[1] earn a little bit more money and pay higher taxes. It does not mean that I am really getting ahead[2] financially.

I understand that there may be some type of retirement account that, as a teacher, I can set[3] up with your insurance company. Am I correct that I would not have to pay income tax on money deposited[4] in such an account?

Please give me any information you have on how I can set up a retirement[5] account with you. Sincerely   [105 words]

49.1 Employee Insurance

Dear Mr. Nelson   About seven months ago I appointed a committee to take a good look at our[1] employee insurance program to find out how it compares with the programs of other companies in our industry.[2] Consequently, we will be making some changes in our present plan.

In about three weeks you will receive[3] information that gives all the details of this new plan. The personnel department will also hold meetings at[4] which the new plan will be discussed. Sincerely yours   [89 words]

49.2

Gentlemen   privilege   occasion   worldwide anniversary

writing   published   steady   readership   has been in it

inception   appeared   response   congratulations golden

49.3 Congratulatory Letter

Gentlemen   Digest Magazine has been on my reading list ever since its inception. I have also had the privilege and pleasure of seeing some of my own writing published in it. On each occasion that my work has appeared in Digest Magazine, I have met with a worldwide response that assures me of steady readership.

Congratulations on your golden anniversary. Sincerely yours

49.4 Account Collection

February 10, 19--
Mrs. Helen Lane
316 State Street
Miami, FL 33716
Dear Mrs. Lane   The management of the Smith Department Store has informed us that you have not paid anything[1] on your account since last January. They tell us that they have offered to discuss the matter with you. They also[2] tell us that they

have offered to let you pay your account in installments.

Now the situation has become[3] serious. It is still our hope that you will be able to pay your bill and avoid damaging your credit rating.[4]

Please call our office this week to make an appointment. We are willing to settle this matter in a most fair and[5] equitable manner. Very truly yours Richard M. Ward
Claims Department   [115 words]

49.5   Special Account

August 19, 19--
Ms. Peggy Dean
First National Bank
1965 Hartman Street
Mesa, AZ 85201
Dear Ms. Dean   As the month of November draws near, my thoughts are turning to the holidays. Every year I earn[1] a little bit more money, but I never seem to save enough for holiday expenses.

I understand that[2] there may be some type of holiday savings account that I can set up with your bank. Please give me any[3] information you have on how I can set up this special holiday savings account with you. Sincerely[4]
Lynn Olson   [82 words]

LESSON 50

50.1   Audit Completion

Dear Mr. Leslie   Last Tuesday our staff completed the audit of your books. They will not, therefore, be reporting[1] to your offices until you call for their services again.

Enclosed is a copy of our contract and a[2] report of operations we have prepared for your company for the period of July 1 to December[3] 31. Other reports will be forwarded to you as soon as they are completed.

I hope we will have[4] the opportunity to service your company in the future. Sincerely yours
[95 words]

50.2

Dear Mr.   loading   furniture   emotional
United States

onto people strain carefully efficiently we cannot services of course we can we are in the it will be

50.3   Family Move

Dear Mr. Henry   Moving from one home to another will involve more than loading your furniture onto a truck and driving off. For many people, moving results in emotional strain. Of course, we cannot take away the stress of moving, but we can help make it a little easier.

We are ready to move you at any time to any town in the United States. When you trust your move to us, you can relax knowing that it will be done carefully and efficiently.

Call us the next time you need our services. Sincerely yours

50.4   Office Furniture

September 11, 19--
Ms. Pamela Winston
Monroe Manufacturing Company
1989 Empire Street
Cincinnati, OH 45202
Dear Ms. Winston   In January you asked for prices on office furniture. A considerable length of time[1] has gone by, and I have not heard from you. Although we have seen rising costs in our industry, I will hold to my[2] original price quotation.

The prices of the furniture in that quotation were for two executive[3] chairs, $350; four visitor chairs, $300; and one three-drawer file cabinet,[4] $150. If you decide to place your order, we can promise delivery within three days.[5] Yours very truly
Mark James
Customer Service   [108 words]

50.5   Price List

August 15, 19--
Ms. Mary Adams
Cooper Manufacturing Company
14 Monroe Street
Springfield, IL 62708
Dear Ms. Adams   You will be pleased to know that our new price list will be ready for mailing in January.[1] We will mail copies of our price list to your customers as a free service. Our price list will consist of a list[2] of our products and the price of each product. We will also let them know that our

products can be purchased at your store.[3] This enables us to sell our goods at your store by providing free advertising for your store.

We are eager[4] to send our price list to your customers but cannot do so until you send us their names and addresses. May[5] we have this important information soon? Yours truly
Henry Bradford
Marketing Services   [117 words]

LESSON 51

51.1   Credit Consideration

Dear Mrs. Black   Please consider this letter your invitation to apply for a Grant Stores credit card. It is[1] one of the most widely used credit cards in this country. If you apply within 14 days, we will send you a[2] valuable free gift. You will be able to make purchases in hundreds of Grant Stores around the United States.[3]

Will you please take a moment now, Mrs. Black, to complete the information requested on the enclosed card and[4] return it to us. Sincerely yours
                                      [87 words]

51.2

promises   resources   professional   public   immediately

discount   effective   one of the   will be   we will have

bookstore   outstanding   people   employees   many   of the

51.3   Bookstore Opening

To the Staff   Our new bookstore on Park Avenue will open on March 20. The store promises to be one of the outstanding book resources for professional people.

This store will service our employees as well as the general public. Your employee discount of 50 percent will be effective immediately at the new store.

On March 15 at 5 p.m. we will have a preview of the store for our employees. Come in and see the many features that we believe make this store outstanding.

51.4   Rifle Club

July 4, 19--
Ms. Sally Decker
National Rifle Club
436 Commerce Road
Watson, OK 74963
Dear Ms. Decker   For many years I have visited some friends of mine who are members of the National Rifle[1] Club. They seemed pleased with their memberships and have often encouraged me to join. Also, I have seen several[2] issues of the magazine that comes with membership in the club, and I am very impressed with it.

Would you please[3] send me an application form so that I may become a member of your club? I am sure that I will enjoy the[4] fellowship of belonging to an organization of people who share my interest. Very truly yours[5]
Maria Morales   [104 words]

51.5   Advertising Appropriation

March 22, 19--
Miss Louise Rowe
Advertising Manager
Gates Advertising
20 Court Street
Stamford, CT 06901
Dear Miss Rowe   As you know, the demand for our goods has fallen very badly in the last few months. A large part[1] of the decrease can be traced to the cut in our advertising appropriation.

When we talked about the[2] advertising appropriation last April, I predicted that the demand for our goods would decrease if we[3] reduced our advertising. The demand decreased between 10 and 15 percent.

I earnestly recommend that we[4] increase the number of advertisements for June, July, and August. I feel this action will help regain our[5] competitive advantage. Yours truly
David Klein
General Manager
cc: A. H. David   [111 words]

LESSON 52

52.1   Seasonal Sale

Dear Mrs. Jones   Most stores have sales in July to

give the public the opportunity to buy merchandise[1] at reduced prices. We will soon be having our July sale.

If you do not have a charge account with us, this[2] would be an excellent time to open one. Our charge account gives you the advantage of buying according[3] to your present needs without having to pay for your purchases all at one time.

If you apply for this card[4] immediately, you will be able to take advantage of this sale. Yours very truly   [97 words]

52.2

clients national investment past financial arrange

staff   new   qualify   dreams   of the   in the you will be

business   card   interview   convenience   to you we will

52.3 Investments

Dear Mr. Jackson   Because of the great number of clients the National Investment Company has added in the past six months, we are expanding our offices in Los Angeles. To staff these new offices, we need people with a solid financial background.

If you qualify as one of our representatives, you will be in business for yourself. The amount of your income will be limited only by your own dreams.

If this career is attractive to you, fill out and mail the enclosed card. We will arrange an interview for you at your convenience. Cordially yours

52.4 Book Supplies

April 23, 19--
Mr. Boyd Oliver
25 Olive Street
Lawrence, NE 68957
Dear Mr. Oliver   In our continuing effort to meet the needs of our customers, we are always open[1] to suggestions. As the director of the business department of Tate College, you are in the best position[2] to know the books that the members of your staff would like to see on the shelves of our store for their students. You also[3] know what books we ought to carry in order to meet the needs of your own students.

Would it be possible[4] for you to send us a list of books that you would recommend for general read-

ing by the students? We look forward[5] to hearing from you. Sincerely
Sharon Dillon
Purchasing Supervisor   [114 words]

52.5 Graduation Preparation

September 28, 19--
Mr. Allen Klein
Principal
Fenton High School
42 Alfred Street
Lansing, MI 45387
Dear Mr. Klein   We are writing to ask whether you can tell us how many caps and gowns you will need this June.[1] We would like to have this information now so that we may give you the best possible service.

If it is[2] impossible to give us the date of your graduation, please do not hold up the order. Let us know[3] approximately how many caps and gowns you will want and the sizes.

If you would prefer to have us send these[4] items on open account, we will do so. Sincerely yours
Russell Mann
National Products
cc: Bruce Andrews
Class[5] Adviser
bcc: Donald Rubin
School District Chairman   [111 words]

LESSON 53

53.1 Car Service

Dear Mr. Becker   It is not uncommon for many of your customers to complain whenever they do not[1] receive the service they demand. But the same customers seldom pay a compliment when the service they receive[2] is outstanding.

That is why it gives me great pleasure to tell you how delighted I was with the service I[3] received on my car recently. My damaged fender was quickly repaired, and the charge was very reasonable.[4]

You can be assured that I will always take advantage of your terrific service. Sincerely yours
                                                            [98 words]

53.2

holidays   approaching   hundreds   suggestions
December

form with the you are you will in the on the to do

doubt ideas catalog choose list guarantee delivery

53.3 Holiday Shopping

Dear Mrs. Kirk With the holidays approaching you are no doubt looking for ideas for gifts that you will give to your friends and family.

You will find hundreds of suggestions in the enclosed catalog. Choose the items you want, list them on the order form on the last page of the catalog, and send the form to us. If we receive your blank by December 1, we will guarantee delivery before the holidays.

We are sure you will agree that this is the easy way to do your holiday shopping. Sincerely yours

53.4 Potential Customer

January 15, 19--
Mr. George Harrington
National Heating Incorporated
15 Henry Street
Lexington, KY 42501
Dear Mr. Harrington
Subject: Heating System
The heating system in my home has not been giving me very good service during the past[1] few years. It is expensive to operate. The house is also not very comfortable during cold weather.[2] I think it is time for a change.

The type of heating system I have in mind is one that will heat all of the rooms[3] evenly. The new system must also use a type of fuel that is not too expensive.

Please have one of your[4] representatives call me to set up an appointment to visit my home and advise me. Yours truly
Ralph Burns   [99 words]

53.5 Car Purchase

August 4, 19--
Miss Marilyn Jacobs
1940 York Street
Willis, OK 73462
Dear Miss Jacobs
Subject: Car Purchase

Congratulations on your recent graduation from high school! Right now you are[1] no doubt making plans to attend college or perhaps get a job. You will need a means of dependable transportation[2] no matter what your plans.

During this month we are making a special offer to new high school graduates.[3] If you purchase a new car, we will give you a free stereo.

Come to our sales offices on Main Street to[4] take advantage of our offer. Sincerely yours
Arnold Lewis
Sales Representative   [96 words]

LESSON 54

54.1 Overdue Account

Dear Mr. Vega For the past six weeks we have become increasingly concerned about your account. You have been[1] sent three requests that you pay your overdue bill.

We have given you every opportunity to explain why[2] you have not mailed us your check. Also, we have given you a chance to ask for special consideration. Unfortunately,[3] you have not replied to any of our letters. Now the situation is serious.

Please let us[4] hear from you soon. We hope that you will avoid damaging your financial reputation. Sincerely yours   [99 words]

54.2

reservation airport arrived American company every

available computer that will to do for you you can

car reserve waiting always we will have one of our

54.3 Car Rental

Dear Miss Allen Have you ever made a reservation for a car at an airport only to find that the car was not available when you arrived? That will never happen when you reserve a car from the American Car Rental Company.

At any time all you have to do is call and we will have a car waiting for you when you want it. Our computer can always locate every one of our cars.

When we tell you that we have a car for you, you can depend on it. Sincerely

54.4 Accounting Publication

November 21, 19--
Smith and Davis
1985 Baxter Street
Fowler, MI 48835
Attention: President of the Company
Dear Sir or Madam   As the owner of an accounting firm, you are no doubt concerned that your staff take a[1] professional interest in their work.

I am the editor for a small publishing house that has just begun[2] publishing a magazine called Accounting Weekly. The people who have subscribed to it early already[3] acknowledge it as the new leader in the field of publications for accounting firms.

You can send our magazine[4] to your employees each week by mailing the enclosed form. This is one benefit that pays big[5] dividends. Sincerely yours,
Dale Dempsey, Editor   [106 words]

54.5 Request for Recommendation

October 5, 19--
Dr. Milton Fisher
721 Farley Avenue
Akron, OH 44305
Dear Dr. Fisher   I am planning to graduate from college next year, and I am starting to get my placement[1] file in order. I would like to request you to write a letter of recommendation for me at your[2] convenience. Please send it to the Planning and Placement Office at Smith College.

I found the shorthand[3] classes which I attended to be very enjoyable. I am sorry that my study of shorthand has been[4] completed. It was a lot more exciting than other classes I have taken. I am sure the skills I have[5] developed in shorthand will help me throughout my life. Very truly yours
Wendy Lewis   [112 words]

LESSON 55

55.1 Employee Discount

Dear Ms. Lowe   Thank you for your letter in which you asked about a special discount for your employees at our store.[1]

The Cunningham Furniture Company will be glad to give the Ames Company employees a special discount.[2] We agree with you that such an arrangement would be good for the people of both companies.

After carefully[3] considering the matter, we have concluded that 10 percent is an appropriate discount. Please keep your[4] people well informed about our new special discount policy. Cordially yours   [94 words]

55.2

dresses   caused   apparently   flaw   acceptable from the

recent shipment concern color faded credit account

material   quality   merchandise   of these we have been

55.3 Clothing Shipment

Dear Miss Quinn   The most recent shipment of dresses from your plant has caused us much concern. Apparently, the material you received from the mill had a flaw in it. The color is faded in several places. Not one of the 35 dresses covered by Invoice 1940 is acceptable to us.

We are returning all of the dresses to you. Please credit our account for the full price of these dresses.

In the past we have been pleased with the quality of your merchandise, and we know that you will be willing to correct an unfortunate mistake. Cordially yours

55.4 Speaking Invitation

December 1, 19--
Rachel Barr, Ph.D.
The National Express
600 Elm Street
Los Angeles, CA 90052
Dear Dr. Barr   As a foreign correspondent for a national newspaper, you have had many exciting[1] experiences. Therefore, I would like to invite you to speak at one of our student press club meetings on Tuesday,[2] February 9. The meeting will take place in Room 436 at Davis Hall.

Several members of our group[3] have had the pleasure of reading your newspaper articles and say that you are a delightful writer who can[4] deliver a powerful message. We would like to have you speak for about 20 minutes on any topic[5] that you think would be of interest to our members.

Please let me know as soon as possible if you are available.[6] Very truly yours
Morris Nichols
Dean of Education   [131 words]

55.5 Communications Seminar

January 10, 19--
Gerald Davis, Ph.D.
Parker Company
70 Larson Street
Baltimore, MD 21260
Dear Dr. Davis
Subject: Seminar on Telephone Techniques
The New York Telephone Company has offered to give a seminar on telephone[1] techniques in our office on Tuesday, May 5; Wednesday, May 6; and[2] Thursday, May 7. I want all the members of your staff to attend one of these sessions. The purpose of the[3] seminar is to review proper ways to use the telephone. I feel all of us will profit by the[4] advice and information we will receive from this session.

Please advise your staff that it has been scheduled for the[5] May 7 session at 10 o'clock. If you have any questions about this seminar, please let me know.[6] Sincerely yours
Ralph T. Charles   [125 words]

LESSON 56

56.1 Flight Trouble

Dear Mr. Brooks   Your travel agent has written us about your unfortunate experience on your return[1] flight from Italy to New York. Upon checking into the matter, I find that at the last minute the plane that[2] was scheduled for the flight developed engine trouble. There was no other plane available to take its place.

Please[3] accept our apologies for the inconvenience you have been caused. We are confident that your next flight will be[4] a pleasant one. Very truly yours   [87 words]

56.2

Parker   during   recent   examination   records frankness

discovered   account   something   you have not we would

request   moment   reasons   happen   reply   may be we have

56.3 Account Inquiry

Dear Mrs. Parker   During a recent examination of our records, we discovered that you have not used your charge account at our store for over a year. We wish to keep up to date and therefore request that you take just a moment to fill out the enclosed form.

We understand there may be many reasons why you have not used your charge account. If we have done something to displease you, we would appreciate knowing about it so that it does not happen again. We will appreciate your frankness in your reply. Sincerely yours

56.4 Problem Tires

Date: October 11, 19--
To: Jack Taylor
From: Jennifer Brooks
Subject: Messenger Service
Our messenger service, The General Service[1] Company, has been having some financial difficulty lately. The officers of the company tell us[2] that they have experienced great increases in their costs during business,[3] they must increase the rates they charge their customers. The new rates will go into effect January 1.

We are[4] expecting to receive the new schedule of rates by December 1. We will post the schedule as soon as we receive[5] it.   [101 words]

56.5 Purchase Order

May 7, 19--
Ann Wilson, Esquire
45 Lake Street
Pittsburgh, PA 15260
Dear Miss Wilson   Thank you for your order for one of our electric blankets.[1] It will be shipped just as soon as you let us know which color you want. This model electric blanket has been made[2] available in five exciting colors. They are listed on the enclosed circular.

We want to make sure that your[3] order is handled properly. Therefore, we are asking you to check the color you want on the enclosed card and[4] return the card to us. We will, of course, fill your order as soon as we receive it. Yours very truly
James T.[5] Mack Jr.
Customer Service   [105 words]